Modern American Drama: Playwriting in the 1970s

DECADES OF MODERN AMERICAN DRAMA: PLAYWRITING FROM THE 1930s TO 2009

Modern American Drama: Playwriting in the 1930s
by Anne Fletcher

Modern American Drama: Playwriting in the 1940s
by Felicia Hardison Londré

Modern American Drama: Playwriting in the 1950s
by Susan C. W. Abbotson

Modern American Drama: Playwriting in the 1960s
by Mike Sell

Modern American Drama: Playwriting in the 1970s
by Mike Vanden Heuvel

Modern American Drama: Playwriting in the 1980s
by Sandra G. Shannon

Modern American Drama: Playwriting in the 1990s
by Cheryl Black and Sharon Friedman

Modern American Drama: Playwriting 2000–2009
by Julia Listengarten and Cindy Rosenthal

Modern American Drama: Playwriting in the 1970s

Voices, Documents, New Interpretations

Mike Vanden Heuvel

Series Editors: Brenda Murphy and Julia Listengarten

methuen | drama
LONDON • NEW YORK • OXFORD • NEW DELHI • SYDNEY

METHUEN DRAMA
Bloomsbury Publishing Plc
50 Bedford Square, London, WC1B 3DP, UK
1385 Broadway, New York, NY 10018, USA
29 Earlsfort Terrace, Dublin 2, Ireland

BLOOMSBURY, METHUEN DRAMA and the Methuen Drama logo
are trademarks of Bloomsbury Publishing Plc

First published in Great Britain 2018
Paperback edition first published 2021

Copyright © Mike Vanden Heuvel and contributors, 2018

Mike Vanden Heuvel has asserted his right under the Copyright,
Designs and Patents Act, 1988, to be identified as author of this work.

For legal purposes the Acknowledgements on p. x constitute
an extension of this copyright page.

Cover design: Louise Dugdale
Cover photo © Richard Corkery/NY Daily News Archive via Getty Images

All rights reserved. No part of this publication may be reproduced or
transmitted in any form or by any means, electronic or mechanical,
including photocopying, recording, or any information storage or retrieval
system, without prior permission in writing from the publishers.

Bloomsbury Publishing Plc does not have any control over, or responsibility for,
any third-party websites referred to or in this book. All internet addresses given
in this book were correct at the time of going to press. The author and publisher
regret any inconvenience caused if addresses have changed or sites have
ceased to exist, but can accept no responsibility for any such changes.

A catalogue record for this book is available from the British Library.

A catalog record for this book is available from the Library of Congress.

ISBN: HB: 978-1-4725-7175-5
PB: 978-1-3502-1547-4
ePDF: 978-1-3500-2259-1
eBook: 978-1-4081-4512-3
Pack: 978-1-4725-7264-6

Series: Decades of Modern American Drama: Playwriting from the 1930s to 2009

Typeset by Fakenham Prepress Solutions, Fakenham, Norfolk NR21 8NN

To find out more about our authors and books visit
www.bloomsbury.com and sign up for our newsletters.

CONTENTS

List of Boxes ix
Acknowledgements x
Biographical Note and Notes on Contributors xi
General Preface Brenda Murphy and Julia Listengarten xiii

1 Introduction to the 1970s *Mike Vanden Heuvel* 1
　Overview 1
　Living in the decade 2
　　Domestic life 2
　　Work life 6
　Society 7
　　Crime and punishment 7
　　Feminism and gay rights 8
　　Sex and porn 9
　　Race 10
　Culture 11
　　Music 11
　　Books 15
　　Art 17
　　Architecture 18
　　Film 19
　　Sport 21
　　Travel and leisure 23
　　Fashion 23
　Political events 24
　　Contexts 24

Events by year 27
 Media 33
  Television 33
  Radio 36
  Print 36
 Science and technology 36

2 American Theatre in the 1970s *Mike Vanden Heuvel* 39
 Setting the stage: The political and social context 39
 American theatre(s): Devolution and evolution 42
 Broadway: Infrastructure 45
 Off-Broadway: Infrastructure 48
 Off-Off-Broadway: Infrastructure 51
 Regional theatre: Infrastructure 55
 Playwriting and production: Broadway 58
  The Broadway musical 64
  Broadway imports 67
 Playwriting and production: Off-Broadway 69
 Playwriting and production: Off-Off-Broadway 73
 'Black is beautiful on Broadway': Contextualizing identity-based theatre of the 1970s 74
 The women's movement and theatre 82
 New writing/new performance theatre 83
 Home away from home: Regional theatres and the resident playwright 87
 Conclusion 88

3 'An Idiom that is a Kind of Vision of the World': David Rabe's Plays of the 1970s – *The Basic Training of Pavlo Hummel* (1971), *Sticks and Bones* (1971) **and** *Streamers* (1975) *Jon Dietrick* 91
 Introduction 91
  The Basic Training of Pavlo Hummel 97

Sticks and Bones 101
Streamers 106
Minor works and conclusion 110

4 Sam Shepard: *Curse of the Starving Class* (1977), *Buried Child* (1978) and *True West* (1980) *Mike Vanden Heuvel* 113

Introduction 113
Curse of the Starving Class 120
Buried Child 126
True West 133
Conclusion 139

5 Ntozake Shange: *For colored girls who have considered suicide/when the rainbow is enuf* (1975), *spell #7* (1979) and *boogie woogie landscapes* (1979) *Neal A. Lester* 141

Introduction 141
for colored girls who have considered suicide/when the rainbow is enuf 144
spell #7 148
boogie woogie landscapes 155
Conclusion 158

6 Richard Foreman: *Sophia = (Wisdom) Part 3: The Cliffs* (1972), *Pandering to the Masses: A Misrepresentation* (1975) and *Rhoda in Potatoland (Her Fall-Starts)* (1975) *Geoffrey King and Craig Werner* 165

Introduction: Cogito ergo boom – Richard Foreman's Ontological-Hysteric Theatre 165
A cross between a (white) college professor and an acrobat 169

How to activate a space (at a distance) 170
Manheim as muse: The Lillian Gish of the avant-garde 174
Thinking against oneself: Language 176
Politics and the dialectics of consciousness 179
Sophia = (Wisdom) Part 3: The Cliffs 182
Pandering to the Masses: A Misrepresentation 185
Rhoda in Potatoland (Her Fall-Starts) 188
Conclusion: Foreman since 1981 (the established avant-garde) 190

Afterword *Mike Vanden Heuvel* 193

Documents 207
David Rabe 207
Sam Shepard 215
Ntozake Shange 223
Richard Foreman 229

Notes 241
Bibliography 267
Index 277

LIST OF BOXES

Box 1.1: Food fads appearing in the 1970s 5
Box 1.2: American crime in the 1970s 7
Box 1.3: Bestselling fiction books of the decade by year 17
Box 1.4: Emerging film stars of the 1970s 19

ACKNOWLEDGEMENTS

I am first very grateful for the colleagues who contributed their excellent essays to the volume: Jon Dietrick, Geoffrey King, Neal Lester and Craig Werner. Their enthusiasm for their selected playwrights and the period was matched only by their patience during a year's worth of emails. I thank them for the rigour of their scholarship and the clarity of their thought. As well, I thank Julia Listengarten and Brenda Murphy, not only for inviting me to participate in this series but for initiating the project in the first place. Thanks as well are due to Mark Dudgeon at Bloomsbury Methuen Drama for his support and vision in seeing the entire eight-volume project through.

I gratefully acknowledge research support provided by a summer research grant from the University of Wisconsin-Madison Office of the Vice Chancellor for Research and Graduate Education.

Preparation of this volume was sadly interrupted in 2015 by the death of my elder brother, Stephen, and so I dedicate the work to him as well as to his daughter, Jessica, and his grandchildren, Lane and new arrival Eloise. Steve came of age in the 1970s, and the only criticism I have of the drama of the period is that none of it would have been adequate to capture his spirit in its entirety. As I stumbled into the decade as an impressionable teenager, he introduced me to Hendrix (too late), the mullet cut (much too early) and muscle cars (just in time). He continued to be a source of my laughter – though unlike him I didn't learn to direct it at myself nearly often enough – and my love for the rest of his days.

To Tracy, who continues to bless my days: T, M, & D. Ever so.

BIOGRAPHICAL NOTE AND NOTES ON CONTRIBUTORS

Mike Vanden Heuvel is Professor of Interdisciplinary Theatre Studies and a member of the Department of Classics and Near Eastern Studies at the University of Wisconsin-Madison, USA. Author of *Performing Drama/Dramatizing Performance: Alternative Theatre and the Dramatic Text* (1991) and *Elmer Rice: A Research and Production Sourcebook* (1996), Vanden Heuvel's current research concerns the intersections between science and performance.

Jon Dietrick is Associate Professor of English at Babson College, USA, where he teaches modern drama and modern American drama. He is author of *Bad Pennies and Dead Presidents: Money in Modern American Drama* (2012). His studies concerning the intersections of business and American drama have appeared in *Twentieth-Century Literature* and *American Drama*. Dr Dietrick also co-directs the Empty Space Theatre at Babson.

Geoffrey King is making a life study of flawed words and stubborn sounds: he co-founded Abreaction Theater with David Bailin (*Disparate Acts, Confessions of a Conformist: The Lists*) and collaborated with Craig Werner to create, compose, direct and produce a performance and recording for radio (*Game Theory*). Geoffrey King currently lives and writes in Queens, NY, USA.

Neal Lester is Dean's Distinguished Professor of English at Arizona State University, USA, and Director of 'Project Humanities'. His teaching encompasses African-American drama, children's literature, folklore, cinema and culture. Author of *Ntozake Shange:*

A Critical Study of the Plays (1995) and *Understanding Zora Neale Hurston's 'Their Eyes Were Watching God'* (1999), Professor Lester is a renowned discussion facilitator and Distinguished Public Scholar of the Arizona Humanities Council.

Craig Werner is Professor and Chair of the Department of Afro-American Studies at the University of Wisconsin-Madison, USA, where he teaches music history, literature and cultural history. A member of the Nominating Committee for the Rock and Roll Hall of Fame, Werner is the author of *A Change is Gonna Come: Music, Race and the Soul of America* (2006) and *Higher Ground: Aretha Franklin, Stevie Wonder, Curtis Mayfield and the Rise & Fall of American Soul* (2004). His most recent book, with Doug Bradley, is *We Gotta Get Out of This Place: The Soundtrack of the Vietnam War* (2015), named Best Music Book by *Rolling Stone* for 2015.

GENERAL PREFACE

Decades of Modern American Drama: Playwriting from the 1930s to 2009 is a series of eight volumes about American theatre and drama, each focusing on a particular decade during the period between 1930 and 2010. It begins with the 1930s, the decade when Eugene O'Neill was awarded the Nobel Prize for Literature and American theatre came of age. This is followed by the decade of the country's most acclaimed theatre, when O'Neill, Tennessee Williams and Arthur Miller were writing their most distinguished work and a theatrical idiom known as 'the American style' was seen in theatres throughout the world. Its place in the world repertoire established, American playwriting has taken many turns since 1950.

The aim of this series is to focus attention on individual playwrights or collaborative teams who together reflect the variety and range of American drama during the 80-year period it covers. In each volume, contributing experts offer detailed critical essays on four playwrights or collaborators and the significant work they produced during the decade. The essays on playwrights are presented in a rich interpretive context, which provides a contemporary perspective on both the theatre and American life and culture during the decade. The careers of the playwrights before and after the decade are summarized as well, and a section of documents, including interviews, manuscripts, reviews, brief essays and other items, sheds further light on the playwrights and their plays.

The process of choosing such a limited number of playwrights to represent the American theatre of this period has been a difficult but revealing one. In selecting them, the series editors and volume authors have been guided by several principles: highlighting the most significant playwrights, in terms both historical and aesthetic, who contributed at least two interesting and important plays during the decade; providing a wide-ranging view of the decade's theatre, including both Broadway and alternative venues; examining many historical trends in playwriting and theatrical production during the decade; and reflecting the theatre's diversity in gender and ethnicity, both across the decade and across the period as a whole. In some decades, the choices are obvious. It is hard to argue with O'Neill, Williams, Miller and Wilder in the 1940s. Other decades required a good deal of thought and discussion. Readers will inevitably regret that favourite playwrights are left out. We can only respond that we regret it too, but we believe that the playwrights who are included reflect a representative sample of the best and most interesting American playwriting during the period.

While each of the books has the same fundamental elements – an overview of life and culture during the decade, an overview of the decade's theatre and drama, the four essays on the playwrights, a section of documents, an Afterword bringing the playwrights' careers up to date, and a Bibliography of works both on the individual playwrights and on the decade in general – there are differences among the books depending on each individual volume author's decisions about how to represent and treat the decade. The various formats chosen by the volume authors for the overview essays, the wide variety of playwrights, from the canonical to the contemporary avant-garde, and the varied perspectives of the contributors' essays make for very different individual volumes. Each of the volumes stands on its own as a history of theatre in the decade and a critical study of the four individual playwrights or collaborative teams included. Taken together, however, the eight volumes offer a broadly representative critical and historical treatment of 80 years of American theatre and drama that is both accessible to a student first encountering the subject and informative and provocative for a seasoned expert.

> Brenda Murphy (Board of Trustees Distinguished Professor
> Emeritus, University of Connecticut, USA)
> Julia Listengarten (Professor of Theatre at the University of
> Central Florida, USA)
> Series Editors

1

Introduction to the 1970s

Mike Vanden Heuvel

Overview

The seventies are just the garbage of the sixties.

ROBERT PATRICK, *KENNEDY'S CHILDREN*[1]

Disco balls, streakers and stayin' alive. Oil shock, long lines for gas, and auto design misadventures like the Pacer, Volare and Pinto. Personal space, personal consciousness and the first personal computers. Latchkey kids, POSSLQs and palimony. Archie Bunker, tying yellow ribbons 'round the old oak tree, and the Bicentennial celebrations. Hardhats beating on Hippies, more hardhats – this time with long hair and Afros ('the industrial Woodstock') – striking at the GM plant in Lordstown. Jimmy Carter's personal relationship with Christ. *Wheel of Fortune*, *Roots* and *Saturday Night Live*. The rise of the Sunbelt, the ascent of the redneck and the 'southernization' of America.[2] Prop 13 in California and propping up South Vietnam. Skateboarders, bored housewives and Microsoft's first motherboard. The rise of the Imperial Presidency and Gerald Ford's (or was it Chevy Chase's?) pratfalls. The Me Decade, 'getting it' at Esalen and getting mad as hell and not taking it anymore. White flight to the suburbs following the Milliken decision, a Skylab in space and the flight of a white seagull named Jonathan. Jesus freaks,

Krishnas, Moonies and the 700 Club. The first age of terrorism for Americans. Fallen torches and torched helicopters, initially in Saigon as America retreated from its first military defeat and then, at decade's end, burning in the Iranian desert.

Living in the decade

Domestic life

The entire period was mired in stagflation – the unique situation of rampant inflation existing simultaneously with high unemployment – and rising prices acted as a multiplier to further dampen purchasing power. At the same time, the 1970s saw the rise of the money revolution and dramatic increases in consumer debt with the aggressive marketing of credit cards and the signifying of debt as something other than moral turpitude. Baby boomers were entering their teen years, causing family expenses to skyrocket. Consumer debt exploded in 1975 to $197 billion and then doubled to $315 billion in just four years. In the face of high interest rates and rising costs, many Americans shifted from acting like bankers frugally managing their money to investors and speculators – utilizing the gradual deregulation of the financial sector to explore every option from money market funds to discount stock brokerage firms and mutual funds – whose aim was to create wealth that at least kept pace with inflation.

A perfect storm of economic factors caused a simultaneous decline in American productivity, trade and wages. When the oil embargos hit in 1973 and 1979, the economy was in no shape to rebound and so economic stress was widespread. Healthcare costs were an issue then as they are today: after Canada passed its single-payer system in 1971, there was interest across both political parties to do the same in America. Progress stalled, although the HMO Act became law in 1973.

In 1970, fully 61 per cent of Americans were classified as middle class (the number in 2015 is 50 per cent, with the majority slipping into the ranks of the lower middle class). Oil prices, not surprisingly, represented the biggest shift in consumption. While in 1950, 38 per cent of America's energy was produced by petroleum, by 1975 this had risen to 45 per cent. When the Middle

East consortium OPEC embargoed oil to the US, the shockwaves were felt across all sectors of the economy. Prices jumped from 30 cents per gallon to $1.20 (this during a decade when wages rose but 0.05 per cent while prices rose at an average of 8.5 per cent). Soon after 1975, American dependence on petroleum products as the source of energy began slowly to erode, and by 2012 they were closer to 1950 figures (38 per cent of total energy).

Things we bought

Average yearly salaries across the decade were only $7,500, but the cost of living was of course much lower: first-class stamps were 6 cents, steak went for under $1.20 per pound, and coffee – by the pound – cost a fifth of what a latte does in 2015. The popular Hot Wheels toy vehicles were about 70 cents apiece, and one could buy furniture for Barbie's house – inflatable! – for about $2. Real cars were running around $3,500 in 1970, and this climbed to $6,000 by the end of the decade. One could invest in the more fuel-efficient (but woefully underpowered) disasters that appeared after the oil crisis, like the Ford Pinto, and only shell out $3,000 in 1979. Cadillacs were the power car of choice, and the Lincoln Continental Mark III could, if memory serves, take up the space of the Pacer, Gremlin and Vega combined. Among other adult toys, those with greater disposable income invested in the first portable phones, though, as their nicknames attest ('Brick Phones'), they were not especially mobile.

For the kids, Americans continued to buy dolls for girls until the middle of the decade, when the rise of women in the labour force and the nascent women's movement caused toys to be advertised without the strong gender marking that characterized post-war culture. By the end of the decade, 'man dolls' for boys were widespread and included G. I. Joe, Stretch Armstrong, Evil Knievel and Colonel Steve Austin, aka the Six Million Dollar Man. Similarly, toy marketing for girls often featured women as doctors, office workers and scientists. Indeed, toys are much more strongly marketed by gender in the twenty-first century than in the 1970s. As in any decade, there were fads that produced must-have items: Pet Rocks were hot mid-decade, but were soon supplanted by Cabbage Patch Kids in 1978. The Rubik's Cube rounded out the decade, arriving in 1979.

More traditionally, the Etch-A-Sketch was still popular, as was Lego (though they didn't make movies based on them as they do today). Board games, along with the venerable Monopoly, Candyland, Stratego and Scrabble, included Mastermind, Mousetrap, Battleship and Boggle. (Remarkably, many of these games enjoy a digital afterlife as contemporary apps.) With Dungeons and Dragons, however, the nature of the board game changed forever: between the elaborate role-playing and the competition to reign as Dragon Master, the game swept the country after 1974.

While electric toys – train sets, Easy-Bake Ovens, those vibrating football games and the like – opened the decade, by 1979 toys were increasingly electronic. Top of the line video games, like Pong, Space Invaders and Galaxian, could only be played at arcades, as home gaming equipment was in its infancy: the Atari 400 would not debut until 1979. Still, plenty of LED-encrusted games were available for home use, ranging from the Lite-Brite board, Simon (a Q&A game with moving, lighted panels) and the first toy calculators for parents wanting education mixed in with the fun. As environmental awareness increased following the first Earth Day celebration in 1970, and concerns grew after the Love Canal scandal of the mid-1970s (in which a school was found to be built on 22,000 tons of toxic waste), concerned parents could purchase a Johnny Horizon Environmental Test Kit.

Americans were beginning to learn how to overstuff themselves: the average diet consisted of 3,300 calories per day, up 300 calories from the leaner 1950s and indicative of trends today (3,800 calories). Red meats were in, eggs were in decline and the movement to consume more fresh fruits and vegetables was still two decades away: Americans ate 13 per cent more canned vegetables in the 1970s than they would by the end of the century. With more women moving into the workplace, traditional family dining and the hierarchy of domestic labour were altered. The appearance of toaster ovens and eventually the commercially produced home microwave oven (for the latter, between 1970 and 1975 sales jumped from 40,000 to over a million) made it simpler to reheat precooked foods at home. But it was also a golden age of fast food, and as more Americans dined out they drank less milk but more than made up for it in increased cheese consumption. In 1970 there were about 30,000 fast food locales in the county, but by 1979 this jumped to 140,000 (some of the long-retired franchises included Biff Burger, Burger Chef and – in the wake of the success of Kentucky Fried Chicken – Mahalia Jackson's Glori-Fried Chicken). Between fast food parlours and conventional restaurants, Americans spent roughly 25 per cent of their food budget dining away from home in 1970: by 1999 that number was 48 per cent. Still, the carbonated beverage market was relatively narrow by comparison, and as a result Americans received only 16 per cent of their refined and added sugars via sodas, compared to 22 per cent today.

Still, with the rise of the environmental movement, 'natural' was in and granola made its appearance alongside the first salad bars and home woks. The Atkins diet created a stir in 1972, and pumpkin and apple pie had to make room for zucchini bread. Organically raised beef helped per capita consumption of red meat reach its highest total ever in 1976 (94 pounds per year) at a time when meats were not lean by today's standards (35 per cent fat on average).

BOX 1.1: FOOD FADS APPEARING IN THE 1970s

Orville Redenbacher Gourmet Popping Corn (1970)
Hamburger Helper (1970)

Snapple (1972)
Stove Top Stuffing (1972)

French bread pizza (1974)
Soft frozen yogurt (1974)

Pop Rocks – along with the urban legend that they could explode stomachs when consumed with carbonated colas (1975)

Starburst Fruit Chews (1976)
Jelly Belly Jelly Beans (1976)

Ben & Jerry's Ice Cream (1978)
Perrier bottled water (1978). By 1997, American consumption of bottled water had increased 908 per cent.

Work life

Few decades have seen the fortunes of the working class rise and fall so dramatically. The 1970s began with labour seeming to be solidly behind the Democrats and poised to make huge gains, but ended with working class movements in disarray and the lower working class shifting politically to the New Right. Essentially labour was caught between the support it received from the Democrats with regard to its economic and workplace struggles, and on the other hand the animosity felt by its rank and file toward liberalism's cultural politics: race and gender, the war in Vietnam, the environment and the perceived erosion of America's manifest destiny. As Jefferson Cowie notes, jazz musician Gil-Scott Heron illuminated the conflict with the line 'America don't know whether it wants to be Matt Dillon [the straight-shooting hero of the television series *Gunsmoke*] or Bob Dylan.'[3] Nixon expertly mined the discontent and incorporated labour into his 'Silent Majority', as evidenced by the huge (and initially violent) 1970 demonstration of 'hardhats' in Manhattan against Hippies in support of Nixon's policies in Vietnam. The president won his landslide 1972 re-election over the pro-labour George McGovern in part by carrying the lower middle class vote. Despite transformative gains by the working class in striking against large corporations such as GM and unionizing the intransigent South in the first half of the decade (particularly the J. P. Stevens plant in Roanoke Rapids, NC, later dramatized in the Academy Award-winning film *Norma Rae*), the recession of 1974–5 all but ended labour's hope of expanding its political and economic influence. The landmark Humphrey–Hawkins Full Employment Act languished under President Carter and died a slow death at the hand of both free-market conservatives and liberal economists.

The other seismic shift in American labour was the increasing number of women entering the workforce. In 1970, 30 per cent of women with children were working outside the home, but the number leaped to 43 per cent by 1976 and continued to climb well into the next decade.[4] The weak economy, which shifted job opportunities from manufacture to the service sectors, created a double-edged sword for women: more jobs opened that did not require advanced training but also did not provide anything close to equal pay or equal opportunity for advancement.

Society

Crime and punishment

The decade had its share of high-profile crime and introduced the image of the serial killer to mainstream media.

> ### BOX 1.2: AMERICAN CRIME IN THE 1970s
>
> David Berkowitz, aka 'The Son of Sam', terrorized New York City for over a year, killing six and wounding seven with a high-powered handgun while sending taunting letters to the authorities that kept the city in constant fear. The San Francisco-based Zodiac killer, whose murders began around 1962, continued and achieved national attention until they ended abruptly in 1978. In a titillating high-profile abduction case, heiress Patty Hearst was kidnapped by the Symbionese Liberation Army in 1974 and within a month appeared (as 'Tania') with her captors as part of a bank robbery in San Francisco.

More generally the 1970s are remembered as a time when urban crime exploded and America's cities – particularly in the Rust Belt, but New York City as well – were perceived as descending into something close to lawlessness. Crime rates soared: compared to 1960, 225 per cent more robberies, a 145 per cent increase in rapes, and murders up more than 100 per cent, much of it youth crime. White flight to the suburbs and Sun Belt and the loss of up to 40 per cent of manufacturing jobs (in cities like Detroit) reduced populations in America's major cities and caused widespread disinvestment in urban retail and housing. The decrepit infrastructure, prominent red-light districts and graffiti-covered subways became the emblem of such decline, and the best anecdotal evidence of the chaos is the widespread looting and violence that occurred during the Northeast blackout of 1977 (which did not happen during the first great blackout of 1965).

But the biggest events related to crime actually were judicial. In 1972 the Supreme Court made consistent application of the death penalty mandatory, which in the short run created a moratorium on executions based on 8th Amendment issues pertaining to cruel and unusual punishment. In 1976, however, *Gregg v. Georgia* provided guidelines for adhering to that clause and opened up use of the death penalty in states that still carried it. Abortion was decriminalized with *Roe v. Wade* in 1973, with a 7–2 vote affirming the due process clause of the 14th Amendment guaranteeing the right to privacy. Penal strategy moved from rehabilitation to deterrence via presumptive and more punitive sentencing as courts responded to the rising crime rate by returning to the mandatory sentencing policies of the past.

Feminism and gay rights

Energized by the initial political progress gained by the civil rights movement, American second-wave feminism was launched in the 1960s and expanded exponentially in the 1970s, supported by sweeping changes in federal and state laws. Sex discrimination was recognized as part of the 14th Amendment in 1971, and in 1974 the Fair Housing Act was amended to include discrimination by gender. Initially, the focus was primarily workplace equality. Gloria Steinem launched *Ms.* magazine in 1971 for professional women, and a 1973 Supreme Court ruling prohibited sex-specific want ads. The percentage of American women working outside the home increased from 27 per cent in 1960 to 54 per cent in 1980. The Equal Pay Act was amended in 1970 to keep employers from changing job titles to justify lower wages for women.

California led the nation by enacting a no-fault divorce bill in 1969 and by 1977 another nine states followed suit. Marital rape laws were written in several states, while the Pregnancy Discrimination Act became law in 1978.

On the cultural front, by 1970, San Diego State University and Cornell hosted the first Women's Studies programmes. Strikes and sit-ins were common, whether in protest against women's magazines (such as *Ladies Home Journal*) seen as perpetuating the 'feminine mystique' or in opposition to discriminatory employment and pay practices (AT&T, among others). Feminist art periodicals such as *Feminist Art Journal* proliferated, but the meeting of the Combahee River Collective in 1974 brought attention to the exclusion of women of colour from NOW (National Organization of Women) and other feminist organizations.

The Equal Rights Amendment, penned by Alice Paul in 1923, was passed in Congress in 1972 and sent to the states for ratification. After concerted efforts by Phyllis Schafly's STOP organization ('Stop Taking Our Privileges', which eventually drove the National Organization for Women to mount an economic boycott of states refusing ratification), the amendment died in 1982 after failing to achieve ratification by the minimum 38 states. However, the Title IX Education Amendment, prohibiting gender desegregation at all levels of the college experience, was passed (1972), and professional schools and athletic programmes saw huge leaps in female participation. By mid-decade, feminism had grown so powerful that the UN declared 1975 'International Women's Year'. In 1979, the first Susan B. Anthony coins were minted.

Lesbian and gay liberation did not enjoy the legal progress accorded to feminism, but 1970 saw the first gay pride parade when thousands flocked to Central Park in New York to commemorate the Stonewall riots of 1969. The American Psychiatric Association removed homosexuality from the list of mental illnesses in 1973, and the following year Kathy Kozachenko of Ann Arbor, MI, became the first openly gay American elected to public office. Ironically, the decade is mostly recalled for two setbacks: first, when Anita Bryant, a former Miss Oklahoma, formed the anti-gay rights 'Save Our Children' campaign in 1977 and succeeded in repealing progressive Florida anti-discrimination laws (earning a retaliatory cream pie to the face at a media event in 1977); and second, with the murder of Harvey Milk, the gay rights activist and San Francisco Commissioner, in 1978. But the 1970s ended with the huge National March on Washington for Lesbian and Gay Rights in 1979 and the Democratic Party's decision to end discrimination against homosexuals.

Sex and porn

If 1960s America experienced the sexual revolution vicariously through the counterculture, the 1970s brought it into daily life.

Restrictions on sexual content and language in films, and then television, were relaxed, and the print industry supplied a steady stream of cheap pornography as well as 'artistic' porn (as when *Playboy* decided, in 1972, to show its models fully nude rather than topless). With contraception more widely available and standards relaxed, pre-marital sex was not only on the rise but accepted by much of the urban population. The highest rates of divorce in American history came during the decade, and a film like *Deep Throat* was discussed and defended on the late-night talk shows as a 'cleansing' experience for moviegoers. The public face of the new porn ranged from the red-light districts of Times Square in New York and the bathhouses of San Francisco to the boulevards of Santa Monica (CA), Wells Street (Chicago) and Hennepin Ave. (Minneapolis).

The backlashes were loud and regular. James Dobson's Focus of the Family went public in 1976 and became a foundation of the New Right and its defence of traditional family values and gender roles as well as its antipathy for abortion rights.

Race

Racial politics in the decade began promisingly when the Supreme Court, in *Swann v. Charlotte-Mecklenburg Board of Education* (1971), recognized that de facto segregation still existed in school districts, and afforded federal courts the right to use busing to rectify the inequalities. After modifications were instituted in the landmark *Milliken v. Bradley* decision (1974), many communities instituted court-ordered busing to desegregate their school districts. An immediate and often violent backlash ensued, particularly in Boston, where ROAR (Restore Our Alienated Rights) sent baseball bat-wielding Southies into black districts while blacks retaliated with stabbings and beatings. The infamous photograph ('The Soiling of Old Glory') depicting one such (though ambiguous) incident created a firestorm and won the Pulitzer Prize for the *Boston Herald American*. Riots occurred, sometimes instigated by the Klan, in Miami, Louisville and small towns across the South.

The rise of black nationalism near the end of the 1960s, aligned with the rise of affirmative action programmes in business and education, created a climate in which even the well-intentioned hiring of qualified black civil servants (firefighters, police officers, state bureaucrats) often resulted in charges of 'reverse discrimination' and lawsuits seeking to re-establish majoritarian rights for whites. The Bakke case (1974–8) became a touchstone for the resistance to affirmative action, but it ended without a majority decision and continues to influence challenges to race-based college admissions into the twenty-first century.

But in the 1970s, race relations were not restricted to black/white. After the 1965 reform acts, dramatic increases in Asian, Latin American and West Indian immigration were seen. Bruce Schulman argues that these shifting demographics were an important influence on the change from an integrationist model of race relations to one based on diversity:[5] 'Over the course of the 1970s, the rationale for affirmative action and the contours of civil rights programs slowly metamorphosed ... Affirmative action was now supposed to promote and celebrate differences rather than eliminate distinctions' (Schulman, 68). A conservative historian like David Frum, of course, saw things differently: he reads the *Griggs v. Duke Power* ruling of 1971 as the point at which equal treatment before the law gave way to entitlements based on race, gender, sexual preference, disability and other 'differences' that would lead inevitably

> not [to] the elimination of laws that denied equality, but the enactment of laws to require companies to pay the costs of remaking the world so that inequality would no longer matter. The civil rights laws that once modestly tried to protect people from irrational hatreds had been inflated into an audacious guarantee that the state would eliminate any obstacle between the citizen and the fulfillment of his dreams.[6]

Culture

Music

The 1970s music scene began not in renewal but in death: in the space of less than two years, in 1970 and 1971, Jimi Hendrix,

Janis Joplin and Jim Morrison all perished by drug overdose. Representing another kind of death, the Beatles officially disbanded in 1970, the same year Simon and Garfunkel released their last album (*Bridge Over Troubled* Water) and – less disquieting perhaps – the Monkees split up. In the wake of Beatlemania, the former Fab Four went on to do remarkable solo work and the 'quiet Beatle', George Harrison – after issuing the revelatory *All Things Must Pass* album – mounted the first global celebrity benefit rock concert, the Concert for Bangladesh (1971). Elvis's death in 1977, although it received worldwide attention, felt more like an afterthought. The Rolling Stones, decamped to France as tax evaders, maintained the British invasion with the release of *Exile on Main Street* in 1972.

Original rock and roll was long gone, but the larger global category of rock crossed into the mainstream, dominating popular culture as never before and influencing high culture (fashion and museum art, mostly through David Bowie and later Deborah Harry) as well popular culture and fashion via Richard Hell's Punk-inspired self-cut, bleached hair and ripped, safety-pinned clothing. Parallel to the rights movement of the 1970s, rock widened its ambit to explore marginalized subgroups with unique expressions of sexuality and gender, new relations between populist and 'art' rock, and crossovers with other genres. Indeed rock, like ethnicity, was now defined by how it was mashed or hyphenated: prog-rock (Traffic, Jethro Tull), acid-rock (Pink Floyd, Iron Butterfly), hard-rock (Cream, Led Zeppelin), glam-rock (Bowie, Elton John, Queen), Southern-rock (Graham Parsons, Lynyrd Skynyrd) and dozens of crosshatched variations. In most instances, and for the first half of the decade, the music conformed to the mood of crisis and even despair seen in the culture more generally. Bob Dylan was still electrifying folk music (*The Basement Tapes*, 1975), but 1979's *Slow Train Coming* initiated his evangelical stage and launched the development of his mordant ballad style. The 'California Style' arrived out of Doug Weston's West Hollywood Troubadour Club, featuring strong songwriting and soulful lyrics that propelled the careers of Jackson Browne, the Eagles, James Taylor, Kris Kristofferson and Linda Rondstadt. One of its signature songwriters, relatively unknown except as part of the 'Goffin-King' brand credited on scores of hit records, retreated to her Laurel Canyon home and produced the biggest-selling album of the decade, Carol King's *Tapestry*.

Follow the money

Despite the malaise expressed in the music, the industry as a whole had little to mourn: by 1973 Americans were spending more than $2 billion annually on records, or roughly three times the expenditure on all spectator sports combined and almost twice what was spent on movies. Elton John and Rod Stewart carried forward the 'second British invasion' and charted numerous No. 1 songs. Stadium rock, embraced by bands as diverse as Fleetwood Mac, Grand Funk Railroad and pre-eminently England's Led Zeppelin, generated huge profits for the artists and their labels. Berry Gordon's Motown operation expanded after he began to cede more creative control to his artists, beginning with Marvin Gaye's stunning concept album-cum-political protest *What's Going On?* (1971) and reaching a zenith with Stevie Wonder and the Jackson 5. The latter dominated the charts (the Michael Jackson-led quintet had four consecutive No. 1 songs, while Wonder ruled the Grammys for the entire decade) and led the charge to bring danceable music back into pop. Funk and Latin, with their lighter groove, stayed relevant throughout the period (Santana's *Abraxas* debuted in 1970 and George Clinton's Funkadelic was active throughout the decade).

By mid-decade funk combined with glam to counter the heavy beats and phallic guitar solos of most 'cock rock' to form disco. The cathartic release from concept-album tendentiousness and rock angst into the fluid, world beat rhythms and black- and gay-infused dance party culture arrived in America by the middle of the decade with the Trammps' *Disco Inferno* and Van McCoy's 'The Hustle'. The 1977 film *Saturday Night Fever* (which introduced John Travolta) arrived with its signature disco soundtrack by the Australian band the Bee Gees, and the frenzy was on as massive dance halls like Steve Rubell's Studio 54 in New York drew celebrities such as Warhol, Grace Jones and Bianca Jagger. The movement immediately drew fire from the male-dominated and straight, white world of traditional rock. By 1979 a 'Disco Demolition Night' held at Comiskey Park, Chicago, as part of a baseball game promotion descended into a riot by fans wearing 'Disco Sucks' T-shirts, who caused the game to be forfeited to the visiting team.

Naturally, as stadium rock grew increasingly remote and stagey and disco fed on its own flamboyance, countercultural responses to the perceived excess occurred. Fed by the existing alternative art and club culture scene in New York (particularly the DJ-curated dance parties at David Mancuso's Loft in Manhattan and the earliest expressions of hip-hop culture emanating from the South Bronx), artists sought to strip away the excesses of a music industry and club culture seen to be increasingly corporate. The epitome of this revolt was the ballad rocker Bruce Springsteen, whose rise to fame by 1975 was fuelled by a return to the origins of rock and roll's rhythms and authenticity ('heartland rock'), as well as his bleak assessment of 'the darkness on the edge of town' and his lyrical paeans to an American dream lost in Vietnam. The other urge to strip back down to basics was expressed by Punk (MC5, Iggy and the Stooges, Television, the New York Dolls, the Ramones, the Dead Kennedys), which rather incongruously flourished alongside disco and aligned with new wave music in its rejection of conventional production, marketing and distribution. The Ramones delivered their stripped down punk props at CBGBs in New York alongside art-rockers like Devo, Blondie and the Talking Heads. Less loudly than Springsteen or Punk, Reggae established a foothold in America as a musical form of political protest, and country music was revived by its affiliations with pop and rock, producing the 'outlaw sound' of Willy Nelson and Waylon Jennings.

On the horizon

By the end of the decade, new wave beats and disco sampling culture were morphing into something radically new: the Sugarhill Gang released 'Rapper's Delight' in 1979, and enthusiastic fans like the eight-year-old Ahmir Khalib Thompson rushed out to buy the record featuring the catchy line, 'the hip, the hop' (Thompson would later become better known as Questlove). In the same year, Funkadelic's *Uncle John Wants You!* went deep into the charts, and the beginnings of hip-hop culture were spawned.

In classical music and jazz of the 1970s, minimalism jumped from an experimental art into the mainstream. Philip Glass ('Music in Twelve Parts', 'Einstein on the Beach') and Steve Reich ('Drumming' and 'Music for 18 Musicians') brought their studies in non-Western music to bear on new works. Jazz artists also imbibed the global music scene, particularly Latin influences as seen in Carlos Santana and Chick Corea. Jazz and rock/soul, heavily influenced by Hendrix, made sustained connections for the first time to produce fusion jazz in the work of Weather Report: Miles Davis led the way with the otherworldly *Bitches Brew*.

Books

Fiction and poetry of the period reflected the general sense of crisis and unease, and even non-fiction writers projected a host of dystopian futures: the decade began with Alvin Toffler's *Future Shock*, followed by Garrett Hardin's books on overpopulation (*Mandatory Motherhood, The Limits of Altruism*), Stephen Schneider on the fears of a new Ice Age (*The Genesis Strategy*), and even critiques of the destructive new narcissism and atomized individualism launched by Tom Wolfe's period-defining essay 'The "Me" Decade and the Third Great Awakening' in 1976. This was followed by Christopher Lasch's *The Culture of Narcissism* (1979, and subtitled 'American Life in an Age of Diminishing Expectations'), which helped fuel the new cynicism with regard to politics that began after the 1974 publication of *All the President's Men* following Nixon's resignation. Other work attempted to alleviate the burdens of such self-examination by reassuring the reader *I'm OK, You're OK* (Thomas Harris's 1972 bestseller).

On a more utopian side of non-fiction writing, the self-help book craze was established by the 1972 *The Joy of Sex* and Wayne Dyer's *Your Erroneous Zones*, while Jim Fixx's *The Complete Book of Running* authorized jogging as the new sex (at least until his death by a heart attack – while jogging – in 1984). David Reuben's *Everything You Wanted to Know About Sex but Were Afraid to Ask* was the top non-fiction seller in 1970, and Shire Hite's 1976 *The Hite Report on Female Sexuality* promised to alleviate the decade's unease with the women's movement, but in the long run probably caused more anxiety than even the more apocalyptic tracts. Little wonder that self-help books (like Albert Ellis's *A Guide to Rational Living*) began to displace cookbooks and devotional literature. Alex Haley's *Roots* (1976) became a non-fiction phenomenon after its release as one of the most significant television events of the decade. But the biggest-selling work of non-fiction was Hal Lindsay's *The Late, Great Planet Earth*, which used the Book of Revelation to predict geopolitical events.

Fiction responded to the decline in optimism by introducing a new breed of existentialist anti-hero, best captured by John Updike's Rabbit Angstrom (in his *Rabbit, Redux* [1971]). The first of his 'Scarlet Letter' novels, reflecting on marriage, adultery and divorce, *A Month of Sundays*, appeared in 1975. Existentialist themes were also prominent in eco-fiction, with Edward Abbey's exploration of the ethics of complaisance versus sabotage in *The Monkey Wrench Gang*, and in the novels of minority experience such as Maxine Hong Kingston's *The Woman Warrior* and Leslie Marmon Silko's *Ceremony*. James Dickey's *Deliverance* opened the decade with scenes of sexual violence that would become more commonplace as censorship laws were relaxed. Joyce Carol Oates's *them*, which analysed the deadening effects of the 1960s on the American psyche, received the 1970 National Book Award. Kurt Vonnegut's absurdist depiction of contemporary life, established by the popularity of earlier works among the counterculture – especially *Slaughterhouse-5* (1969) – continued through the science fiction and time-travelling themes of *Breakfast of Champions* (1973) and *Jailbird* (1979). E. L. Doctorow slyly incorporated America's past heroes and heroines into *Ragtime* to put an irreverent slant on its history (and incidentally created a revival of Scott Joplin's music). William Styron revisited Auschwitz and European history in the 1980 National Book Award winner, *Sophie's Choice*. Saul Bellow continued to promote his brand of honourable intellectualism and humour (and to reap awards) with *Mr. Sammler's Planet* (National Book Award, 1971) and *Humboldt's Gift* (1975, Pulitzer Prize in the same year Bellow received the Nobel Prize). The self-conscious, meta-fictional and parodic style of American Postmodernism culminated with John Barth's *Chimera* (1972). It was followed the next year by Pynchon's *Gravity's Rainbow*, which would align Postmodernism with paranoia as its defining characteristic. Tim O'Brien's *Going after Cacciato* was the first award-winning novel of the Vietnam War (National Book Award, 1979). The arrival of Toni Morrison, with her explosive trilogy of 1970s novels (*The Bluest Eye*, *Sula* and *Song of Solomon*), marked the arrival of the post-Updike generation of American fiction.

Paperbacks became increasingly prevalent and pushed the sales of the decade's most popular fiction. The return to straightforward storytelling brought success to such period pieces as Erich Segal's *Love Story* and the decade-long bestseller by Richard Bach, *Jonathan*

Livingston Seagull. Paperback sales made names for William Peter Blatty (*The Exorcist*), Joseph Wambaugh (*The Onion Field*), Erica Jong (*Fear of Flying*), John Irvine (*The World According to Garp*), Herman Wouk (*War and Remembrance*), as well as Arthur Hailey, John le Carre, Peter Benchley, James Michener, Michael Crichton and – following the success of *Carrie* (1974) – a former Maine schoolteacher named Stephen King. Garry Trudeau won a Pulitzer in 1975 for his comic strip *Doonesbury*, the first cartoonist ever so honoured.

BOX 1.3: BESTSELLING FICTION BOOKS OF THE DECADE BY YEAR

Erich Segal, *Love Story* (1970)
Arthur Hailey, *Wheels* (1971)
Richard Bach, *Jonathan Livingston Seagull* (1972, 1973)
James Michener, *Centennial* (1974)
E. L. Doctorow, *Ragtime* (1975)
Leon Uris, *Trinity* (1976)
J. R. R. and Christopher Tolkien, *The Silmarillion* (1977)
James Michener, *Chesapeake* (1978)
Rod Ludlum, *The Matarese Circle* (1979)

Art

A plethora of new styles succeeded the dominance of Abstract Expressionism and Pop, and movements that gathered around ideologies more so than style or content marked the decade. New outlets for training and exhibitions opened and arts schools flourished, for example the Dia Art Foundation (established in 1974). The National Endowment for the Arts (NEA) reported that between 1970 and 1980 the number of artists as part of the American labour force increased by 81 per cent with expansion in all 50 states (though actual earnings from the arts declined along with most salaries during the period of recession). The Endowment was committed to bringing art and culture to the general population through greater funding of arts projects (the NEA's budget doubled between 1970 and 1971 and grew through the first half of the decade) and more educational television programming. Environmental art (Robert Smithson, James Turrell, Gordon Matta-Clark), graffiti art (SAMO, aka Jean-Michel Basquiat), feminist art (Judy Chicago), photorealism (Ralph Goings) and performance art (Vito Acconci, Joan Jonas, Cindy Sherman) all flourished, even as Pop (Roy Lichtenstein, James Rosenquist), Colour Field (Helen Frankenthaler) and Minimalism (Donald Judd, Richard Serra) continued to thrive. Warhol remained active in various fields (the *Mao Zedong* series appeared in 1973) and as cultural provocateur across the decade. Alexander Calder and Man Ray passed away in 1976 and Norman Rockwell died in 1978. Near the end of the decade, arts funding began to decline and the seeds were sown for Reagan's several attempts to defund the NEA and NEH (National Endowment for the Humanities) during the 1980s.

Architecture

High Modernism and the Postmodern existed in uneasy dialogue with one other, as the ill-fated World Trade Tower went up the same year (1972) that Robert Venturi and colleagues published the first edition of their anti-Modernist manifesto *Learning from Las Vegas* (the more widely read version appeared in 1977). With every Modernist Sears Tower that arose in clean perpendicular lines, another Postmodern, faux-historic ziggurat appeared like the Transamerica building in San Francisco. Houston's 'less is more' Penzoil Place, by High Modernist guru Philip Johnson, was countered by the bric-a-brac 'less is a bore' of Charles Moore's Piazza d'Italia in New Orleans. In faraway Santa Monica, Frank Gehry designed a house that influenced Postmodern styles into the next century. Mass-produced housing from the period, exemplified by the omnipresence of the one-storey ranch design, is today featured in many retro design movements (though few of these comply with the average 1,700-square-foot size of 1970s homes).

In terms of interior design, the 1970s are sometimes called 'the decade that taste forgot', but this actually indicated a significant shift in consumption from a generic Modernism to the more individualist pastiche of styles developed to serve emerging lifestyle choices.[7] One ancillary result was the growth of Interior

Design degrees offered at American colleges. As self-awareness and expression assumed the primary role in creating social identities, more experimentation could be expected in both corporate and domestic design as businesses and individuals sought a unique look. This sometimes reached exorbitant lengths, as with the characteristic DayGlow colours of everything from Saarinen Tulip chairs to bathroom fixtures (and yes, shag-covered toilet seats were a thing). Just as often, an enviro-friendly vibe would be sought and the design might feature macramé wall hangings and muted afghan rugs. (A nice balance of corporate and domestic period styles can be seen in the 2014 film *American Hustle*.)

BOX 1.4: EMERGING FILM STARS OF THE 1970s

Ellen Burstyn
Robert DeNiro
Robert Duval
Harrison Ford
Jody Foster
Gene Hackman
Diane Keaton
Harvey Keitel
Jack Nicholson
Al Pacino
Robert Redford
Meryl Streep

Film

The decade-long economic slump provided an unexpected boon to Hollywood in the first half of the decade as the conventional studios and their dominant production model began to collapse, ceding creative control to more independent directors. The 'new Hollywood' welcomed the work of Sidney Lumet (*Serpico, Dog Day Afternoon, Network*), Robert Altman (*M*A*S*H, Nashville, McCabe and*

Mrs. Miller), Martin Scorsese (Taxi Driver), Roman Polanski (Chinatown) and Francis Ford Coppola (The Godfather). Such films echoed, as Bruce Schulman notes, Bob Dylan's cry that 'the dream is over, the American Dream is over'[8] and emphatically displayed the growing cynicism toward traditional sources of authority, particularly the government, military and overly-simplified histories of the American West (Arthur Penn's *Little Big Man*, Tom Laughlin's *Billy Jack*) and the American family (Mike Nichol's *Carnal Knowledge*, Bryan Forbes's *The Stepford Wives*).

By decade's end, however, global corporations reasserted control over the studio production system and the hunt turned toward the blockbuster. The first of these, Steven Spielberg's *Jaws*, appeared in 1975 and was then topped by George Lucas's *Star Wars* in 1978. Both films (as was Spielberg's *Close Encounters of the Third Kind* [1977]) were accompanied by the first televised film advertisements and the saturation marketing of souvenirs and tie-ins with everything from fast food chains to toys to fashion. The successes of blockbusters like these and earlier hits like Lucas's *American Graffiti*, conversely, made directors like him and Spielberg increasingly independent, and both went on to form their own studios.

A decade dramatized by both rising crime rates and the white backlash against the rights movements was bound to produce its share of vigilante films, and the 1970s gave us Charles Bronson in *Death Wish* and the beginning of the *Dirty Harry* series with its signature tagline 'Do you feel lucky, punk?'. Scorsese's *Taxi Driver* was the self-conscious exploration of this genre and raised the form to art. But the genre also opened up possibilities for the first fully-independent black filmmakers by reversing the race polarities of the vigilante film to produce 'blaxploitation' films. The first was Melvin van Peebles' *Sweet Sweetback's Badasssss Song* (1971), while the most successful was Gordon Parks' *Shaft* (1971) featuring Richard Roundtree as the ultra-hip detective battling white criminals.

And if street revenge didn't satisfy the need to see contemporary crises played out as melodrama, one could turn to the spate of disaster movies – some of the highest-grossing films of their time – that began with *Airport* (1970) and continued unabated with *The Poseidon Adventure*, *The Towering Inferno*, *Earthquake* and *The Swarm*. The decade's experience with failed government and terrorism brought human-made disaster to the screen as well in *The China Syndrome*, *The Parallax View* and *Black Sunday*.

After the success of *The Godfather*, ethnically based stories saw renewed popularity, laying the groundwork for Sylvester Stallone's megahit, *Rocky* (based on a real promotional fight between Muhammad Ali and the hapless Chuck Wepner). The decade's strangest success story partakes of this genre, as *Saturday Night Fever* used the return of disco as the escape path for its hero, Tony Manero, from the cultural repression of his Italian heritage.

The 1970s also marked the regular appearance of feature-length films on television, beginning with *Gone With the Wind* in 1976, which drew huge home audiences. More insidious for the film industry's long-term prospects was the arrival of Home Box Office and the Betamax tape player, both in 1975. By 1977, VHS had become the standard tape format and the first commercial VCRs were available. As more and more films became obtainable for home viewing, consumers could catch them at their convenience. Hollywood countered by making their libraries available for distribution, and reaped huge profits in the short run.

Sport

The 1970s was a time of expansion and profitability for the major American sports (football, baseball, basketball) and featured some of the most memorable Olympics in modern history, although not always for athletic achievement. Money dominated as television contracts for local and national coverage of Major League Baseball, the NFL, NCAA football and professional and college basketball skyrocketed. In 1970, the Supreme Court dismissed Curt Flood's challenge to baseball's reserve clause, which dictated that ownership of the player's contract lay with the team. Momentum from the suit, however, eventually led to the concept of free agency for players, thus rewriting the relations between athlete and organization. As a result, by the end of the decade player salaries (sometimes tied to television profits) rose steeply, with many athletes earning more than $100,000 a year and some – like baseball's Pete Rose – negotiating contracts in excess of $1 million. With greater wealth came increased celebrity, and the decade saw an upsurge in athlete endorsements, perhaps most famously by football quarterback Joe Namath (everything from shaving cream to panty hose).

Baseball was dominated by the dynasties of the fledgling Oakland Athletics (consecutive championships in 1972–4) and then the Cincinnati Reds (1975–6). With the advent of free agency, George Steinbrenner used lucrative TV money to begin building a powerhouse with a revived Yankees team. Hank Aaron broke Babe Ruth's home run record with his 715th career blast, and Frank Robinson became, at the end of his illustrious playing career, the first African-American manager in the major leagues. In American football, dynasties came and went – the Vikings, Dolphins, Steelers, Raiders – but what is most remembered is a brand: the Dallas Cowboys assumed the mantle of 'America's Team' just as the 'rednecking' of the country reached its apex and the Sun Belt (along with country music and fried food) began to flaunt its cultural power.

The 1972 Munich Olympics entered history as the only Games to date invaded by terrorists when Palestinian gunmen killed two Israeli athletes and abducted nine others. The remaining captives and all but two of the terrorists were killed in a rescue attempt: sportscaster Jim McKay's doleful 'They're all gone' ended the continuous television coverage of the tragedy. Before that calamity, Mark Spitz (USA, swimming) and Olga Korbut (USSR, gymnastics) made history by their performances. Politics of another kind reared its head when the Soviet Union's contested defeat of the American basketball team (which had never lost the gold previously) turned into a political firestorm. The subsequent 1976 Games, held in Canada (Montreal) for the first time, were not spared, as South Africa was banned as a penalty for its continued enforcement of apartheid: this caused the boycott of an additional twenty-two African countries. In the meantime, the Romanian Nadia Comăneci produced electrifying performances in gymnastics, earning the first ever perfect score – and then six more perfect 10s. The boycott plague continued when the US refused to attend the 1980 Games in Moscow in protest against the Soviet incursion into Afghanistan. (The Soviet Union and a number of its satellites would return the favour by boycotting the 1984 Games in Los Angeles.)

The Winter Olympics, held in Sapporo, Japan in 1972 and Innsbruck, Austria in 1976, fared better politically. The 1976 Games are remembered in America primarily because Denver, reeling like many American cities from the recession despite the Bicentennial, pulled out for economic reasons from acting as host after it had been selected.

Professional boxing enjoyed its best (and perhaps final) comeback as Muhammad Ali continued to dominate the heavyweight division after coming out of forced retirement in 1970. His battles against the current champion, Joe Frazier – and produced by the impresario Don King – became part of boxing lore. The 1974 'Rumble in the Jungle' (vs. George Foreman) in Zaire not only went down as one of the sport's great fights, but as the first television programming to be continually broadcast via satellite. In other weight classes, Sugar Ray Leonard and Roberto Duran drew large audiences for their televised welterweight bouts.

An offshoot of the jogging craze begun by Jim Fixx, the New York Marathon, premiered in 1970 – it is now the largest race held in the world – and spawned hundreds of urban lookalikes. Billie Jean King defeated Bobby Riggs in the much-hyped 'Battle of the Sexes' tennis match in 1973.

Travel and leisure

Despite some horrific air disasters – crashes and hijackings – the decade was considered a golden age of air travel. The Boeing 747 took its maiden flight in 1970, enlarging capacity to over 500 and creating a business travel environment never surpassed. The sheer size of the 'Queen of the Skies' created lower fares, especially for overseas travel. In the meantime, the age of airport security also began as hijackings peaked in 1969 (82) and continued to plague carriers throughout the decade. Camping and beach vacations remained popular despite the gas pinch – it was the first decade when driving averages declined nationally – and when Americans drove cross-country they now often checked in with fellow drivers and truckers via CB radio. These skyrocketed in popularity after C. W. McCall's song 'Convoy' hit the airwaves in 1975 (fantasizing a working man's revolt against The Man) and the Burt Reynolds *Smokey and the Bandit* films premiered in 1977.

Fashion

Perhaps the greatest shift in fashion appeared with the first successful rhytidectomies after 1976: the improved modern facelift. But the 'Me Decade' produced numerous fashion trends – some painful to recount – and launched the careers of notable designers and brands such as Ralph Lauren and Calvin Klein (the latter introducing the concept of designer jeans). The period was dominated by the mainstreaming of the 1960s counterculture fashion: bell-bottomed jeans, leisure suits, platform shoes and the occasional mood ring. For men, wide was in: ample collars, lapels and ties. At the same time, men's clothing became tighter, more fitted, even more so after the introduction of polyester. For both sexes, hair tended to be big and expressive: longer locks, afros, fuzzy sideburns, exposed chest hair for men, stacked, permed or blow dried for women. The feathered 'Farrah' cut based on the star of *Charlie's Angels* created a million variants of flipped and flicked wings. College women experimented with hip-hugger bellbottoms and short skirts, while professional women went in the other direction and sported colourful pant suits, the shoulders of which built up steadily until becoming the outlandish sign of women's workplace equality in the 1980s.

Political events

Contexts

The 1970s presented a series of challenges to the values and cultural practices of the 'liberal consensus' that had held sway in America since Roosevelt's New Deal. This broad accord shaped the nation's domestic and foreign policy under both Republicans (such as Eisenhower and to some degree Nixon) and Democrats (Kennedy and especially Johnson).[9] Given its global economic and military dominance immediately following the war, the US could afford to sustain both high military spending (which climbed by 300 per cent beyond pre-Second World War levels and funded initiatives like NATO), low unemployment and generous social welfare programmes such as social security, public housing and – eventually – federal support for civil rights and programmes like the War on Poverty. Such gradual recalibrations, rather than substantial structural changes to capitalism and the social values it upheld, were seen as contributing to the eventual perfectibility of the American Way and consequently (quoting the title of a seminal study of the liberal consensus by Daniel Bell published at the outset of the 1960s) 'the end of ideology'.[10] Held together by anti-communist sentiment and policy as well as by classical liberalism's attachment to the values of competitive individualism and free markets – all of which mitigated the differences between liberal Democrats and moderate Republicans – the liberal consensus dominated the social, economic and cultural life of America between roughly 1948 and 1968. It produced the overweening confidence associated with America's global pre-eminence during the period, but also the 'Quiet Generation' of the 1950s, defined by its self-assured complacency and unwillingness to question seriously the nation's imperialist and sometimes racist policies, and to focus instead on personal status and the challenges to it.[11] Such foci help explain the almost single-minded attention paid in American drama during the period to social mobility, themes of belonging and alienation, and to the family as the barometer of personal development.

But hugely significant changes in the demographics of American society (massive migrations of minorities into American cities, an explosive population growth in the conservative Sun Belt, record numbers of women entering the workforce, among others) and, eventually, the fallout from the Vietnam War placed substantial pressure on the liberal consensus and led to its erosion. In its immediate wake during the 1970s, not only a great deal of public dissensus but also the increasing distance between American political parties originated at this time. The New Left emerged in the 1960s, made up of an unstable alliance between more radical Democrats previously connected with the Old Left socialists (drawn mostly from liberal Protestant traditions); the emerging student protest organizations (such as the Students for a Democratic Society); urban blacks and other minority groups; women's groups; and anti-war activists. While the arrival of the New Right had to wait until the later 1970s, the seeds were being planted across the decade for a revived populism focused on the values of patriotism alongside an ultraconservative desire to limit government by rolling back the welfare state and public sector unions and to support American Cold War defence budgets and military police actions abroad.[12] The beginnings of the New Right, which would emerge fully after Ronald Reagan's first election in 1980, issue from the powerful moneyed class from the Sun Belt, which saw itself as symbolizing the rebirth of the frontier spirit, retrieving American values of hard work and the conservation of traditional family values from the advocates of the welfare state located 'back East'. The dramatic sign of the so-called 'sunburning' of America, where economic and political power began to shift from the Northeast to the Sun Belt and its values, was the surprise elevation of businessman and Arizona senator Barry Goldwater as the Republican nominee for president in 1964.[13] A divisive figure in the history of the GOP, Goldwater was rejected by many prominent 'Rockefeller Republicans' who supported the liberal consensus, and lost the election to Lyndon Johnson in a landslide. But at an Ecumenical Prayer Breakfast in Los Angeles during the campaign, the political neophyte Ronald Reagan delivered a speech in support of Goldwater that so electrified the conservative base of the party that it was repeated for television. 'The Speech', as it came to be called (it was ranked alongside William Jennings Bryan's 1896 'Cross of Gold' oration), catapulted Reagan toward a successful 1966 California gubernatorial race and created the platform for the rise of the New Right. The 1964 election marked the return of bedrock American conservatism, but also what Richard Hofstadter – defending the liberal consensus now under siege – called the 'paranoid style' in American political thought.[14] In the wake of the rebelliousness and even lawlessness of the 1960s and early 1970s, the anti-liberal agenda would continue to gain strength and give Richard Nixon both a so-called 'Southern strategy' to propel him into the White House in 1968 as well as a putative 'silent majority' of conservatives to pit against the New Left during his presidency.[15] And after Nixon, every US president until Barack Obama would hail from the Sun Belt.

Perhaps as a consequence of this unweaving of the homogeneity of American culture, the decade is also regularly said to mark the recognition of the end of the 'American Century' and the arrival of cynicism and malaise with regard to political representation and the role of America on the world stage. One litmus test of this transformation might be found in the rise of American paranoia, as reflected in conspiracy theories, punk rock, films that proliferated in the 1970s like *Chinatown* and *The Parallax View*, and the increasing public suspicion regarding the threats of Big Government.[16] But not all the paranoia was based on fiction: like our own time, the 1970s existed under the shadow of worldwide terrorism, as evidenced by the activities of the Red Brigade and other terrorist groups in Europe. Closer to home, the Weathermen, New World Liberation Front and Symbionese Liberation Army all made regular US headlines and in 1974 alone there were 2,044 actual or attempted domestic bombings.

Thus, if we need not accept the stereotypes of the 1970s whole cloth, we can with hindsight see that several strands of the complex historical weave remain essential to understanding the period. First and foremost, the 1970s brought an end to the optimism and confidence that characterized America since the end of the Second World War. Referred to in histories of the decade as the 'death of the American Dream', 'The End of the Great American Ride', the 'Fallen Torch' and similar melodramatic metaphors, this turn toward despair, cynicism and sometimes apocalyptic foreboding is the result of numerous intersecting factors. Certainly America's defeat in Vietnam and the subsequent soul-searching that followed the final retreat weakened the sense of national exceptionalism. The flagging of the global economy and the rise of both high inflation and low employment ('stagflation'), fuelled by the two OPEC boycotts in 1973 and 1979 and increasingly high prices for oil, deprived many Americans of their characteristic hope for a better future. Nixon's disgrace after Watergate and the related scandals associated with high political office erased whatever remained of the idealistic belief that government was trustworthy and working in the people's best interests – and this would have far-reaching implications for the shift away from the liberal consensus and toward varieties of neoliberal, conservative and fundamentalist alternatives.

Events by year

1970

America's population exceeded 200 million for the first time, but the decade's low birth rate marked the end of the baby boom. Postal workers struck in March, flouting the existing law against federal workers taking part in industrial action. In April, the world watched with suspense as Apollo 13 aborted its planned landing on the Moon following an oxygen tank explosion and returned safely to Earth. On 4 May, National Guardsmen in the small college town of Kent, Ohio, shot and killed four, and wounded nine, unarmed students protesting against an escalation of the war in Vietnam. Exactly two weeks later, two students were killed and twelve wounded at Jacksonville State College (now University) in Mississippi. More than four million students and faculty across the nation went on strike to protest against the shootings. Earth Day was celebrated for the first time, the Corporation for Public Broadcasting came into operation and *Doonesbury* premiered. In September, 'Skyjack Sunday' saw Palestinian terrorists hijack four planes with more than 300 people taken hostage. Kate Millett published *Sexual Politics* while Germaine Greer contributed *The Female Eunuch*. Bela Abzug was elected to Congress and the London 'Miss World' contest was interrupted by feminist protesters. Alvin Toffler published *Future Shock* and introduced the notion of 'information overload' to describe the new post-industrial society awaiting Americans.

1971

President Nixon ended the Gold Standard monetary policy that had existed since 1944, thus severing the links between currencies and actual commodities and thereby unleashing enormous speculation in international currencies. Intended to combat growing inflation, the move is today generally seen as having contributed in the short term to the 'stagflation' that bedevilled the decade, and in the long term to having initiated the explosive growth of the financial sector in the American economy. At the Attica prison in New York state, inmates seized control and demanded political and humanitarian rights. After negotiations broke down, police stormed the prison, leaving thirty-three prisoners and ten correctional officers dead. The Surgeon General issued the first warnings regarding possible links between smoking and an increase in lung cancer. The 26th Amendment was passed and ratified, giving the vote to Americans eighteen years of age and older. *All in the Family* premiered on CBS in January, the first episode preceded by a prologue stating that the show 'seeks to throw a humorous spotlight on our frailties, prejudices and concerns. By making them the source of laughter, we hope to show, in mature fashion, just how absurd they are.' Lieutenant William Calley was found guilty on twenty-two counts of murder in the 1968 My Lai Massacre, and sentenced to life in prison: he served just three years before being released.

1972

Nixon enjoyed a roller-coaster year that began with his unexpected trip to China in February and the eventual normalization of relations between the two powers, followed by the May signing of the first Strategic Arms Limitation Treaty (SALT 1) and the first Anti-Ballistic Missile Treaty with the Soviets. Later in the year, on 17 June, five men were arrested during a burglary of the Democratic National Headquarters in the Watergate office complex in Washington, DC. In May, Arthur Bremer shot conservative Democratic presidential candidate George Wallace five times, paralysing him for life and effectively ending a campaign that was picking up steam. *Ms.* magazine was founded and the Equal Rights Amendment sent to states for ratification that never came. Capital punishment was ruled arbitrary and a violation of the 8th Amendment governing cruel and unusual punishment by the Supreme Court. Over 600 death sentences were commuted and the death penalty suspended until being reinstated in 1976. Shirley Chisholm became the first African-American female presidential candidate, but Nixon was re-elected by a landslide over George McGovern and Wallace in November. Apollo 17 returned safely to Earth and became the last manned mission to the Moon to this point in human history. Widespread strikes hit General Motors, especially at the Lordstown, OH, plants where workers asked for more humane working conditions. For the first time, the Sun Belt saw the highest population growth.

1973

The Supreme Court, in *Roe v. Wade*, ruled that abortion is legal and cannot be banned by individual state laws. In February, activists with the American Indian Movement (AIM) occupied the town of Wounded Knee on the Pine Ridge reservation in South Dakota. They remained for 71 days, during which deadly gunfire was exchanged regularly with FBI agents and US marshals. America's twelve-year ordeal in Vietnam came to a formal close with the signing of the Paris Peace Accords in January (the Accords were never ratified by the US Senate). Watergate quickly escalated into the political scandal of the century: Nixon's secret Oval Office tapes were discovered soon after the Watergate hearings began, and led to the 20 October 'Saturday Night Massacre' in which one special prosecutor (Archibald Cox) was fired and two Attorneys General (Eliot Richardson and William Ruckelshaus) resigned. Vice-President Spiro Agnew was forced to resign for separate acts of malfeasance (tax evasion and an ensuing cover-up) and Congressman Gerald Ford of Michigan was named vice-president. Late in the year, the oil consortium OPEC announced an oil embargo of the Unites States in retaliation for the support the US had given Israel during the Yom Kippur War. Oil prices immediately soared from $3 to nearly $12 per barrel. In May, Skylab was launched into low orbit, where it hosted four missions; however, due to increased solar activity, the vehicle (scheduled to last for ten years or more) suffered a degraded orbit and plunged to Earth in 1979 – a not uncommon metaphor for the decade's aspirations.

1974

Daylight Savings Time began in January in response to the oil embargo, as did mandatory 55-mph highway speed limits. Also in January the House Judiciary Committee voted for three Articles of Impeachment: in July the first was recommended and on 9 August Nixon resigned. Vice-President Gerald Ford became president and on 8 September pardoned Nixon. A federal judge ordered mandatory busing in Boston in order to desegregate its schools, and the city and nation roiled in some of the worst racial conflicts since the early civil rights movement. In Kanawha County, West Virginia, a massive school boycott set urban secularists against rural conservatives (whose children were being bused to Charleston) when controversies over school textbooks inflamed local school boards and pastors. Miners went on strike in support of the boycott and several schools were bombed. The economy officially moved into recession, taking away the last hope of labour to sustain its efforts to improve workplace conditions and pay.

1975

In response to oil insecurity, construction of the Trans-Alaska pipeline began. The situation in South Vietnam continued to deteriorate after America formally withdrew, and on 30 April Saigon fell to the North Vietnamese communists. Images of the panicked retreat of American civilians and military and CIA operatives still in the country were broadcast around the world and left a lasting scar on the American psyche. President Ford survived two assassination attempts, the first by Lynette 'Squeaky' Fromme, a holdover from the Charles Manson cult of the 1960s. The CIA was judged complicit in the 1973 overthrow of Chilean president Salvador Allende, who died in the coup. California passed the Agricultural Labour Relations Act, bringing to fruition years of organizing and work stoppages by César Chávez and the United Farm Workers. At the same time, unemployment peaked at its highest rate nationally since 1941. New York City teetered on the edge of default after President Ford first refused a federal bailout before relenting late in the year. Apollo and Soviet Soyuz astronauts linked up and docked vehicles in space. American military academies were opened to women for the first time, and 44 per cent of married American women were employed throughout the economy.

1976

In the year of the American Bicentennial, Jimmy Carter upset Gerald Ford to become the 39th president. The first personal computer, the Commodore PET, appeared in retail stores, and 'Micro-soft' became a registered trademark. The first Son of Sam casualty was discovered in New York City. The initial outbreak of Legionnaires disease killed twenty-nine conventioneers in Philadelphia. *Time* designated 1976 the 'Year of the Evangelical'. The death penalty was reinstated.

1977

The Northeast suffered a massive blackout during which – unlike the 1965 event – widespread looting and violence occurred, providing more images of an America whose social fabric had decayed. Soon after, President Carter created the cabinet-level Department of Energy, but protesters delayed the opening of the Seabrook Nuclear Power facility (the Trans-Alaskan pipeline, however, was completed). Carter pardoned the majority of Vietnam War draft dodgers. Apple Computers, founded in a Los Altos, CA, garage, was incorporated by Steve Jobs and Steve Wozniak: but on 'Black Monday' (19 September), the Campbell Steel Works of Youngstown Sheet and Tube shut its doors, heralding the steady decline of American manufacturing. The convicted murderer Gary Gilmore was executed by firing squad in Utah after demanding his sentence be carried out – the first state execution in ten years.

1978

The Senate voted to return the Panama Canal to Panamanian control despite strong opposition from Ronald Reagan, who had used the issue to raise visibility for his failed bid for the Republican presidential nomination in 1976. The *Bakke* case was heard by the Supreme Court, which upheld the principles of affirmative action but weakened its implementation. President Carter helped broker the Camp David Peace Agreement between Israeli prime minister Menachem Begin and Egyptian president Anwar Sadat. Carol Wotyla was elected pope, becoming the first non-Italian pope since the Renaissance. In an unexpected victory, Howard Jarvis led the California state ballot initiative known as 'Prop 13' to a landslide victory, thus mandating lower property taxes in the state. It was the first step in the 'Tax Revolution' that would help sweep Ronald Reagan into office two years later. In Guyana, the Reverend Jim Jones led more than 900 of his cult followers in mass suicide when they collectively drank cyanide-laced Kool-Aid.

1979

In early March, just twelve days after the film *The China Syndrome* opened, the Three Mile Island nuclear power plant in Pennsylvania suffered a partial core meltdown, the worst nuclear power accident in the world until Chernobyl. Chrysler successfully negotiated a bankruptcy bailout from the Federal government. Ninety Western hostages (sixty-three American) were taken at the American Embassy in Iran in retaliation for the US allowing the recently deposed Shah to seek cancer treatment in America. The event marked the beginning of a 444-day ordeal that would play out until the day of Ronald Reagan's inauguration in January 1981, and initiated a second energy crisis and oil embargo. President

Carter addressed the nation mid-year and diagnosed a 'crisis of confidence' in the electorate owing largely to the energy crisis. Although he did not use the term, the televised talk quickly became known as the 'malaise' speech and an indictment of the Me Decade. The Strategic Arms Limitations Treaty (SALT 2) was signed, but in December Soviet forces entered Afghanistan to quell a nationalist uprising and America refused to ratify the agreement. After America helped arm the Muhajideen, Russian forces remained for ten years and suffered heavy casualties. The prime interest rate hit 21.5 per cent, the highest in history. George Wallace proclaimed he was born again and apologized to black civil rights leaders for his 1963 stand at the schoolhouse door at the University of Alabama in support of school segregation. Jerry Falwell announced the formation of the Moral Majority, whose primary aim was to defeat liberal candidates for local, state and national office. In a fitting end to the decade, Francis Ford Coppola's *Apocalypse Now* won the Academy Award for Best Picture.

Media

Television

Until the middle of the decade there were only three nationally broadcast channels of entertainment and news: the three syndicated national networks (ABC, CBS and NBC). Larger cities had one or more local channels, and the Corporation for Public Broadcasting (PBS) began to generate content in 1970 and displaced National Education Television as the largest distributor of educational programming. PBS not only introduced *Sesame Street* (beginning in November 1969) but carried live coverage of the Watergate hearings. The first crack in the domination of the national networks appeared in 1972, when a small cable-TV operation in the Northeast broadcast blacked-out sporting events to its subscribers as well as films like the 1971 *Sometimes a Great Notion*. Eventually broadcasting from satellite, Home Box Office (HBO) was available in all fifty states by 1980 and was quickly followed by Showtime, the Movie Channel and other cable- and satellite-based stations. Cable also fed the growing interest for niche content, feeding, among other interest groups, the ascending Christian Right.

The decade began with the launch of Norman Lear's comedy *All in the Family*, which for most of the decade was a flashpoint for many pressing social issues: race and the white backlash, Vietnam, rising crime and the growing conservative tide. Although intended to skewer Archie Bunker's overt racism and misogyny, many viewers (including President Nixon) empathized with the character as a spokesperson for the silent majority. A year later, in 1972, the Korean War became the setting for *M*A*S*H*, based on Robert Altman's thinly veiled anti-Vietnam War film (itself based on the Richard Hooker novel of 1970). While lacking the acerbic wit and absurdist tone of the film, the television version kept the memory of Vietnam and American military misadventures in mind. It received numerous awards and its finale (a two-and-a-half-hour movie broadcast in 1983) garnered the largest audience in the history of television broadcasting to that date (125 million). Flip Wilson became the first African-American to host a nationally broadcast variety show (*The Flip Wilson Show*, 1970–4), which arrived just as the iconic *The Ed Sullivan Show* ended its dominance. The year 1973 brought the first reality show with the debut of *This American Family*, featuring the Louds of Santa Barbara, CA. During the show's run, one son came out as gay, the husband was revealed as a serial adulterer and the final episode featured the wife demanding a divorce. Joining the shift away from rural-based comedies and melodramas (CBS spent the decade fleeing its reputation as the 'hillbilly channel' of *The Beverly Hillbillies*, *Green Acres* and *Hee-Haw*) to the younger and more urban sensibilities of *The Flip Wilson Show* and *M*A*S*H*, the improvisational sketch comedy *Saturday Night Live!* premiered in October 1975. The show reached a share of 39 per cent by 1978 and its antic tone made stars of Chevy Chase, Dan Ackroyd and John Belushi, while also bringing uncharacteristic attention to its female comedic artists, Lorraine Newman, Gilda Radner and Jane Curtain.

These exceptions notwithstanding, however, the decade retained continuity with television's past, filling up the daytime hours with game shows and soap operas and the evening with detective serials (*Mannix*, *Ironside*, *Baretta*) and situation comedies (*Bridget Loves Bernie*, *Happy Days*, *Three's Company*), even as the staple Westerns (like *Gunsmoke* and *Bonanza*) began to decline. But even traditional shows skewed contemporary, with afternoon soaps increasingly addressing topical themes such as women's liberation, birth control and abortion; detective shows featuring the disabled Ironside and the wisecracking anti-hero of *The Rockford Files*; and situation comedies relocating from the suburbs and rural areas (*The Dick Van Dyke Show*, *Petticoat Junction*) to cities like Minneapolis. It was there that *The Mary Tyler Moore Show* (its eponymous star played Van Dyke's wife) made TV history by focusing on the travails and triumphs of a single woman whose life was determined by work and friends rather than love interests and homemaking. Counterbalancing such progressive fare was the advent of 'jiggle TV' such as *Charlie's Angels* and *Three's Company*. Out of nowhere, seemingly, Robin Williams appeared as Mork on *The Mork and Mindy Show* in 1978 and revolutionized television comedy.

The network news shows retained their basic structure: an authoritative and objective white male (Walter Cronkite, John Chancellor) reading the news with sparse media breaks or outside reports. However, the 'news magazine' that arrived with *60 Minutes* in 1968 (and which filled the void left by the decline of mass-circulation magazines) expanded in popularity and breadth (*20/20* premiered in 1978) and welcomed female reporters like Barbara Walters, who went on to become the first female co-anchor of a national nightly news broadcast.

Out of the circuit of regular programming, special broadcasts like the successive Moon landings dominated the schedule. After a significant decline in viewership between the first and second missions, the Apollo 13 disaster of 1972 brought a different kind of spectatorship to NASA. Thereafter the remaining missions (Apollo 14–17) drew fewer and fewer viewers, and television was not much affected by the budget-based cancellations of Apollo flights 18–20. Another TV special, based on a novel by Alex Haley, created a more lasting impression: the new genre of the 'telefilm' (or miniseries) appeared with *Roots* (1977), nominated for 37 Emmys and responsible for bringing both black history and family genealogy into vogue. But the longest-lasting innovation in special programming was the arrival of *Monday Night Football* in 1970. The event made stars of broadcasters Howard Cosell and Don Meredith and forever changed the definition of the weekend.

Radio

Higher-fidelity FM radio increased in popularity and impact, eventually surpassing AM stations and leaving the latter to host mostly talk and news programming. Casey Kasem premiered *American Top 40* in 1970, and by 1980 the show was carried by more than 500 stations. The splintering of popular music styles was reflected by the niche broadcasting formats that emerged: stations devoted solely to country, gospel, soul, disco, rock, religious broadcasts, folk, jazz and the newly-minted 'easy listening'. In 1970, fewer than ten formats existed, but by the end of the decade this had grown to 133.

Print

Newspapers were still the primary vehicle for daily news, although televised news became more popular. Bernstein and Woodward's uncovering of the Watergate scandal brought prestige to news reporting during a decade when civic trust in institutions was generally flagging. Nevertheless, spurred on by Spiro Agnew's public indictments of the 'liberal media', news organizations eventually fell prey to suspicion from both the Right and Left. Women made inroads into the male-dominated and clubby environment of journalism. Katherine Graham turned the *Washington Post* into a major news organ and approved the release of Daniel Ellsburg's Pentagon Papers after courts denied the right to the *New York Times*. Hunter S. Thompson revamped the 'New Journalism' of Tom Wolfe and others from the 1960s to develop his unique brand of 'gonzo journalism' – highly subjective and distorted reporting (often under the influence of benzedrine) that laid the groundwork for later 'docu-fiction'.

Science and technology

NASA, still riding the success of the 1969 manned Moon landing, sent ten more men to the lunar surface and successfully returned the damaged Apollo 13 craft to Earth with no fatalities. The unmanned Voyager I and II probes were sent beyond the outer planets of the solar system, the second carrying the iconic Golden Record bearing a greeting to other life forms (in 2015, Voyager II stood 1.62×10^{10} miles from the Sun). In 1976, Viking I landed on Mars and sent back the first images of the surface of the red planet.

But from NASA and elsewhere, new inventions defined the decade in terms of its technological advances. The first digital watches and pocket calculators appeared, and microwave technology entered American homes. After the development of the first general microprocessor (the Intel 4004, 1971), the 'C' programming code and Unix operating system followed. The age of home computing began with the arrival of the iconic Apple I (1976) and Apple II (1977) computers, along with the Commodore PET and Atari 400/800 – the latter making possible the golden age of video games. New developments in fibre optics transformed global communications.

In biology, the first DNA genome was sequenced and the first genetically altered bacteria were produced. Medicine saw the first use of MRI technology while the development of PET (positron emission tomography) revolutionized cancer research. Smallpox was declared eradicated globally in 1979. The first test tube baby produced by in vitro fertilization (IVF), Louise Joy Brown, was born in the UK in 1978. In 1972, after decades of controversy over the viability of amygdalin-based Laetrile as a cancer drug, the US Food and Drug Administration refused to approve it and shut down clinics advocating its use. In a decade filled with conspiracy theories, advocates for the drug asserted that the FDA had colluded with Big Pharma and the medical community to suppress the cancer cure in the name of profits: the questioning of science that erupted, often funded by conservative libertarian groups, still crops up today with regard to climate change and vaccines.

In 1975, a relatively unknown researcher at IBM working on problems ranging from fluid dynamics to price fluctuations in cotton markets and information theory coined the word *fractal* to describe geometrical figures whose irregular shapes evinced patterns of self-similarity. He published some of his ideas on such 'orderly disorder', first in France and then, in 1977, in the US under the title *Fractals: Form, Chance and Dimension*. Two years later, Benoit Mandelbrot used a powerful computer to generate the fractal that would forever bear his name, the Mandelbrot Set, and revised his book as *The Fractal Geometry of Nature* (1982).

A decade that began in disorder ended in a new understanding of the orders within chaos, an interpretation that – like much of the dramatic literature produced in the period – seemed to revel in irregularity while also disclosing deep and complex pockets of order.

2

American Theatre in the 1970s

Mike Vanden Heuvel

Setting the stage: The political and social context

Like every period broadly designated by decade or linked causally primarily by major events, the 1970s in America produced its share of iconic images and stereotypes. The most robust of these present a decade characterized by a benign period of lassitude, broken up by brief eruptions of strife and discontent, marking a holding action between the tumultuous 1960s and the 'new day in America' that heralded the Reagan revolution and the rise of the political Right in the United States beginning in the 1980s. But striking images and abridged narratives produce simplified historical readings and risk creating narratives that retrofit tidy ideological patterns. Thus an otherwise readable and wide-ranging book like David Frum's *How We Got Here: The Decade that Brought You Modern Life (For Better or For Worse)* quite explicitly takes as its target for everything that happened in the 1970s the general dumbing-down and waning of American common sense: but it does so to better construct a salvationist account centred on the rise of the New

Right and Reagan's accomplishments.¹ In a similar vein, historians like Todd Gitlin cannot help but narrate the 1970s as a falling off from the passion and politics of the 1960s (as provided in the moving *The Sixties: Years of Hope, Days of Rage*), with the Left thereafter wandering in the desert of identity politics while Reagan and the Right dominate until the revival of 'Occupy activism' in more recent years.² For labour historians such as Jefferson Cowie and Aaron Brenner, on the other hand, the 1970s can only be read as a disastrous decade that, despite the more than 5,000 labour strikes it saw, resulted in historical setbacks for organized labour.³

The simple fact is that the 1970s was never so simple: for Beth Bailey and David Farber 'the 1970s may be our strangest decade ... an era of incoherent desires, and even a fair amount of self-flagellation'.⁴ Certainly American art, and American playwriting in particular, could be defined by similar terms. Perhaps for this reason a truly nuanced picture of the decade could not be realized immediately, and instead the 1970s became a catchword, even before the decade's end, for emptiness, vacuity, 'stagflation' and ennui: a 'Pinto of a decade' according to Howard Juncker, aptly comparable to that 'perfect Seventies symbol ... the Pet Rock, which just sat there doing nothing'.⁵ Before going on to complicate such narratives, Bruce Schulman characterizes the 1970s as 'an eminently forgettable decade', an era of 'bad clothes, bad hair, and bad music impossible to take seriously'.⁶ Only after several decades' worth of hindsight have historians been able to produce more complete and complex views of the period that show how pivotal the decade has been in the development of American culture.

In fact, the 1970s ushered in a great historical transformation by mollifying the radical utopianism of the 1960s and redirecting its central message of personal liberation toward what George Packer calls 'the sovereignty of the free market and private life'.⁷ This set the stage for not just the Reagan revolution but the ensuing neoliberal culture that dominates American social and political life in the twenty-first century. During the 1970s both the American Left and Right, perhaps out of simple weariness with the fraught violence and roiling politics of the 1960s, each found ways to forge a separate peace with that decade by transforming its radical rebellious spirit into a less threatening ethos of individualism. Political ideology came to be defined as whatever created the best means by which to exercise individual freedom, and identities formerly established by political beliefs and social class were transformed into lifestyle choices. Thus, the 1960s counterculture's animus against corrupt government could be co-opted by the New Right and converted into a movement to remove government interference from otherwise free markets, as well as from legislating morality. Once wedded to the rising Christian Right, this rejection of the liberal consensus that had shaped American life since the Second World War laid the foundation for the rise of neoconservatism and the evangelical-based Tea Party that began in the 1990s. For the Left, the countercultural lifestyle alternatives promoted in the 1960s formed the new barometer of political health, as fresh opportunities to exercise choice became entwined with political rights. Class struggle lost its primary position in radical politics, to be replaced by affiliations with one's ethnic, gender, sexual preference or subculture group, and the battles – in the 1970s fought more often in the courts than in the streets – emphasized the freedom to choose such associations and to identify one's politics with the liberty to express them. To this day, the brightest line dividing Americans remains whether one decides to support 'freedom from' or 'freedom to'; and yet, as Packer wrote, 'By the end of the 70's, the self-liberations that had originated in the 60's were merely "lifestyle choices," and they easily fused with the Sun Belt spirit of individualism.'[8]

The progress initiated by the civil rights movement of the 1960s also led to unexpected consequences during the 1970s, as the idea of 'integration' seemed to fail in light of the desegregation efforts in public education and the furore over school busing. Eventually, the ideal of integration would give way, in Schulman's phrase, to the concept of 'diversity'.[9] The earlier civil rights model that envisioned all races (and by extension ethnicities and subcultures) having the equal right to assimilate as 'Americans' was gradually transformed by the broadening rights movement until it found itself displaced by the new focus on 'difference' and identity politics. While in an earlier play like *A Raisin in the Sun* (1959) the merits of integration were a given, following the increasing violence of the civil rights movement, the emergence of Malcolm X and the Black Panthers and the assassination of Martin Luther King in 1968, a trajectory toward separatism and cultural nationalism was well established by the opening of the 1970s. Rather than validating progress by the metric of integration, which to many non-whites, women and gay citizens increasingly appeared to be a fatal compromise that confirmed the dominant culture, the focus turned instead toward raising consciousness of one's own difference from the mainstream and to restoring pride and historical place to that position of alterity. In addition to endorsing ethnic rights for blacks, Latinos, Asian-Americans and Native Americans, movements gathered support promoting women's rights as well as gay and lesbian identities (if not yet those for transgender individuals), among others, as well as political, economic and cultural rights for special interest groups like the disabled and the aged. Even the environment was said to have rights that could not be superseded, leading to the first Earth Day celebration in 1970 and the growing environmental movement across the decade. The arts, including theatre, played an important role as the cultural arm of the black power movement, a site for women's liberation and consciousness-raising, a rallying point for gay liberation and movements initiated on behalf of Chicano/a, Native American and Asian-American identity formation.

Collectively, then, America in the 1970s would sometimes feel itself being pulled apart from exacerbating tensions both internal and external to the country. Yet in the long run, these centrifugal forces would serve to enhance and dignify the diversity of its people and its art.

American theatre(s): Devolution and evolution

Like the sometimes blithe comparisons made between the radical events of the 'years of hope/days of rage' of the 1960s as opposed to the seemingly more quiescent 1970s, accounts of American theatre often draw invidious comparisons between the vital period of experimental, political and Off-Off-Broadway theatre that characterized the earlier decade as distinct from what evolved out of it during the 1970s. Matthew Roudané catches the tone perfectly when he writes that 'many dramatists felt that the idealism of the 1960s was all over for a wayward America whose children increasingly seemed buried in some deep political pit'.[10] Mark Fearnow, in an otherwise excellent overview of 1970s theatre, goes so far as to say that, following 'a drama of radical questioning and idealism' during the 1960s, '[t]he 1970s flooded those dream estates with pessimism, ushering in what might be called a "drama of malaise"'.[11]

But if the break-up and questioning of the national consensus is the dominant motif of the decade, then in American theatre as well as society the result was an exciting moment of reconfiguration and a dynamic period of expansion and change as everything from funding to audiences and aesthetics could be rethought. The 1970s saw the decline and rebound of Broadway theatre; the further evolution of the Off- and Off-Off-Broadway movements; the emergence of a new generation of playwrights who experimented with, and ultimately altered, the long-standing dominance of American realist theatre; the explosive growth and maturation of the resident professional theatre movement; and the second and most significant stage of experimental live art performance. As smaller theatres focused on new work and formerly-marginalized voices proliferated, the 1970s saw the coming-of-age of the Black Arts Movement, Chicano theatre, feminist theatre and the first signs of nascent American Indian and Asian-American theatre. As Samuel Leiter points out in his indispensible guide to New York-based theatre of the decade, the period was 'enormously rich in controversies, developments and talent ... fascinating and important changes were being made in every corner of the profession'.[12]

The 1960s left American theatre more fragmented than ever, but also potentially more vibrant. In New York City alone, still widely considered the hub of dramatic activity and the gold standard for theatre professionals, the dominance of Broadway had begun to decentralize slowly during the 1950s and 1960s to Off-Broadway and, later, Off-Off-Broadway. These in turn would feed the more amorphous 'alternative' theatre scene that included in its first stage companies like the Living Theater and the initial crossover performance forms of Happenings and performance art, and in the following years produced Richard Schechner's Performance Group (and later, under Elizabeth LeCompte, the Wooster Group), Squat Theatre, Ping Chong, Charles Ludlam's Ridiculous Theatre, Robert Wilson's Byrd Hoffman School of Byrds and Richard Foreman's Ontological-Hysteric Theatre, among others.[13] This gave proof of a decline in the power of Broadway to shape the theatrical landscape by presenting innovative new work in alternative spaces and paved the way for greater devolution to come.

Yet the allure and prestige of writing for the Broadway stage never disappeared entirely, and the 1970s continued the tradition of earlier playwrights who followed a trajectory from the margins to the mainstream and culminated in the iconic Broadway success. A number of the new cohort of dramatists gravitated to Broadway from the 'Offs', such as two of the playwrights featured in this book (Sam Shepard and David Rabe), along with Arthur Kopit, Lanford Wilson and John Guare; or, alternatively, they arrived from the non-profit residential houses outside New York (David Mamet, Ntozake Shange, A. R. Gurney, Tina Howe, Marsha Norman, Christopher Durang and Romulus Linney). What was different, and quite remarkable, about the appearance of these writers in the commercial theatre was the degree to which they were able to transfer some of the innovation and experimental energy of their pre-Broadway work to the staid and sometimes formulaic fare that dominated Broadway. Even accounting for the signal achievements in form and content launched by O'Neill, Miller and Williams between the 1950s and the 1970s, commercial theatres generally sought out relatively well-made plays that focused on the development of character within a recognizable social milieu, and usually fixated on the internal life and relations of the protagonists at the expense of current social and political events. Plays that evoked nostalgia, rather than a truly critical look at America's history and culture, carried the day and provided an important form of social cohesion (at least for the cadre of social, political and intellectual elites who engaged with serious American drama at a time when both this class and American theatre were densely located in and around the Northeast corridor).

In responding to the turmoil wrought by the 1960s, the infrastructure of American theatre, like the political consensus, began to divide and splinter. The first changes took place in New York, where the relationship between Broadway, Off-Broadway and Off-Off-Broadway was altered in ways that created new paths to access and cultural capital for American playwrights. Modelled on these relationships, the slowly evolving regional theatre movement in America took flight during the 1960s and 1970s to further reduce the centrality of Broadway as the ultimate site of new dramatic writing. Finally, forms of performance with little or no relationship to Broadway, but with strong connections to movements in related arts such as film, dance and installation art, began to emerge in the 1960s and developed during the 1970s into the phenomenon of performance art.[14] Collectively, these and other forces would alter forever the status and function of Broadway and make room for the incredibly diverse worlds of theatre and performance that dominate the American cultural sector today.

Broadway: Infrastructure

Even as the significance of Broadway as the sole crucible for new work and ideas lessened, ticket prices increased regularly to support rising labour and production costs. What diversity there was in audiences was reduced even further to an increasingly narrow slice of upper middle-class (and white) spectators and the occasional tourist group. The infrastructure of the theatre district also declined dramatically as New York faced bankruptcy by 1975: pictures and media coverage from the period notoriously featured red-light porn shops, massage parlours and a city fabric that was all but shredded by crime, vagrancy and neglect.[15] In the first three years of the decade the area was almost dark on some nights as the energy crisis forced the dimming of the few marquee lights in use. Leiter hardly overstates when he reports that 'Times Square was the blighted symbol of the putrid mess into which the Broadway district was evolving. Garbage was piled high on Broadway's once fabled streets; pornography, prostitution and drugs were easily available on sidewalks and in the doorways ... theatrical producer Leo. H. Shull called [the Broadway District in Times Square] "Slime Square".'[16] Audiences often feared to enter the playhouse district at night: in 1975, when Mayor Ed Beame was threatening to lay off 10,000 officers of the NYPD, its union published and distributed a pamphlet entitled 'Fear City: A Survival Guide for Visitors to the City of New York', which instructed tourists on the rising crime rates, recommended that no one walk in the city (while also advising everyone to 'avoid public transportation') and suggested a 6 pm curfew.[17] The unheard-of notion of beginning plays earlier than the sacrosanct 8.30 pm schedule was considered mainly to avoid post-show muggings. During Game 2 of the 1977 World Series at Yankee Stadium, ABC-TV's cameras cut to one of the many fires ignited in vacant buildings by arsonists for insurance purposes, and Howard Cosell notoriously announced, 'There you have it ladies and gentlemen: the Bronx is burning.'[18]

As the infrastructure crumbled and audiences turned to less expensive forms of entertainment such as television – which remediated the most popular forms of American performance like the variety show and the revue – theatres darkened and did not reopen. In 1971 the Lincoln Center for the Performing Arts Board overseeing the sprawling complex of arts venues considered turning the Vivian Beaumont Theatre (open for all of six years) into a complex of movie houses. Historical theatres closed and city government was forced to stem the decline by offering incentives (such as zoning variances to build higher towers) to construct, not new theatres, but more often mixed-use, high-rise buildings that housed theatre facilities on the ground floor. Profits dropped 18 per cent in the first half of the decade, and both the number of shows and the average length of performance runs plummeted. In the wake of the Baumol Report of 1972,[19] reduced-price ticketing policies were put into effect to bring in new audiences with middling impact, although the arrival in 1973 of the TKTS booth in Duffy Square on 42nd Street, supported by the Theatre Development Fund (established in 1968), marked the origin of an iconic structure. Artists and theatre labourers all took part in massive anti-pornography marches to push the X-rated houses out of Times Square, and various city planners proposed new configurations for 42nd Street; but Broadway remained for most of the decade a far cry from today's gleaming and Disneyesque public space of upscale theatres, restaurants, IMAX houses and high-end retail outlets selling, in addition to jewellery and fashionable clothing, the tie-in merchandise that now appears alongside every successful musical spectacle.

Still, there appeared signs of life in the commercial theatre by the second half of the decade. New methods for financing productions emerged, sometimes soliciting large numbers of small donors ('angels'), but more often depending upon the economic muscle of corporate theatre owners like the Shuberts to leverage combinations of private and public subsidy. Sponsorship of shows and theatres was advertised by corporations in show programmes and ads. Sunday matinees became more widespread, bringing in new suburban audiences on a day when theatres were traditionally dark. As Off- and then Off-Off-Broadway performance spaces proliferated, 'The Street' at first faced increased competition for the niche market of audiences interested in the latest developments in playwriting and performance practices. Rather than compete with the Offs, most Broadway theatres doubled down on the strategy of sifting through a combination of tried-and-true hits to revive (often British), musicals to develop into moneymakers, and transfers of recognized Off- and Off-Off successes to produce for long runs and thereby cover production costs and realize profits. However, those same alternative theatres also helped to create a new generation – and a new diversity – of spectators, a percentage of whom moved up to Broadway shows as the offerings became marginally more diverse in terms of content as well as ethnic and gender representation. These included transfers of the biggest Off and Off-Off musicals such as *Hair*, which came to Broadway in 1968 directed by Tom O'Horgan, long a fixture in the Off-Off scene. For these and a variety of economic and cultural reasons, Broadway first struggled back to life by mid-decade and then experienced an adolescent surge of growth as theatre houses reopened or were newly-built, audiences began to flock back into the District and the number of new openings – if not new work – increased dramatically.

But this would turn out to be a prolonged pubescence, one for which few would venture the opinion that much growing up actually took place. Instead, buoyed by just enough hits to offset the still-considerable rate of failed shows, Broadway producers took note of the formula for their success and recognized that the risk associated with opening new work was not necessary to bring in sufficient audiences. Indeed, the 1970s might be recognized as the period during which the transformation of Broadway into solely a commercial venture with no pretence of operating as a cultural institution culminated, or at least began to be acknowledged widely as such (recall that the original film satirizing the economics of Broadway, Mel Brooks's *The Producers*, appeared in 1968). Gerald Berkowitz quotes from a 1996 interview with the producer Alexander Cohen describing the situation that arose in the 1970s:

> The Shuberts do not originate projects. They look at projects. They go to London and say, 'Oh, it's *Skylight* [by David Hare] – one set, three characters; that ought to do it. Let's put up the money.' And they put up the money, and then the London producer, in this case the National Theatre, sends the show over, supervises it, and puts it on.[20]

As one result, during this decade Broadway turned away from its historical role as an important incubator of a specifically American drama (perhaps stunned by the 1973–4 season, during which, as Leiter reports, 'not a single American play was a commercial success')[21] and sought, without national bias, to showcase commodities from other parts of the globe, particularly Britain. When it did stage new American work, one could be sure it had premiered successfully elsewhere before Broadway producers would risk inflating its production costs and salaries for star performers to bring it to their large houses for lengthy runs. The few new American plays that succeeded under these circumstances and which premiered on Broadway or followed the tried and true routine of opening on the east coast before hitting 42nd Street are few, and seldom recognized in the pantheon of substantial works of American drama (for instance, Ira Levin's *Deathtrap*). As Gerald Berkowitz summarizes his definition of the 'post-Broadway age':

> By the 1970s a new young playwright might have his first play produced Off Off-Broadway [sic], his second in Los Angeles or Chicago, and his third on Broadway; or he might make the same journey in reverse. Established Broadway dramatists were produced Off-Broadway or in regional theatres, while regional or Off Off-Broadway hits transferred to Broadway for commercial runs.[22]

Although these are obvious signs of Broadway turning ever more to an economically elite audience, it's hard to argue with the raw numbers: between the 1970–1 and 1979–80 seasons, Broadway's gross income rose by 187 per cent.[23]

Off-Broadway: Infrastructure

The history of New York City theatre in the 1970s was no longer only the history that happened on or near 42nd Street. The now-established Off-Broadway and Off-Off-Broadway movements, and the explosion of 'alternative' theatres that altered the landscape beginning in the mid-1950s (with the founding of Julie Bovasso's Tempo Theatre about the same time Judith Malina's and Julian

Beck's Living Theater commenced regular productions) continued to thrive and expand during the 1970s.

The development of smaller theatres outside Times Square that began in earnest in the 1940s culminated in an Actors Equity agreement in 1949 that established Off-Broadway as theatres with under 300 seats (revised to 499 seats in 1974). The new legal definition of Off-Broadway was consequential, since it not only legitimized the movement but also made apparent, in Arnold Aronson's view, that 'members of this new Off-Broadway movement were not rebelling so much against the aesthetics of Broadway as against the restrictive nature of its economically driven production structure'.[24] This made it a model for a revolution in theatre beyond Broadway, indeed, beyond New York: as Berkowitz writes, 'it directly or indirectly spawned other alternative movements throughout the country. Off-Broadway broke the Broadway monopoly in the public perception and created room for other possibilities.'[25]

Since its emergence in the 1950s, Off-Broadway had typically been described as everything from the anti-Broadway to Broadway's smaller twin. For a time, Off-Broadway hosted innovative work, mostly by European authors and particularly Beckett, Ionesco and the dramatists of the Theatre of the Absurd. Less often, it supported new work by American playwrights and launched productive careers. For instance, Off-Broadway provided Edward Albee with his breakout work, *The Zoo Story* (1960), a play influenced by absurdism. Ironically, the success of the production brought greater investment and subsidized non-profit institutional structures, higher production costs (accompanied by actor strikes) and mainstream attention to Off-Broadway. Although for a time the movement could sustain the pretence that it was founded in revolt against mainstream aesthetic taste and provided a home to innovators and radically experimental theatre – with Albee as evidence – eventually it emerged as what Aronson calls 'a shadow Broadway' (106), producing relatively mainstream work at lower costs and for more intimate audiences than Broadway could provide.

A devastating Actors Equity strike at the opening of the 1970s made explicit that the borders between Broadway and Off-Broadway, whatever they may have been, had to all intents and purposes collapsed. From the union's view, Off-Broadway's business model was not distinct from the prevailing profit-driven logic that existed in the bigger theatres, and it no longer accepted the view of Off-Broadway as an incubator of upcoming talent and promising new work. The subsequent rise in salaries for Off-Broadway performers not only lowered the tolerance for risk on new shows, but drove playwrights and producers to aim either for the minimal costs associated with Off-Off-Broadway or to risk Broadway. The 1974 agreement sought to ameliorate the situation by increasing the number of seats defining an Off-Broadway house from 299 to 499, but the actual impact was negligible.

As a result of the weakening of Off-Broadway's role in mounting new work, four main outlets – a specific element within Off-Broadway, the still-active Off-Off-Broadway scene, the expanding network of resident professional theatres and a burgeoning alternative art movement allied with new developments in dance, visual art and film – provided opportunities for provocative and sometimes even experimental work. Within Off-Broadway, Joe Papp's New York Shakespeare Festival ('Shakespeare in the Park') continued to expand after opening in 1959, first with a permanent outdoor structure (the Delacorte Theatre in Central Park, built in 1961) and then moving eventually into the landmark Astor Place Library in 1967 as a multi-stage venue intended to serve Papp's goal of making theatre for the masses. Here, the several theatre spaces collectively came to be known as 'The Public' (and, after Papp's death in 1991, the Joseph Papp Public Theater). By 1970, according to Christopher Bigsby, the Public 'employed more actors than any other institution in the country',[26] and provided a training ground for a generation of notable performers: Bea Arthur, Jack Palance, Faye Dunaway, Frank Langella and Meryl Streep. Papp, an iconoclast producer, became one of the most significant figures in non-commercial theatre, and in fact is credited with initiating the reversal that resulted in most new work emanating first from the institutional, not-for-profit theatres, rather than Broadway. From the beginning, Papp gravitated toward supporting new, emerging playwrights (including David Mamet, John Guare, Dennis Reardon, Wallace Shawn and – especially – David Rabe), minority dramatists (Charles Gordone, Miguel Piñero, Ed Bullins, Adrienne Kennedy, Ntozake Shange) and to a lesser extent female playwrights (Myrna Lamb). He emphasized 'rainbow casting' and thereby helped more fully integrate the New York stage by casting actors of colour even in classical roles. Although by the end of the decade the Public was losing some of its radical lustre,[27] for much of the period it provided a springboard for many of the most important playwrights of the 1970s. Papp was, in Mel Gussow's estimation, 'the soul and constantly-shifting center of Off-Broadway'.[28]

But during the 1970s, Papp and Off-Broadway also worked both sides of the aisle, bringing to the Public and other venues successful plays and directors from the resident regional and Off-Off theatres while also angling for commercial transfers of successful Off-Broadway shows to the big houses on 42nd Street (such as Guare's *House of Blue Leaves* and Lanford Wilson's *Hot L Baltimore* [sic], discussed below). Sometimes the transfers were extremely profitable: Papp's New York Shakespeare Festival was, Leiter notes, 'sustained for over a decade by the cash coming in from its monster hit, *A Chorus Line*'.[29] Even so, the practice of Off-Off houses and – even more so – the resident professional non-profit theatres outside New York engaging in for-profit transfers incited the wrath of playwrights/producers such as Edward Albee and critics like Martin Gottfried: the latter pointedly stated that 'there is a danger in the commerce between these two kinds of theatre in that it connects the resident theatre to the commercial theatre in a profit-sharing sense. In its own way it turns the resident theatre's play selection process toward the potentially popular rather than the potentially artistic.'[30] Ultimately, the transformation wrought by Off-Broadway cut both ways, as Berkowitz summarizes:

> It was not so much that Off-Broadway, having had its experimental fling, had retreated back into the theatrical mainstream. Rather, the mainstream had been altered and expanded so that artists and sensibilities that had once been peripheral now made up a significant part of the center.[31]

Off-Off-Broadway: Infrastructure

The big developments in Off-Off-Broadway (OOB) in the 1970s concerned scale, visibility and funding.[32] Whereas in the mid-1960s only 15–20 OOB theatres consistently produced plays, after 1968 the scene exploded and by 1974–5, 150 OOB theatres produced over 500 plays. Despite a diaspora of OOB theatres from the original East Village area after it started showing signs of gentrification, lower Manhattan buzzed with experimental theatre activity during the 1970s. In 1974, the Off-Off-Broadway Alliance (OOBA) even hosted a 'Coming Out Party' in the form of a parade and a festival celebrating its cultural and economic impact on the city. But the downside to this growth, what Stephen Bottoms calls 'off-off-Broadway's suicidally rapid expansion',[33] would eventually contribute to its decline at the end of the decade.

Some of the more successful companies were upgrading by moving into spaces vacated by Off-Broadway theatres that, facing rising production costs, had gone under. Given the expanding scale of the enterprise, it soon became necessary to provide institutional organization and support. First, in 1971, the OOBA began to represent practitioners, later (in 1972) superseded by the Alliance of Resident Theatres/New York. After a decade or more of operating either as a pass-the-hat circuit or opting to form (like La MaMa ETC) as subscription theatre clubs operating on shoestring budgets, by the mid-1960s Lyndon Johnson's Great Society eventually came knocking and federal, corporate and private foundation arts funding poured in. The National Endowment for the Arts, founded in 1965, funded state arts councils and thereby provided further impetus to the decentralization of American theatre. Within New York City, corporate funding had an especially unsettling effect on OOB, long a bastion against the commercialization of art. In the most outstanding example of such changes, Ellen Stewart, the founder of La MaMa in 1961, had overseen several relocations and reconfigurations of the performance venue during the 1960s, but in 1969 she moved the club to East Fourth Street (where it remains to this day after Stewart's passing in 2011). Using an annual $60,000 grant from the Ford Foundation, she also opened three spacious rehearsal halls in the East Village and began inviting Off-Off writers and companies to work there during residencies, hosting Mabou Mines, the Ping Chong Company and many other luminaries during the decade. Many decried the loss of the all-for-one-and-one-for-all DIY ethos that prevailed during La MaMa's poor theatre period, but the quality of work it supported during the 1970s is a testament to Stewart's commitment to develop roots for the alternative theatre movement she helped seed in the 1960s.

Another significant change, which altered forever the cultural capital of experimental theatre in America, was the greater press, publishing and scholarly attention paid to productions premiering away from Broadway. Once the *Village Voice* created a critical mass of counterculture readers, by 1966 New York City's respectable weeklies followed and eventually even the *New York Times* was devoting columns in its Sunday arts supplement to the 'Pass-the-Hat Theatre Circuit'.[34] (This contrasted with 1965, when Ellen Stewart had to send a company to the European festival circuit to garner reviews.) This was followed inevitably by editions of selected OOB plays and even a 1966 anthology (*Eight Plays from Off-Off-Broadway*, edited by Nick Orzel and *Voice* critic Michael Smith). By 1972, the Albert Poland/Bruce Mailman comprehensive *The Off-Off-Broadway Book* provided an aerial view of the developments in alternative playwriting, directing, acting and design from the Village.

Given even a small sampling of published texts on which to work, American arts schools and even universities began to incorporate the history and development of alternative theatre into their curricula.[35] From there, it was a small step to hosting residencies and developing performance projects with artists from Off- and Off-Off-Broadway; and, to complete the cycle, graduates of university and art college programmes then streamed into New York seeking lives built around the making of non-commercial art. The University/Resident Theatre Association (U/RTA) was founded in 1969 to enable professional standards in university theatre productions and to create collaborations between campuses and resident professional companies. University campuses sometimes even became an alternative to the regionals, where students and faculty energized by the developments in adaptation, directing, acting and design that erupted during the 1960s now began to parse that legacy and study its potentialities through projects and productions. Further, universities and arts colleges (also benefiting from foundation and federal support for the economic value of the arts) witnessed the influx of huge numbers of baby boomers into their ranks near the end of the 1960s, many of whom arrived with first-hand experience of the political and cultural tumult of that decade. National tours of edgy Off-Off-Broadway plays and musicals, as well as productions by alternative theatre companies like the San Francisco Mime Troupe and Richard Schechner's Performance Group, energized a generation of newly politicized students. Soon, university theatre departments were patronizing residencies by artists who had once denounced the schools as havens of the Quiet Generation. By 1975, the producing company A Bunch of Experimental Theaters specialized in arranging residencies and performances at a number of private and state schools. And in the inevitable outcome of this process, by the 1980s and 1990s many OOB and alternative theatre artists had themselves become affiliated with various colleges and universities – most notably at New York University – as part-time and even permanent faculty. This development would prove foundational for the next generation of American alternative theatre, whose ranks would be dominated by degree-wielding students thoroughly immersed in the history and aesthetic practices of the earlier avant-garde, which they would adapt, deconstruct and remake in the later 1970s and throughout the 1980s and beyond.

But eventually the decade-old white flight from the city,[36] combined with the recession of 1974–5, weakened the audience base for alternative theatre at the same time that corporate and federal funding dried up. As well, OOB became a victim of its own success as more theatres opened and more of its shows transferred to Off-Broadway (and sometimes up to Broadway itself, following the success of *Hair*) along with some of its most productive artists. With that success also came greater involvement of unions like the Actors Equity Association (AEA), which had negotiated the first showcase agreements that allowed union performers to act in Off-Off shows at a fraction of their normal scale. In 1975, with the AEA looking now to capitalize on OOB's expansion, a new agreement was forged that established minimum AEA salaries pegged to a theatre's total operating budget. This made paying performers a hardship for many of the smaller and mid-sized companies, and they thus resisted the changes. After years of fruitless haggling, in 1979 the AEA established a tier system that contained the contentious demand that future subsidiary rights of a play be tied to the use of AEA actors.[37] This led to a number of playwrights refusing to open work on OOB and, combined with other forces, produced a significant drop in productions. Christopher Olsen notes that 'by 1980, OOBA [Off-Off-Broadway Alliance] reported that their theatres used half as many Equity members and opened 60 per cent fewer shows ... playwrights and producers working in Off-Off Broadway were calling it "The End of an Era"'.[38]

As America's political landscape grew more conservative and its economic policies focused on urban growth, cities like New York turned increasingly to attracting new corporate and retail tenants who often displaced fledgling theatre companies. (When the influential Hungarian expat company Kassak Studio relocated near the famous Chelsea Hotel in 1977, they altered their name to Squat Theatre in recognition of their living conditions, which saw them living communally in the space while producing their plays in the attached storefront.) By the end of the decade, New York's OOB was in decline; however, the movement had contributed to the decentralization of Broadway and established the basis for a new network of substantial, non-profit theatres across the country investigating cutting edge performance practices and provocative content that commercial companies in New York could not afford to attempt. Although the original OOB spirit is now part of history, even today in 2016 there are more than 350 member theatres in the Alliance of Resident Theatres/New York.

Regional theatre: Infrastructure

Between the late 1940s and early 1960s, artists and producers also began looking beyond the geographical confines of New York City and sought to establish non-commercial, subsidized, professional resident theatres in medium to large urban communities. There existed a few precedents, such as the Cleveland Playhouse (whose roots go back to 1916), but only after Margo Jones established Theatre '47 in Dallas (1947), followed by the opening of the Alley Theatre in Houston the same year and the Arena Stage in Washington, DC, under Zelda Fichandler (1950), did the so-called 'regional theatre' movement begin in earnest. Funded largely by the Ford Foundation under the leadership of W. McNeil Lowry, the regional movement accelerated the decentralization of Broadway and its 'circuit' – the hundreds of local theatres, summer stock companies and opera houses around the country, usually part of a franchise owned by theatre powerhouses like the Schuberts, Ehrlangers and Frohmans – that remounted Broadway hits for the masses.[39]

Significantly, these new regionals appeared about the same time that Off-Broadway was making headlines in New York following the epochal success of José Quintero's production of Tennessee Williams' *Summer and Smoke* at Circle in the Square (1951). Many regional theatres, while recognizing Broadway as the ultimate mecca of American theatre, thus developed their institutional structures and seasons on the model of Off-Broadway rather than Broadway. With intimidating production costs and the pressure of speculating in for-profit theatrical schemes somewhat allayed by lower costs and public and private subsidy, regional theatre producers and artists could venture into non-canonical work from home and abroad as well as new dramas by playwrights who had not yet made a name for themselves.[40] Theatre '47, for instance, immediately established itself as a venue to launch new work by lesser known American dramatists and international playwrights not often seen in the US.

In the wake of success in Texas, regional theatres sprung up in Milwaukee, Pittsburgh, Minneapolis, Los Angeles and San Diego, among others. However, as regional theatres proliferated, the tendency was to back away from the original impulse to present new work: as Joseph Zeigler summarizes, 'for the most part of the twenty year period between 1947 and 1967, American regional theatres reversed [Margo Jones's] doctrine, concentrating on classics instead of new writing'.[41] However, after the Arena Stage, at considerable risk, staged Howard Sackler's *The Great White Hope* on a grand scale in 1967, the tide began to turn. The resident professional theatres, increasingly confident in the quality of productions and talent, while secure in the knowledge that Broadway would seldom risk mounting work by unknown writers, began to premiere new work with an eye toward taking it to New York. In other cases, in fact, authors and producers with plays that likely would succeed on Broadway chose nevertheless to give their plays to regional resident theatres out of a general distaste for Broadway's commercialism.[42]

By the 1970s, the tradition that saw Broadway originating new work by American playwrights and the touring circuit bringing these to the hinterlands began to transform. As Philip Kolin and Colby Kullman summarize, a regional theatre movement that 'was once marginal or too small to compete with Broadway became center stages producing some of the most important plays of the 1970s. What was once marginal theatre gave the nation its mainstream plays by the end of the decade.'[43] The source for producing the majority of new American dramatic writing had thus been reversed. The success of the first-generation regional theatres led to new repertory companies appearing in the 1970s, such as the McCarter Theatre Center (Princeton, NJ), Steppenwolf Theatre, Victory Gardens and Wisdom Bridge Theatre (all 'Off-Loop' theatres in Chicago), American Repertory Theatre (Cambridge, MA), Wolf Trap (Vienna, VA) and rep houses in Denver, Seattle and Indianapolis. Los Angeles alone reported more than a hundred diverse 'off' theatres featuring everything from Hollywood acting showcases to fringe political groups and ethnic theatre companies. And it was during the 1970s that these and older resident theatre companies began to assume the role of incubator of new directing, acting and design talent.

As Leiter notes, 'Approximately 530 works appeared on Broadway during the decade. Of this number, at least 120 were produced in resident theatres before coming to New York.'[44] Included in that total are the astounding 285 musicals that played at some point in the ten-year span, many of which ran only for weeks before closing. Add to that the number of revivals, transfers from Off-Broadway and Off-Off Broadway and imports from abroad, he concludes, and 'we get a total of 290 Broadway shows out of 535 – or 55 percent – that began elsewhere than on Broadway'.[45] The 1970s was thus a dynamic decade for the regional theatre movement, so much so that the term 'regional' finally went out of fashion as connoting a secondary status to Broadway and unable to capture the spirit of theatre as an institution connected to its own community. Its replacement, 'resident', began to proliferate in the mid-1960s, and by 1966 the League of Resident Theatres (LORT) was formed in order to facilitate regional productions utilizing Equity and other union staff, bringing a higher degree of professionalization to these houses by the 1970s.[46]

Thus, between Off-Broadway, Off-Off-Broadway and the emerging regional theatres, 'all the best dramatic writing in America from the late 1960s on was first staged someplace other than Broadway'.[47] But the history of the regional/resident professional theatre peaked in the 1970s before the steep cuts in federal arts funding during the Reagan administration, as well as the culture wars over funding by the National Endowment for the Humanities in the 1990s. These would render the possibility of maintaining a true resident theatre like William Ball's American

Conservatory Theatre in Pittsburgh unsustainable.[48] Since 1980, when a business model emphasizing sustainability and self-sufficiency became the norm (this for organizations with legal status as non-profits), very few theatres have been able to sustain a resident company that performs a steady repertory of titles, some of which may come from relatively unknown playwrights. The dream of extending an Off-Off ethos beyond New York encompassing urban America has, like the Off-Off movement itself, been constantly deferred but never abandoned.

Playwriting and production: Broadway

Broadway playwriting at the outset of the 1970s was also decentralized and no longer dominated by an authoritative dramatic voice, as Eugene O'Neill and Arthur Miller provided in the 1940s and shared with William Inge and Tennessee Williams in the 1950s. Miller, capitalizing on his dominance of Broadway throughout the 1950s, returned with *After the Fall* (1964), *Incident at Vichy* (1965) and *The Price* (1968), which, though a strong trio of plays, did not capture the nation's moral pulse as had his earlier work. Perhaps embittered by the failure of *The Creation of the World and Other Business* (1972), which sunk quickly not only as a play but bombed as a musical (as *Up from Paradise*), Miller thereafter mostly avoided opening his plays on Broadway during the decade, which he thought had become too commercialized, and turned to more appreciative audiences in Washington, DC, and, more frequently, in London, for his premiers.[49] Williams, though he remained prolific, entered his period of steep decline during which his only moderate successes in New York were the revised version of *Summer and Smoke* (retitled *Eccentricities of a Nightingale*), mounted at the Morosco Theatre in 1976 for just 24 performances despite warm reviews, and *Small Craft Warnings*, which had a decent run Off-Broadway in 1972. Both playwrights, along with O'Neill, maintained strong reputations by regular revivals of their better-known works, by public scandal (mostly Williams) or via their non-dramatic writing (Miller's *Theatre Essays* appeared in 1978); yet the vacuum created by their absence from Broadway was palpable.

Edward Albee's Broadway success of the early 1960s (*Who's Afraid of Virginia Woolf?* [1962]), which arrived after the Off-Broadway success of *Zoo Story* (1960) and *The American Dream* (1961), was not followed by other Broadway hits. Both *Tiny Alice* (1964) and the 1967 Pulitzer Prize-winner, *A Delicate Balance*, fared poorly with audiences. The playwright, whose partnership with Richard Barr and Clinton Wilder in forming the Playwright's Unit at the Cherry Lane Theatre in 1963 reinvigorated Off-Broadway theatre and provided a welcome home to Off-Off playwrights like Sam Shephard, Adrienne Kennedy and Arthur Kopit, continued however to exert considerable influence on upcoming American playwrights. But by the beginning of the 1970s he was exploring a more abstruse style focused on what Brenda Murphy terms his 'threnodies', resulting in the short Broadway run of *All Over* (1971, directed by John Gielgud) and *The Lady from Dubuque* (1980).[50] There were regional theatre productions of *Listening* (1976) and the one-act *Counting the Ways* (1977). As Albee explored options away from a Broadway theatre, he often hectored American mainstream theatre in the press. Still, he crossed over successfully to Broadway once more with *Seascape* (1975), a lighter play Albee directed himself that addressed themes of personal and social evolution. It featured Frank Langella as one of the human-sized sea creatures commiserating with the human figures, garnering him a Tony, and Albee – despite poor box office – his second Pulitzer. Generally, however, Albee's affair with Broadway in the 1970s was an uneven one and his constant battles with the commercial theatre conducted through the media stand as testimony to how mutually corrosive the relationship between playwright and Broadway could become.

There were still playwrights who honed their craft and established strong reputations away from Broadway and then – when the content of the work was directed at more mainstream audiences – moved up to 42nd Street. Arthur Kopit perhaps best characterized this haphazard path, having tasted brief Broadway success in the early 1960s (*Oh Dad, Poor Dad ...* [1962]) before falling off the grid until 1969 when *Indians* brought him back to Broadway after a London premiere. The play can be seen as either the last gasp of the 1960s flirtation with 'primitive' cultures or the opening salvo of the 1970s and its long, torturous engagement with Vietnam and its aftermath. Kopit continued his mordant analysis of American values in successful plays that did not reach Broadway but nevertheless received intelligent regional productions (such as *Secrets of the Rich*, produced in 1976 at the O'Neill Theatre in Connecticut) and publication. However, he landed a hit on Broadway with another kind of play, the 1977 *Wings*, which won him a Pulitzer. The play followed the usual route of a Kopit play to Broadway, with its genesis at the regional Yale Repertory Theatre, followed by a run Off-Broadway and only then moving up to the Lyceum in 1978. Here, Kopit devised a clever route into the commercial theatre by altering themes that characterized his absurdist pieces in their exploration of the failure of verbal communication. In this instance, however, Kopit took the opposite tack, showing how the loss of language following a debilitating stroke by the protagonist, the aviatrix Emily Stilson, deracinated language and identity. The play dramatized her struggle to regain speech and a sense of subjectivity, thus making the play more amenable to mainstream audiences. Kopit continued to produce works for regional stages (becoming a fixture at the annual Humana Festival in Louisville) and realized a second life as a successful composer of books for successful musicals such as *Nine* (1982) and his attempt to 'correct' Andrew Lloyd Weber with his own *Phantom* (1991).

Similarly, Terrence McNally and Lanford Wilson might establish a reputation with an early Broadway show, step off what Ruby Cohn memorably called 'Broadway's tightrope' without fear of disappearing entirely, and then return when the material suited mainstream tastes. McNally was a significant presence in the Off-Broadway and OOB scenes in the 1960s, adapting works like Dumas's *The Lady of the Camellias* (which moved up to Broadway for a brief run in 1963) and penning original one-acts like *Morning, Noon and Night* (1968). He returned to Broadway in the 1970s, first with a pair of one-acts entitled *Bad Habits* (1974) and then more successfully with the acclaimed *The Ritz* (1975), a rare gay-themed farce that enjoyed more than 400 performances, garnered a Tony for Rita Moreno and was made into a film in 1976. Though the play traffics in stereotypes (reviews commented drily that gay men were wittier, better built and more sexually active than heteros), the play introduced McNally's particular brand of gay theatre, one that could appeal to heterocentric audiences by arousing an empathy based in tolerance and basic human dignity and using farce as the great leveller. Having endeared himself to a gay and straight cross-section of New York playgoers, McNally was welcomed into the Manhattan Theatre Club in the 1980s, where he would see his most significant plays (*Masterclass, Love! Valor! Compassion!* and *Lips Together, Teeth Apart*) produced to ever-growing audiences and critical acclaim.

Lanford Wilson, since his arrival in New York City in 1962, put in his time at various Village venues, producing what Christopher Bigsby describes as 'an astonishing deluge of works' at Caffe Cino and other sites.[51] *The Madness of Lady Bright* (1964) put Wilson on the map, not only garnering the first review of an Off-Off-Broadway play by the mainstream press, but also touring internationally and at Ellen Stewart's La MaMa. Other successes such as *Balm in Gilead* (1965, La MaMa) and *The Rimers of Eldritch* (1966, Cherry Lane Theatre) established Wilson's dramatic voice and style of lyric naturalism that laid a path to Broadway, which he reached at the end of the 1960s when *Gingham Dog*, his treatment of the decline of an interracial marriage, transferred for a short run. Soon after, he was invited along with his Caffe Cino crony Marshall Mason and others to form the Circle Rep (which survived until 1996). As Bigsby says, 'It would be difficult to over-emphasize the importance of the Rep to Wilson or of Wilson to the Rep.'[52] It provided the playwright with a safe place to experiment and refine the lyricism of his early work and to establish a sustained collaboration with Mason, who became his long-time director. Based on the successes the team had with Rep productions of the 1970 *Serenading Louie, The Hot L Baltimore* (1973) and *The Mound Builders* (1975), Wilson would later find welcoming audiences on Broadway at the end of the decade with his Talley trilogy (*Fifth of July* [1978], *Talley's Folly* [1979, Pulitzer Prize] and *Talley and Son* [1985]). The first play in the series, which represents the latest chronological point in the trilogy, was suffused with an atmosphere of regret over the American loss of prestige and idealism after defeat in Vietnam. Mark Fearnow believes that '[i]f American drama of the 1970s can be said to have a masterpiece, it is surely *The Fifth of July*'.[53] The remaining two plays, with increasing realism and a waning of Wilson's landmark lyricism, reveal moments of individual self-realization and connection set against a broader landscape of decline and lost opportunities for redemption.

John Guare, another child of the Off and Off-Off scenes, began his inexplicably slow rise to prominence with *The House of Blue Leaves* (1971), which opened at the Bowery's Truck and Warehouse Theatre and won an Obie and Drama Desk Award (the 1984 Broadway revival garnered four Tonys). A farce in the style of the popular British playwright Joe Orton, the play ridiculed the American obsession with fame, which by the 1970s had clearly departed from the earlier quest for an American Dream of middle-class aspirations and economic stability. He followed this with a popular rock musical adaptation of *The Two Gentlemen of Verona* that opened in Central Park before moving to Broadway to claim the Tony for Best Book. His signature style of frantic, absurd farce culminated in the first play he wrote for the resident Nantucket Stage Company, *Marco Polo Sings a Solo* (1976), which eventually played at the Public (1977). Possibly as a result of leaving New York and focusing on more intimate plays for his new adopted home in Nantucket, the rest of the decade saw Guare refining his art by tempering its farcical elements with deeper considerations of the American way of death (*Landscape of the Body*, 1977) and the real pain emanating from lives lived, as Bigsby describes them, like 'performances, texts' (*Bosoms and Neglect*, 1979).[54] Guare's second ascent began early in the 1980s with *Lydie Breeze* (1982) and was capped by the 1990 *Six Degrees of Separation*.

Although David Mamet would find his New York roots Off-Broadway (see below), his *American Buffalo* transferred first from the Goodman Theatre in Chicago to the Theatre of St Clement's Church in 1976 (directed by Gregory Mosher, whose career would rise alongside Mamet's) before arriving at the Ethel Barrymore Theatre the following year in a version directed by Ulu Grossbard. Mamet's first foray into Broadway earned the play a decent run (122 shows) and widespread critical recognition. David Krasner calls *American Buffalo* 'the representative play of the era', recognizing its profound connections to the 1970s American *zeitgeist* of paranoia, opportunism and growing white rage.[55] In this 'simple play about simple men who cannot pull off a simple robbery',[56] a vitriolic but insecure junk shop owner (ironically named Teach) plots with two companions to steal the coin referenced in the title. In the neo-Darwinian universe of the play, these losers attempt to project through broken (yet dazzling) dialogue a sense of mastery that their actions never match. The play almost single-handedly established the 'Mamet-speak' that would characterize his work into the twenty-first century, and this verbosity masking an overwhelming impotence caught the tenor of the time. With a tone not unlike that of Martin Scorsese's film *Taxi Driver* from 1975, Mamet's play both provided a pulpit for the expression of anxious rage and a mode of critiquing the basis of such dispossession. As well as capturing the mood of the decade with unerring pitch and rhythm, Mamet's play provided a platform for a second generation of Method actors: Teach was originally played by Robert Duvall and then Al Pacino in a searing 1981 revival at Circle in the Square, and the role continues to attract top actors such as William Macy (in a Donmar Warehouse production in 2000) and Tracy Letts for Steppenwolf Theatre. *American Buffalo* announced a precocious and controversial new talent, one who followed Sam Shepard into the multiple career track of screenwriter, film director and author of notable fiction and non-fiction works.

For all the historical significance of these nascent careers and movements, by any criteria Broadway playwriting of the 1970s was dominated by a single author, Neil Simon, who continued his 1960s success unabated into the 1970s. Simon's comedies regularly enjoyed long runs and rang up huge box office receipts, and at the outset of his career (during the period known as 'Simon Says') an unprecedented four of his plays ran simultaneously on Broadway. *Barefoot in the Park* (1963), *The Odd Couple* (1965) and *Plaza Suite* (1968) established Simon's signature style of witty banter awkwardly covering up benign neuroses in his protagonists that, in the end, are mollified and recuperated by the generous society that happily receives the misfit back into its fold. The formula held true for Simon's work in the 1970s, which saw an astonishing eight plays mounted on Broadway. He occasionally produced work dealing with weightier themes, such as the successful but critically panned run for *The Gingerbread Lady* (1970); however, he failed spectacularly with *God's Favorite* in 1974. Thereafter he returned to sentimental comedies of a very high order, packed with sufficient gags and one-liners to leaven the potential for mawkishness. The decade included only two true hits (*The Prisoner of Second Avenue* [1971] and *Sunshine Boys* [1972]) as the playwright's attention turned to screenplays after relocating to Los Angeles (where he also began premiering his new plays). But he ended the decade on a high note with *Chapter Two*, a self-study of his lingering grief over his first wife's death enlivened by a brilliant comic turn by Marsha Mason. He then scored big with the book for the revue *They're*

Playing Our Song (based on the love affair of Marvin Hamlisch and the singer Carole Bayer Sager) in 1979.

The Broadway musical

When Neil Simon took time to catch his breath, Broadway turned again and again to musicals capable of returning the growing financial investment in professional productions (though some of the biggest and most expensive bombs in the history of musical theatre – like Gerome Ragni's eco-themed *Dude* – occurred during the 1970s as well). However, unlike the situation that existed during the decades following the Second World War, even the successful shows did little to burnish the reputation of the classical American Broadway musical, which Leiter describes as 'America's most popular and original contribution to world theatre'.[57] The original work, mostly stemming from the collaboration of producer Harold Prince and composer Stephen Sondheim, was rarely popular; and, correspondingly, the most popular work was seldom original. Rarely did new work resonate strongly with the culture at large, evidenced by Raymond Knapp's *The American Musical and the Formation of National Identity*, in which only a single work from the decade (Sondheim's *Pacific Overtures*) is selected as worthy of analysis.[58]

The decade saw the gradual decline or passing of some of the great individual librettists of the 1950s and 1960s (such as Richard Rodgers), composers (Alan Jay Lerner) and creative teams like Kanders and Ebb as well as Strouse and Adams (though Strouse was involved with the throwback sentimental hit *Annie* in 1977). New talent arrived, to be sure, and significant new directions in content were initiated (often first through Off-Broadway musicals), including plays on black, Asian and women's themes, as well as the introduction of rock music (following *Hair*). But for the most part the decade signalled a decline in the inventiveness that characterized the books and librettos of the past. Some of this regression was covered by the extraordinary accomplishments of Prince and Sondheim and by the arrival of a series of accomplished directors/ choreographers whose talents sometimes covered the weaknesses in the books and scores.

Nostalgic mountings of older musicals, oftentimes reprising their original stars – *My Fair Lady*, *The King and I*, *Fiddler on the Roof* – remained a staple, and for a period there was extraordinary interest in reviving titles from the early years of the musical: *No, No, Nanette* from the 1920s (1971), *Irene* (original 1919, remounted in 1973) and even Scott Joplin's 1907 and unproduced *Treemonisha* (1975). *Over Here* (1974) not only revived the music of wartime America from the 1940s but brought back two of the Andrews Sisters to perform. John Degen attributes the nostalgia trend to 'a reaction to the novel elements invading musical theatre … perhaps generated by the tumultuous social-political climate, perhaps by a distaste on the part of traditional theatregoers for the new sounds and subjects'.[59] Among these innovations was the popularization of the rock musical (which, owing to the notoriety of *Hair*, also ushered in nudity and more prominent roles for ethnic minorities), which peaked early with the British import *Jesus Christ Superstar* in 1971. The show made superstars of Andrew Lloyd Webber and Tim Rice as well; their reputations were solidified with *Evita* in 1978 and thus laid the groundwork for Lloyd Webber's ascent to the stratosphere of musical theatre fame. Another mode of nostalgia was produced through the rock musical *Grease* (1972) that returned to the roots of rock and roll and resurrected an anodyne version of the 1950s in much the same way that the popular TV serial *Happy Days* would do later in the decade.

But there were two outstanding and sustained developments in 1970s musical theatre whose legacies continued to influence work beyond the decade. The popularity of the 'concept musical', begun by Brecht and Weill and arriving in America in the 1940s, achieved the status of a substantial movement only near the end of 1960s with shows like *Cabaret* and *Hair*. Shaped by a dominant director/choreographer using found material or improvising from an existing libretto to develop a concentrated mood or set of loosely-aligned themes (often at the expense of linear narrative and sustained character development), concept shows gave the American musical something akin to the phenomenon of the German *regietheatre* and, similarly, troubled the traditional dominance of the book writer and composer in the production hierarchy. 'Light on book, and heavy on production elements tied to unusual theme or approach',[60] concept musicals – which often had their genesis in Off-Broadway productions – could run the gamut of styles: from Sondheim's first stab at the form in *Company* (1970); to Bob Fosse's adaptation of the original book for *Pippin*

(1972) into the existential spectacle it became in its Broadway premiere; to Elizabeth Swados's staging of Jewish kabbalistic ritual practices in *The Haggadah* (Off-Broadway, 1980); and to Robert Wilson's image operas of the period (*Deafman Glance* [1971] and *Einstein on the Beach* [1976, Avignon; American premiere 1984]). Among the *enfants terribles* directing concept musicals, Bob Fosse continued to be as close to a sure thing as one could find, although his tendency to dominate productions and take liberties with the book often aggrieved writers, composers and producers. As a sign of Broadway's weakened status in the early 1970s, when *Pippin* premiered in 1972 Fosse also directed the first television ad for a Broadway musical (which must have been effective, since the show ran until 1977). He added *Chicago* to his credits in 1975, which in its 1996 revival was at one time the longest-running show in Broadway history. He also directed *Dancin'* (1978) and produced and choreographed *Liza with a 'Z'* in 1972, which was televised and thereby popularized the theatre concert form for other comeback recitals in the decade by Diana Ross and Debbie Reynolds.

The most enduring example of the concept musical, however, is *A Chorus Line*, created when Joe Papp gave Michael Bennett unlimited workshop access at the Public to explore the experiences of Broadway's 'gypsy' chorus dancers, the nameless and largely faceless labour upon which the American musical has historically been built. Reflecting the 'Me Decade's' cult of self-improvement and obsession with self-examination, consciousness raising and self-expression, the somewhat thin book by James Kirkwood and Nicholas Dante was based on more than 30 hours of transcripts recording the group therapy-like interactions between itinerant dancers. Having converted these dialogues into memorable lyrics (Edward Kleban) and music (Marvin Hamlisch), all that remained was to conceive the character of the formidable director, Zach. Bennett himself added the outstanding choreography needed for the corps of dancers cast in the piece. After opening at the Public Theater in April 1975, the show moved up to the main Schubert house on Broadway where it won nine Tonys and a Pulitzer Prize and set attendance and longevity records during its remarkable fifteen-year run. It made stars of Robert Lupone, Priscilla Lopez, Kelly Bishop and Sammy Williams.

The second source of innovation in musical theatre of the 1970s was the partnership between Stephen Sondheim and Hal Prince.

The duo continued pressing the borders of the musical theatre form until the catastrophic failure of *Merrily We Roll Along* in 1981. Before that they rolled out, in addition to the already-mentioned *Company*, *Follies* (1971), *A Little Night Music* (1973–4), *Pacific Overtures* (1976) and *Sweeney Todd, the Demon Barber of Fleet Street* (1979). The daring motifs – the ghosts of the showgirls' former selves in *Follies*, the implementation of waltz time for the majority of numbers in *A Little Night Music*, the all-Asian cast of *Pacific Overture* and the exploration of the dark themes in *Sweeney Todd* – would remain a staple of Sondheim's work throughout the 1970s and into his later collaborations with James Lapine and others. A protégé of Oscar Hammerstein II, Sondheim made his name in the 1960s first as a successful lyricist (*West Side Story*) and finally as a 'difficult' composer beginning with *A Funny Thing Happened on the Way to the Forum*. His notorious wordplay and experiments with prosody, along with the complexity of his compositions, assured a relatively small but devoted following during the 1970s that would blossom only in later years into outright popularity with works like *Sunday in the Park with George* and *Into the Woods*. His work is now featured at the London Proms, heard in films, commissioned by Madonna, and the stuff of several popular Sondheim-based revues. In 2010, the Henry Miller Theatre in New York was renamed the Sondheim Theatre.

Broadway imports

While it arrived later than it did on the music scene, Broadway experienced its own 'British Invasion' during the 1970s. As Leiter notes, 'had it not been for the large number of excellently performed, attended and awarded British plays, Broadway would never have had the economic boom it experienced during these years'.[61] While awaiting the next Neil Simon piece or the arrival of an edgy musical from Sondheim or the newest thing from Off-Broadway, producers could depend on transferring the latest London hit, complete with original stars and production team, to 42nd Street for profitable runs. As Laurence Maslon points out, this is precisely what happened before *A Chorus Line* transferred from the Public, when Peter Schaffer's *Equus*, with its imaginative staging, took Broadway by storm in 1974.[62] The 1970s saw the renewed presence of Harold Pinter's work in America, with *Old Times* (1971–2), his first play on Broadway since 1968. This was followed by a typical star vehicle production of *No Man's Land* featuring Ralph Richardson and John Gielgud in 1976 (Pinter also directed several British plays in New York during the decade). Tom Stoppard established a presence on Broadway with the 1967 production of *Rosencrantz and Guildenstern Are Dead*, and brought a handful of new plays (including *Jumpers*, 1974; *Travesties*, 1975; *Every Good Boy Deserves Favor* – with André Previn conducting at the Metropolitan Opera – 1979). Even Noël Coward and Terence Rattigan, both of whom passed away in the decade, had their late work produced in New York. New arrivals included Alan Ayckbourn, who would prove to have lasting appeal on Broadway, Simon Gray, David Storey and Alan Bennett. And Off-Broadway sometimes seemed like London redux, with productions of plays by Caryl Churchill, David Edgar, David Rudkin and David Hare filling the bills (many of them would graduate to Broadway in the 1980s).

In conclusion, despite the severe slump in attendance in the first years of the 1970s, by mid-decade Neil Simon comedies, mega-musicals and British transfers collectively helped to bring back traditional audiences, open the door for new spectators and produce enough hits to re-energize the touring circuit. By the 1975–6 season, profits resulting from the higher ticket prices were soaring despite the lumbering economy, growing at an incredible 20 per cent per year for a time. As business boomed, the surrounding infrastructure of the Great White Way improved, and clips from Broadway and Broadway shows were featured prominently in the wildly successful 'I ❤ NY' campaign. Success, however, came at a price as Broadway increasingly fixated on the sure hit at the expense of any commitment to experimentation and new serious dramatic work. As theatres increasingly became concentrated in the hands of only a few organizations (the Schuberts, Jujamcyn, Nederlanders) and ticket sales became automated, the model built on opening a long-running hit (almost always a musical) and maintaining it for thousands of performances in the same house, while touring shows travelled the circuit reaping extra profits, was established. Box office soared while quality and diversity declined, and Broadway began its slow evolution into the tourist spectacle and corporate-sponsored entity it has mostly become in the twenty-first century.

Playwriting and production: Off-Broadway

As already noted, by the mid-1970s Off-Broadway had lost some of its alternative edge, and a good deal of energy was devoted to mounting shows that might transfer profitably up to Broadway. The biggest shows to stay during the 1970s were musicals that reflected the split personality of Off-Broadway, the Stephen Schwartz adaptation of the Gospel of Saint Matthew, *Godspell* (1971), and the pro-sexual liberation *Let My People Come* (1974). *The Fantastiks* (premiered 1960) continued its preternaturally long life at the Sullivan Street Theatre (closing in 2002). But occasionally Off-Broadway still produced and supported new work by American artists. Albert Innaurato's *Gemini* started at the small Playwrights Horizon in 1976, but after a stopover at Circle Rep it jumped to Broadway and – despite its coming-out theme – ran for almost 2,000 performances. Papp kick-started the career of David Rabe (whose accomplishments are covered by Jon Dietrick in this book) by presenting his 'Vietnam Trilogy' between 1971 and 1976. The first play, *The Basic Training of Pavlo Hummel*, won an Obie and had a major Broadway revival in 1977 featuring Al Pacino. Marshall Mason and Lanford Wilson turned the Circle Rep into a major supporter of new playwriting that pushed the boundaries of realism, despite not having a permanent theatre until 1982. In addition to supporting Wilson (see above), during the 1970s Circle Rep premiered work by Mark Medoff (*When You Comin' Back, Red Ryder?* [1973]), who ended the decade with the hit *Children of a Lesser God*. More mainstream work by Beth Henley and Terence McNally, and imports such as Brian Friel, were produced by the Manhattan Theatre Club under Lynne Meadow. Characteristic of the path that new plays could follow, Ed Bullins received the 1975 Obie and Drama Desk Award for Best American Play when *The Taking of Miss Janie* moved first from the regional Mark Taper Forum in Los Angeles and then to New York at the New Federal Theatre and on to the Public. The Performance Group delivered an environmental theatre version of Sam Shepard's *The Tooth of Crime* in 1973, and all of Shepard's plays of the 1970s (reviewed in a later chapter) saw their first New York productions Off- and Off-Off-Broadway.

It was in the Off-Broadway theatres of the late 1960s and 1970s (and in the similar resident professional theatres: see below) that the transition in dramatic form that would define the future of a broader mainstream American theatre took place. Off-Broadway dramatists, given a wider ambit of production possibilities and without the anxiety of having to create plays for large audiences, were freer to experiment with form and content, and to direct the themes of their plays to the tumult occurring throughout the decade. In terms of content, where Arthur Miller might express a latent foreboding at the prospects for American liberalism by treating it metaphorically (and historically distant) in a made-for-Broadway play like *The Crucible,* by the second half of the 1960s Off-Broadway playwrights were more apt to treat such issues directly, as for instance Israel Horovitz did on the theme of American racism in *The Indian Wants the Bronx* (1968) and Amiri Baraka (then LeRoi Jones) even more scathingly presented in *Dutchman* and *The Slave* (1964). And on the level of form, the dominant domestic realism of the 1940s and 1950s was slowly being altered by the experiments taking place in Off-Broadway theatre, such as the Living Theatre's productions of *The Connection* (1959–60) and *The Brig* (1963). Their work engaged with the new English translation of Artaud's *The Theatre and Its Double* (1958), bringing the work of the historical avant-garde into a position of influence hitherto unknown in American theatre since O'Neill, Elmer Rice and others had experimented with Expressionism beginning in the 1920s. These tendencies, in turn, prepared the ground for international works being featured in New York in unprecedented numbers, beginning with the continental work of the Absurdists (Ionesco most strongly, but Beckett as well) and eventually forms of non-Western theatre and performance that resonated strongly with the anti-imperialist and environmentally conscious elements of the 1960s countercultures.[63] Off-Off-Broadway and the experimental art scene, similarly, contributed new approaches to play creation (communal, devised), staging (environmental, non-matrixed) and acting (epic, improvised, transformational, physicalized, task-based) that contested the hegemony of Method-based dramatic character, strictly linear plotting and neat resolutions of themes and conflicts.[64] As well, the emergence of women's and minority writing that sought to speak to, and for, particular cultures emphatically sought alternatives to a realism that for many seemed the voice and form of the oppressor's language.

These experiments defined two broad trajectories in American theatre: in their 'purer' and most radical form (and abetted by influences from other art forms), they shaped the development of new performance forms and radically unconventional styles of scenographic writing that characterized the alternative arts scene discussed below (see also the chapter on Richard Foreman in this volume by Geoffrey King and Craig Werner). Second, in modified and somewhat attenuated form, the experiments from the 1960s shaped the new variations on conventional realist form that would characterize virtually every significant American playwright in the 1970s and beyond.[65] Gerald Berkowitz maintains that '[t]he number of writers corrupted or discouraged by exposure to companies that did not respect the text is probably matched or exceeded by the number who were inspired to expand their dramatic vocabulary and attempt new styles and techniques as a result of exposure to radical productions'.[66]

To say that those playwrights of the 1970s brought up on the innovations and experimental forms of the 1960s transformed American playwriting overnight would, however, be an overstatement, and Berkowitz is certainly correct to claim that 'a clear mainstream remained ... Whatever the subject, however dominant the social or political agenda, however particular or unconventional the life experience being explored, the overwhelming majority of American dramatists continued to find that their concerns could best be dramatized through the everyday, personal experiences of ordinary characters.'[67] Yet clearly mainstream theatre had adapted some of the experiments in form and content, and found willing producers for such work in the resident professional theatres (including university theatres), in the burgeoning Off-Off-Broadway scene, and at the Public and other Off-Broadway theatres. Some of these even found their way to Broadway, although by the end of the 1970s many believed that the evolving separation between serious dramatic experimentation and Broadway had all but culminated. The careers of the playwrights featured in this book, all of whom to one extent or another self-consciously turned away from conventional domestic realism, are exemplary of the sea change that took place in American theatre during the 1970s and stand as harbingers of a more diverse continuum of dramatic form and content. Among playwrights involved in the reformulation of conventional writing (rather than its overthrow or negligence of it entirely), Off-Broadway hosted Marsha Norman, Charles Fuller, Samm-Art Williams and Wendy Wasserstein, as well as many others.

Thus it seems fitting to conclude this section by looking briefly at David Mamet, who established his career in the 1970s in the new resident professional circuit (Chicago) before moving to Off-Broadway, and then establishing the reputation that would catapult him to Broadway and into the first rank of American dramatists in the 1980s and beyond. His work, like that of the playwrights analysed in the ensuing case studies, explores a modified realism that reveals the impact of previous experiments in performance and shows how such work successfully moved from the margins to the mainstream.[68]

Mamet's arrival on Off-Broadway, after a successful career that began at Goddard College in Vermont before relocating to Chicago, began in 1976 when a double bill of *The Duck Variations* and *Sexual Perversity in Chicago* opened at the Cherry Lane Theatre (the latter winning the Obie for Best Play). These were followed later that year by *American Buffalo* (discussed above) and the stage version of Mamet's earlier radio play *The Water Engine*.[69] His name already established in Chicago, Mamet vied with Rabe and Shepard for pre-eminence in the world of 1970s Off-Broadway. His signature plotless but language-intoxicated plays drove to the core of the self-deceptions that Americans made use of during a period when capitalism seemed poised to falter and national pride appeared to shrink by the day. His realism addresses moments when the 'real' world and its structures of being fail and the self is thrust into modes of performance that become the constitutive, but always unstable, force of existence. Whether investigating casual romantic relationships (*Sexual Perversity*), the dehumanizing effects of consumerism (*American Buffalo*) or the American myth of can-do innovation (*The Water Engine*), Mamet expressed, in Toby Zinman's phrase, 'equal opportunity cynicism'.[70] The plays of this period gave voice to a scathing critique of the self-defining structures of American capitalism: 'about how we excuse all sorts of great and small betrayals and ethical compromises called business. I felt angry about business when I wrote [*American Buffalo*].'[71] Christopher Bigsby rightly recognized that in these plays 'rapacity and greed [are not] presented as the decadent products of history. In America, he implies they were its motor force.'[72] Interestingly, Mamet's later work would reveal, like the 1970s in general, a deeply conservative strain beneath the seemingly liberal, anti-business stance of these plays. In his growing desire to see capitalism not undermined but returned to the days when it manifested American power and dominance, Mamet was already anticipating the 1980s.[73]

Playwriting and production: Off-Off-Broadway

Further downtown, the Off-Off scene was still lively despite some notable departures: Caffe Cino closed soon after the tragic suicide of Joe Cino in 1968, Ralph Cook left Theatre Genesis in 1970 and Tom O'Horgan was often busy with transfers uptown. Michael Smith finally quit at the *Village Voice* (saying 'there was too much going on there ... too many artists') and OOB lost its most acute critic.[74] The Old Reliable Tavern suspended its theatre programming in 1971 and Genesis finally closed in 1978 (Judson Poet's Theatre would follow in 1981). With the greater institutionalization of companies like La MaMa ETC and the dying out of the showcase tradition that allowed Equity actors to perform in a specific number of performances without formal compensation, many began to lament the loss of the 'free theatre' ethos (which Stephen Bottoms characterizes as 'free of charge, free of creative interference from backers, freewheeling, reciprocal collaboration between artists').[75] Yet powerful work by OOB stalwarts Al Carmines, Sam Shepard and Maria Irene Fornes among others continued to draw audiences as well as cautious mainstream critical commentary.

New writers emerged during the decade like Leon Katz (*Dracula Sabbat*, 1970; *The Making of Americans*, 1972) and David Patrick (*Kennedy's Children*, 1974, which played briefly on Broadway and earned Shirley Knight a Tony for best actress; *My Cup Runneth*

Over, 1976). Kennedy, along with Ronald Tavel and Doric Wilson among others, would go on to write and produce some of the first openly gay plays presented to (relatively) mainstream audiences in the 1980s. In 1974, Wilson helped launch TOSOS (The Other Side of Silence) by converting a Church Street bar into a home for gay-themed performances. William M. Hoffman's path-breaking anthology *Gay Plays* appeared in 1979, establishing a foundation for his success in the 1980s with the first queer play on Broadway, *As Is* (1985).

New resident theatres modelled on OOB opened: Jo Ann Schmidman decamped with Megan Terry to form the Omaha Magic Theatre, while alternative regionals like San Francisco's Magic Theatre (magic seems to have been in the air) began to appear. In New York, former Judson Poets' Theatre alumni Larry Kornfield, Theo Barnes and Crystal Field opened Theater for a New City, which still thrives today under Field. Maria Irene Fornes organized the New York Theatre Strategy (1973–8) to facilitate production of work in alternative spaces, such as the 1977 premiere of her self-directed production of *Fefu and Her Friends*. Charles Ludlam separated from the Play-House of the Ridiculous at the end of the 1960s and opened The Ridiculous Theatre Company with *Bluebeard* in 1970, bringing the first salvos of a specifically queer aesthetic to American theatre.

'Black is beautiful on Broadway': Contextualizing identity-based theatre of the 1970s

Along with launching and maintaining the reputations of significant playwrights, perhaps the most important role Off-Broadway and Off-Off-Broadway played during the 1970s was as an incubator for theatres curating shows for marginalized identity groups. Although critics like Meserve and Aronson are dismissive of this trend, citing it as evidence of the break-up of American consensus, a disrespect of dramatic forbearers and signs of an encroaching political correctness, history shows that such artists in the 1970s – and reaching back to immigrant Yiddish, Irish and German traditions

– gave voice to the country's polyglot culture and infused American drama with new forms and content.[76] Hanay Geiogamah, with momentum provided by the Native American Literary Renaissance – initiated when N. Scott Momaday's novel *House Made of Dawn* won the Pulitzer Prize in 1969 – founded the American Indian Theatre Ensemble out of Café La MaMa in 1971 (it later became the Native American Theatre Ensemble). A decade later, he published the first anthology of Native American plays.[77] Asian-American theatre established a toehold in the mid-1960s with the East West Players in Los Angeles and the Asian-American Workshop in San Francisco. By the 1970s these acting troupes were joined by the Northwest Asian Theatre Company, but the first actual repertory theatre devoted to producing Asian-American plays arrived only in 1977 with Tisa Chang's Pan-Asian Rep in New York. Before that, only Frank Chin's *Chickencoop Chinaman* (1972, American Place Theatre, directed by Jack Gelber) was produced in New York. Addressing the stereotypes found in American film and literature, Chin's play broke the ice and laid a foundation for the later work of David Henry Hwang, but it was not successful on stage. Hwang would arrive from the California theatre scene in 1979, when Lloyd Richards selected *FOB* for the New Playwrights Conference at the O'Neill Center in Connecticut. By 1980, the play had reached Papp's Public Theater where it won the 1981 Obie for Best Play. A comic look at the perils and possibilities of assimilation, the play itself – in the emerging Postmodern style of pastiche – assimilates characters from Maxine Hong Kingston's novel *The Woman Warrior* and another play by Chin (*Gee, Pop!*), as well as Asian and American theatrical styles. Writing at the end of the decade, Hwang was fully alert to the changes in the myth of the American melting pot that took place after the civil rights movement shifted toward a politics of difference and identity. Similar themes were explored through the multimedia work of Ping Chong's Fiji Company, resident at Ellen Stewart's new La MaMa spaces and regular performers at art galleries such as Meredith Monk's House Foundation.

Latino/a theatre expanded out from the pioneering work of Luis Valdez's El Teatro Campesino and the Puerto Rican Traveling Theatre Company, both founded in the 1960s and strongly associated with street theatre and agit-prop performance styles seen in work like ETC's 1970 *Vietnam Campesino*.[78] The '*teatro*' structure took root in a number of regional theatres such as Teatro de la Esperanza in Santa Barbara, and national networks were established to support the new theatres.[79] Valdez created controversy within the movement when he elected to produce *Zoot Suit* in mainstream theatres, first at the resident Mark Taper Forum in Los Angeles (1977) and then on Broadway the following year.[80] The Nuyorican Movement produced its first mainstream success with Miguel Piñero's *Short Eyes* (1974), which won the New York Drama Critics' Circle Award. Fornes's presence alone guaranteed higher visibility for Latina drama.

The rise of 'issue theatre' in the wake of the radical politicization of the 1960s, long a staple in the Off-Off and not-for-profit alternative scenes, brought the first tentative crossovers of a recognizably black aesthetic to Broadway and Off-Broadway. As Christopher Bigsby distinguishes it, this shift lay in the emergence of 'a theatre which sought to address directly the realities and myths of black life. It lay in a racially conscious, racially derived and racially directed theatre that, for a time at least, saw itself as the cultural arm of the black power movement.'[81] This marked a radical departure from the well-intended dramas and musicals on black themes written and produced by white artists that peppered the Broadway listings in previous decades: musicals like *Lost in the Stars* (1948), *No Strings* (1962) and *Golden Boy* (1964), and dramas such as *In Abraham's Bosom* (1926), *Take a Giant Step* (1953), *The Owl and the Pussycat* (1964) and *The Great White Hope* (1968). While Broadway could point to the increased integration of its audiences and casts, little evidence existed that the form or content of its playwriting and the purpose of its theatre had changed in the face of America's struggle with race.

Despite Leiter's claims that 'black was beautiful on Broadway' in the 1970s,[82] the majority presence of black artists there during the decade was in musicals and revues. After the singular success of Lorraine Hansberry's seminal *A Raisin in the Sun* (1959), the 1960s saw only a trickle of notable plays by black writers produced on Broadway, including Ossie Davis's *Purlie Victorious* (1961), and at the outset of the 1970s the last 39 performances of Charles Gordone's *No Place to be Somebody* (a transfer from the Public and other Off-Broadway theatres). The trend continued across the decade, which saw only nine dramas by black authors produced by the commercial theatre in New York, which even given the economics and risk-averse environment was a sign of how far behind Broadway had fallen in taking the pulse of American life. One of these was the premiere in 1970 of Lorraine Hansberry's *Les Blancs*, left incomplete at her death in 1965 and completed by her husband, Howard Nemiroff. Perhaps expecting a drama on the virtues of integration in line with *Raisin*, the post-colonial themes and overt Bandung humanism of *Les Blancs* and its more strident condemnation of white power initiated controversy and forced the show to close after only one month. In 1973, Joseph Walker's *The River Niger* transferred from Off-Broadway (uniquely bringing its original black cast, which included Douglas Turner Ward), where it had won the Obie for Best Play. Stewart Lane contends that during the Broadway run, perhaps for the first time, black people made up the majority of the audience, and the production went on to garner the Tony for Best Play.[83] For the rest of the decade, until the unique commercial success of Shange's *colored girls who have considered suicide/when the rainbow is enuf* (1976) and Samm-Art Williams's *Home* (1980), black playwriting was barely visible along the Great White Way.

Instead of mounting new plays by black writers, Broadway often turned to casting all-black revivals of iconic American plays and musicals: following David Merrick's decision to close down the hugely successful and still-running *Hello, Dolly!* and then reopen it with a black cast in 1967, producers followed suit with *Guys and Dolls* (1976) and *Kismet* (as *Timbuktu*) in 1978. In musicals and revues, black progress was seemingly on display. Previous plays by black dramatists, such as Davis's *Purlie Victorious*, were remounted as successful musicals (the 1970 *Purlie*, which ran for almost 700 performances). Virginia Capers electrified audiences in *Raisin*, the 1973 musical adaptation based on Hansberry's two-decade-old breakthrough play, which won a Tony for Best New Musical, while Capers walked away with Best New Actress in a Musical. Following the lead of *Hair*, high-profile original book musicals such as *Jesus Christ Superstar* (1971) and *Pippin* (1972) cast black performers like Ben Vereen in significant colour-blind roles (though his appearance as Judas in *Superstar* caused some controversy). Musical revues were popular, ranging from the experimental *The Me Nobody Knows* (1970, after premiering Off-Broadway), based on stories submitted by children living in New York ghettos, to lavish celebrations of well-loved American performers (*Bubbling*

Brown Sugar [1976], *Eubie!* [1978] and the hugely successful *Ain't Misbehavin'* [1978, Tony Award for Nell Carter]).

However high such work raised the profile of America's black performers (in addition to Vereen and Carter, these shows introduced dancers Maurice and Gregory Hines, Honi Coles and Debbie Allen), without a complementary presence of black playwrights there still lingered, as Arnold Aronson notes, 'uncomfortable echoes once again of minstrelsy'.[84] Winds of change seemed to blow when Melvin Van Peebles brought *Ain't Supposed to Die a Natural Death* from the Black Arts/West stage in California to Broadway for a run of 325 performances and introduced a recognizably soul aesthetic to the American musical.[85] He followed with another successful musical, *Don't Play Us Cheap*, in 1972. These quasi-political musicals expressing black vernacular culture did not sustain their legacy, however, despite their innovative use of popular black music and dance.[86] Instead, as the energy of the Black Arts Movement waned and America grew more politically conservative by mid-decade, Broadway capitalized on new black audiences arriving to see Van Peebles' work by mounting, in 1975, *The Wiz*, which Laurence Maslon charitably describes as 'not the finest hour for black artists'.[87] Despite trading in stereotypes and traditions of black performance that Van Peebles sought to evict, *The Wiz* nevertheless won seven Tony Awards, ran for 1,672 performances (largely by virtue of an activist campaign launched by the black arts community to counter poor mainstream reviews) and succeeded in bringing an even more significant black audience to Broadway.[88]

But for most of the decade Broadway remained closed to emerging black writers, and the most significant (and politically grounded) black playwrights, Amiri Baraka, Sonia Sanchez and Ed Bullins, saw none of their work produced there. Bullins came closest with a notorious production of *Duplex* that moved to Lincoln Center, but the show was mired in controversy when Bullins publicly protested against the play's treatment at the hand of director Gilbert Moses. (All must have been forgiven, as Bullins's 1975 play, *The Taking of Miss Janie*, was directed by Moses and ran briefly in the Mitzi Newhouse Theatre at Lincoln Center as well.) Ironically, the lack of access to Broadway and even to most of Off-Broadway (apart from the Public and theatres associated with the Black Arts Movement such as the New Lafayette) coincided with a final burst of private and federal funding that produced a number of new black theatres and companies. Woodie King, Jr initiated the New Federal Theatre in 1970 and then moved in 1974 to New York's Henry Street Arts Center, specializing in minority drama. Barbara Ann Teer left the Negro Ensemble Company to form the National Black Theatre, and Lou Bellamy followed the wave toward new regional resident theatres by forming Penumbra Theatre in Minneapolis in 1976.

Black theatre's history with Off-Broadway is also an uneven one, though it bears reminding that the longest running non-musical of the 1960s beyond 42nd Street was the St Mark's Playhouse production of Genet's *The Blacks* (1961, more than 1,400 performances). The rotating cast included, besides the omnipresent James Earl Jones, Cicely Tyson, Roscoe Lee Brown, Charles Gordone, Louis Gossett, Jr and Maya Angelou. Off-Broadway also hosted the seminal black play of the 1960s, LeRoi Jones's (not yet Amiri Baraka) *Dutchman* (1964, Cherry Lane Theatre), the play that launched Ed Bullins' aspirations as a writer, spurred development of new black theatre companies in New York (particularly the NEC and the New Federal Theatre) and laid the foundation for the renewal of the Black Arts Movement.[89] Off-Broadway had also supported Alice Childress during the 1960s and produced *Wedding Band* in 1972. Adrienne Kennedy's innovative work (which would influence Ntozake Shange) drew the interest of experimental theatre directors such as Joe Chaikin, who directed her *A Movie Star Has to Star in Black and White* at the small Public Theater Workshop in 1976.[90]

The 1970s saw continued Off- and Off-Off-Broadway support for dramatists associated with the Black Arts Movement that had begun in the 1960s, such as Baraka and Bullins. Baraka opened the decade with the pageant play *Slave Ship*, produced first at Spirit House in 1967 and then mounted by Gilbert Moses Off-Broadway, and to some the play announced the playwright's conversion to black nationalism.[91] The building up of ritual *communitas* by the incorporation of music and other affective techniques certainly signalled a new commitment to the values of black culture and the necessity to reclaim the voice to relate its own history. However, Baraka's denouncement of black nationalism's reformist aims and leaders by 1974 (when he dropped the religious title of Imamu from his name) and turn toward an explicit Marxist-Leninist programme all but negated a future presence on Off-Broadway. *The Motion of History* (1978), which ran for four hours and utilized film projection and other epic techniques, was essentially Baraka's farewell to a mainstream audience he no longer had patience to address.

The New Lafayette Theatre hosted writing workshops that developed plays for productions there by J. E. Gaines (*What If It Had Turned Up Heads?*, 1972) and Richard Wesley (*The Sirens*, 1976). The workshop leader, Bullins, was the prime example of the tensions that existed between even the non-commercial theatre and black playwriting of the 1970s. Often appearing as a footnote to theatrical histories of the time and with work that is rarely produced today, Bullins, in Mike Sell's estimation, 'has persistently shattered critical and theatrical orthodoxy ... recast the basic terms of dramatic criticism, engaged with some of the most pressing issues surrounding race and racial representation, and written provocative, fascinating, and quite often beautiful drama'.[92] During the decade, Bullins exemplified the need to find new production outlets, as he saw his work produced in Off-Off-Broadway houses, Baraka's Harlem-based Black Arts Repertory School and the New Lafayette Theatre (founded in 1968 by Robert Macbeth, and for which Bullins was the first artist-in-residence). After editing the seminal 1968 Black Theatre issue of *The Drama Review* where the Black Arts aesthetic was spelled out clearly in relation to American theatre, Bullins built on his reputation established with *Clara's Ole Man* (1965, Firehouse Rep, San Francisco) and later in New York with *Goin' a Buffalo* at the American Place Theatre (1968). His notable plays of the 1970s are the relatively naturalistic *The Duplex* and *The Fabulous Miss Marie* (both appeared at the New Lafayette Playhouse in 1971), as well as his best-known work, the blues-infused *The Taking of Miss Janie* (1975, New Federal Theatre, Obie Award). In the latter, Bullins cast a cynical eye on the evolution of race relations as fuelled by liberal intentions, and indicted American culture for its failure to address racial inequality during a promising period of social change. Like many Americans during the 1970s, his protagonists are highly evolved in their ability to see and name the history and causes of oppression in the wake of 1960s radicalism, yet portrayed as powerless to effect change.

Charles Fuller, who would win the 1981 Pulitzer for *A Soldiers Play*, established a long-running relationship with the Negro

Ensemble Company during the late 1960s. Although often excoriated by Black Arts Movement members – in part because of its location in Greenwich Village and thus distant from the black communities in Harlem and the South Bronx – the NEC trained many theatre practitioners to a high level.[93] Fuller's best-known play from the 1970s was *The Brownsville Raid*, a procedural drama based on the historical miscarriage of justice against a black company of soldiers in 1906 Texas. As Matthew Roundané writes, by virtue of his juxtaposition of the accounts spoken by the soldiers and by various colonial spokespersons (such as Theodore Roosevelt), 'Fuller effectively asks his audience to become a jury' and thus partakes of the new interest in the 1970s for docufiction.[94] The 1980 *Zooman and the Sign*, similarly, used actual events to explore themes of black-on-black violence.

The exception that proved the rule regarding new work by black writers on Broadway was the 1976 transfer from the Public to the Booth Theatre of Ntozake Shange's choreopoem, *for colored girls who have considered suicide/when the rainbow is enuf* (see also Neal Lester's essay in this book). Emerging from the author's San Francisco group poetry performances (with musical accompaniment) and black dance training, the interconnected stories of seven black women at different points of personal and historical experience was first presented, with Shange performing, at taverns near the Berkeley campus. When Shange went to New York, she continued to show it at clubs before taking it first to the Henry Street Settlement's New Federal Theatre in 1976 and to the Studio Rivbea in July 1977. The buzz surrounding the piece was intense enough to catch Papp's attention and led him to bring it to the Public in June and then transfer it to Broadway's Booth Theatre in September. The hybrid nature of the 'choreopoem' and Shange's own electrifying performance at the Broadway premiere (which, due to illness and her ambiguous response to having the piece played before Broadway audiences, was cut short) created strong responses – many positive, but some, such as John Simon's notorious 'Enuf is Not Enough', quite vituperative and dismissive[95] – and brought a unique black, feminist perspective to American drama.[96] Moreover, Trazana Beverley's Tony for Best Actress was the only such award for a black performer in a straight play for the entire decade.

Shange's presence was maintained with the 1977 production of *A Photograph: A Study of Cruelty* (Public Theatre), later revised to *A Photograph: Lovers in Motion* when it was produced in Houston's Equinox Theatre.[97] Barnard College produced her *From Okra to Greens: A Different Kind of Love Story; A Play with Music and Dance* in 1978, and after revision it appeared as *Mouths* at the Kitchen in New York City in 1981. *boogie woogie landscapes* was produced at the Shakespeare Festival in 1978, and after several revisions appeared on Broadway in 1979 and then at the Kennedy Center for Performing Arts the following year. Shange's amazing run closed out the decade with *spell #7: geechee jibara quik magic trance manual for technologically stressed third world people*, produced by the Public in 1979, and her 1980 adaptation, set in the American Civil War, of Brecht's *Mother Courage and Her Children* (which won an Obie in 1981) also at the Public. The choreopoem form swept through American theatre from Broadway to the regionals and university theatres, and Shange became one of the most produced artists in America by the early 1980s.

The women's movement and theatre

Shange's achievement was especially singular given that between 1969 and 1976 only 7 per cent of all American theatrical productions featured women's writing or female directors.[98] Across the entire decade, Broadway produced six female-authored plays and, as Leiter notes, all were flops.[99] The opportunities rose slightly Off-Broadway (see below): Tina Howe had both *Museum* and *The Art of Dining* produced at the Public, Wendy Wasserstein's *Uncommon Women and Others* had a short run at the Phoenix and Marsha Norman's *Getting Out* transferred from the Louisville Humana Festival for Off-Broadway runs. But the chances of seeing female authors produced were (relatively) greatest Off-Off-Broadway, where plays by Maria Irene Fornes, Rosalyn Drexler and Gloria Gonzalez could be seen and where female directors like Julie Bovasso, Elizabeth LeCompte and JoAnne Akalaitis earned widespread recognition.

With the emergence of second wave feminism in the late 1960s, the first theatres by and for women began to appear, slowly at first and then near the end of the decade more explosively. Susan Yankowitz, an occasional collaborator with the Open Theater, helped launch with others the Westbeth Feminist Collective in New York in 1971.[100] Maria Irene Fornes teamed up with fellow Off-Off-Broadway playwrights Rosalyn Drexler, Megan Terry and Rochelle Owens in 1972 to establish the Women's Theatre Council, dedicated to a repertory of female-authored plays. In its later manifestation as the New York Theatre Strategy (of which Sam Shepard was a member), the Council was responsible for the first production of Fornes's signature play, *Fefu and Her Friends* (1976). The Meisner acting guru, Margot Lewitin, opened her loft theatre, Women Interarts Center, in 1973, and the Women's Project was incorporated into the American Place Theatre in 1978 and later split off as its own producing company. The Women's Experimental Theatre (WET), under Roberta Sklar, Claire Cross and Sondra Segal, began *The Daughters Cycle* in 1976 and produced work into the next decade. Beyond New York, following the lead of such stalwarts as Megan Terry and JoAnn Schmidman – who broke from the Open Theater to go west to form the Omaha Magic Theatre in 1968 – At the Foot of the Mountain was established in Minneapolis in 1974, the same year that Lilith Woman's Theatre opened in San Francisco. Spiderwoman formed in 1976, the first feminist company to address specifically ethnic issues within feminism through 'storyweaving' in pieces like *Lysistrata Numbah!* (the company would eventually splinter, with one part forming the significant 1980s feminist performance collective Split Britches). By the end of the decade, there were scores of women's regional theatre companies, most underfunded and just scraping by but still collectively making it possible for women playwrights to be published and produced while training a generation of female artistic directors. Indeed, the 1970s is often referred to as the golden age of feminist theatre and a formative influence on the next generation of feminist performance.

New writing/new performance theatre

Marvin Carlson helpfully distinguishes an 'alternative theatre' movement in contrast to Off-Off-Broadway, first by virtue of the former's stronger presence in regions outside New York, and second the fact that such work bears little or no relationship (antagonistic or otherwise) to Broadway theatre.[101] With a slightly different emphasis, Ehren Fordyce describes as 'experimental drama' playwriting that exists on a continuum between writers who 'expand' realism in various ways (Tennessee Williams, Adrienne Kennedy, Sam Shepard, David Rabe) and those who disregard conventional realism entirely rather than adapting it. Many of the latter, such as Mac Wellman and Len Jenkin, got their start in the 1970s, producing work at La MaMa and other Off-Off spaces.[102] Such work, which includes the writing of Richard Foreman, exploring the limits of denotation and the dramatic text, would reverberate more profoundly in the 1980s and 1990s, establishing a line to Sarah Ruhl, Charles Mee and Suzan-Lori Parks.

Such alternative theatres tended also (but not always) to form in the 1960s around companies and often as well around alternative politics of a kind. One trajectory of modern American alternative theatre thus passes through the Living Theatre and the Open Theater in New York City, as well as the San Francisco Mime Troupe and El Teatro Campesino in California, and black, feminist and other 'minority' theatres across the nation. Many of these companies dispersed or reformed during the 1970s, and some did not survive long into the decade. Most notably, Joseph Chaikin's The Open Theater produced until 1973 (*The Serpent*, 1960–70; *Terminal*, 1970; *The Mutation Show*, 1972; the unfinished *Nightwalk*, 1973) before disbanding. Meanwhile, the Living Theatre, after its contentious return to the US in 1968, spent most of the decade living and producing collectively abroad (although their work remained vital owing to the publication of Julian Beck's *The Life of the Theatre* and Judith Malina's *The Enormous Despair*, both in 1972). They returned to work briefly in the US (in Pittsburgh) between 1972 and 1974, but relocated to New York only in 1984.

But a new generation of alternative theatre-makers emerged after the initial wave, in this instance drawing sustenance less from anarchist politics than from aesthetics pioneered by Marcel Duchamp and John Cage. Encompassing theatre auteurs such as Richard Foreman and Robert Wilson and mixed-arts practitioners like the Wooster Group, Squat Theatre, Mabou Mines, Meredith Monk, Ping Chong and Laurie Anderson, this trajectory marked more emphatically than any other sector of theatre the dramatic changes taking place in American culture after the decline of the radicalism of the 1960s. An art of extreme subjectivity and self-reflection displaced the more overtly political and issues-oriented alternative theatre of the previous decade, giving rise to performance art, multimedia performance and other paradigm-altering forms that developed a variety of scenographic writing forms.

Although many of these fall beyond this book's focus on playwriting, the productions of Wilson, Mabou Mines and the Wooster Group laid the foundations for significant developments in American theatre well beyond the 1970s. As Carlson notes, these artists focused more upon formal and structural concerns, creating a more abstract theatre with artistic connections to minimalism in the visual arts, certain trends in Modern and Postmodern dance, and the concerns of the creators of live events like the Happenings.[103] Wilson's work in the decade centred on the Byrd Hoffman School of Byrds, which he founded in 1969 to carry forward his work with developmentally disabled performers whose particular forms of consciousness he explored through innovative and image-charged productions that functioned without perceptible plots or embodied characters. *Deafman Glance*, a four-hour-long silent series of stunning tableaux, premiered at the University of Iowa in 1970 before moving to the Brooklyn Academy of Music the following year. When it travelled to France, Wilson's reputation in Europe was established and eventually, after the debacle of the failed production of *The CIVIL warS* by the Olympic Arts Festival in 1984, he would premiere the bulk of his work there. But during the 1970s Wilson's ambitions were still directed at succeeding in New York, with *A Letter to Queen Victoria* produced at the Broadway ANTA Theatre (later the August Wilson Theatre) in 1975 for a short and critically disastrous run. Wilson then collaborated with the dancer Lucinda Childs and composer Philip Glass to produce his best-known work, *Einstein on the Beach*, first overseas in France in 1975 before bringing it to the Metropolitan Opera House for an epochal single performance in 1976. The 1984 revival at the Brooklyn Academy of Music became a launching point for what Bonnie Marranca would later term 'The Theatre of Images' and effectively ushered Postmodern theatre into the American canon.[104]

Mabou Mines emerged from the vibrant San Francisco performance scene stemming from the SF Mime Troupe's work that began in the 1960s.[105] A collective that formed around four core artists (writer Lee Breuer, actress Ruth Malaczech, director JoAnne

Akalaitis and composer Philip Glass), Mabou Mines established an artistic home in New York at the Theatre for a New City, where they premiered a series of works based on Samuel Beckett's late dramatic and non-dramatic writing. In tandem with such High Modernist explorations of inner consciousness, the company created the so-called 'animations' (*Red Horse Animation*, 1970; *B. Beaver Animation*, 1975; and *The Shaggy Dog Animation*, 1978) out of Breuer's typical 1970s preoccupations with self-analysis and interior monologue, presented in a collage of expressive physical actions, painterly tableaux and references to pop culture comic books and films. Collectively and individually, Mabou Mines would produce some of alternative theatre's most inspiring work beyond the 1970s, becoming particularly well known for their deep investigations and deployment of non-Western performance styles.

Perhaps no development in new performance modes best encapsulates the shift from the 1960s to the 1970s than the gradual transformation of the Wooster Group out of Richard Schechner's seminal Performance Group.[106] The latter investigated mythic structures that continued to shape American life and politics, and was performed within environmental staging that aimed to re-establish community and critical democracy, often through audience participation. After its demise, some members re-formed in the same space (the Performing Garage on Wooster Street in the East Village) to explore new acting and performance styles. During the 1970s, their work focused on the autobiographical material of actor Spalding Gray, which was collaged with found material and texts in the manner of Dada; however, in the spirit of the 1970s these materials were often recorded (phonograph records, family slides, film and later video) and played as part of the performance. The decade saw the completion of an informal trilogy of works directed by Elizabeth LeCompte (*Sakonnet Point*, 1974; *Rumstick Road*, 1977; *Nayatt School*, 1979) that established a signature style built on ambiguity and indeterminacy. One result was a mediated, abstract presentation of Gray's emotional crises that produced a distancing effect that would soon be understood as a hallmark of the cool and detached perspective of Postmodern art. While still investigating environmental staging, the new performance milieu projected an industrial feel, with media machinery in full view and performers interacting with it. In contrast to the Performance Group's search for authenticity and mythic roots, the Wooster

Group invited audiences to see themselves as already mediated by technologies of reproduction; and, rather than inviting the spectators to participate, they were distanced by the many layers of screens and found texts that rebuffed attempts to empathize with a central script or character. Still producing cutting edge work in 2016, the Wooster Group is one of America's longest-running alternative theatre companies and its influence on contemporary work has been profound.

Home away from home: Regional theatres and the resident playwright

By the mid-1970s Broadway's domination of American theatre was decisively over. Off- and Off Off-Broadway theatres routinely produced six or more times as many shows as Broadway did each season; and the hundreds of professional theatres around the country together staged many more productions than all the New York City theatres put together.[107]

For the brief period when the resident non-profit professional theatre movement flourished, emerging American playwrights were freer than at any other time in the nation's history to develop and hone their craft through production – sometimes multiple productions with different staging concepts – and to experiment with new content and dramatic forms. The presence of non-proscenium stages in many of the regional theatres encouraged writers to treat space flexibly and to push against the constraints of the kitchen sink or domestic brands of realism. The process of 'workshopping' a play by touring a circuit of resident and university theatres (begun with Jerome Lawrence and Robert E. Lee's *The Night Thoreau Spent in Jail* at the beginning of the decade) allowed playwrights to develop and refine their work.[108] Although in many instances the regional resident theatres were treated (and saw themselves) as the launching pad for transfers to the New York commercial theatre, many continued to promote new work for its own sake, based on artistic merit or the resonance between a play and its regional audience.

With a new boldness, some resident companies sought to define their distinctive vision with an annual festival or by bringing in a resident artist for a season or longer. The signature American resident theatre festival remains the Humana Festival in the heart of the country, where the Actors Theatre of Louisville was founded in 1964. Created in 1976 by John Jory, the Festival was developed, according to Jeffrey Ullom, for two reasons: 'to educate his audience to the aesthetics of new plays and to foster the audience's willingness to support multiple productions'.[109] Part of the plan featured a Great American Play Contest, and in its first year the award went to Donald Coburn's *The Gin Game*, which eventually made its way to New York and won the 1978 Pulitzer Prize. During its ascent, for the second festival Marsha Norman – perhaps not entirely coincidentally a Louisville native – submitted *Getting Out*. Her play, too, would eventually be produced at the Theatre de Lys in New York, and cemented the Festival's reputation for developing new dramatists (an annual anthology of the best plays from Humana are now a staple of new play publishing). In the years to come, the Actors Theatre garnered a Margo Jones Award (1979) and a Special Tony Award for Outstanding Nonprofit Theatre in America (1980).

Conclusion

This overview provides but a glimpse of the variety and breadth of theatrical activity in America during the 1970s. As Broadway for once and all dedicated itself to pursuit of the sure-fire hit or mega-musical, the labour of nurturing emerging talent fell to Off- and Off-Off-Broadway, the booming regional theatre circuit of resident not-for-profit theatres and the broad school of performance art practices that might as likely take place in a museum or university performance centre as a conventional theatre. This devolution produced real losses, as any notion of a national theatre or collective site of America's theatrical arts dissipated, and along with it dissolved that long-sought-after illusion, a unified sense of national identity and history. Moreover, a Broadway singularly devoted to commercial successes at the expense of new work and the development of new playwrights created a theatre culture that, outlandishly, is still understood by many to represent the nation's highest traditions of theatre art.

In the long run, however, the final break-up of Broadway's hegemony over American theatre must be understood as both necessary and fruitful. By intent or by force of history, Broadway developed as an organ of the almost exclusively white, male and upper middle-class audiences that had long patronized it. The break-up of the time-honoured liberal consensus meant as well the fragmenting of that constituency and its power to manage public discourse – both its content and its forms. Following the movements toward civil rights (and its expansion into women's rights, gay rights and rights for all minority ethnic groups and cultures) and the lasting imprint made by the counterculture's search for more radical forms of democracy, maintaining a consensual voice in American theatre would have seemed anomalous and retrograde. The theatre that the 1970s gave to America was sometimes strident and almost always discordant and clamorous: equal to its subject and almost a match for its aspirations.

3

'An Idiom that is a Kind of Vision of the World': David Rabe's Plays of the 1970s – *The Basic Training of Pavlo Hummel* (1971), *Sticks and Bones* (1971) and *Streamers* (1975)

Jon Dietrick

Introduction

David Rabe was born on 10 March 1940 in Dubuque, Iowa. He was raised Catholic, though he has since rejected the faith. He began studies in theatre at Villanova but dropped out and was drafted into the army in 1965, where he served his last eleven months in Vietnam attached to a hospital support unit. He returned to Villanova in 1967, where he earned an MA one year later. Between 1971 and 1976, David Rabe composed and saw staged five plays: *The Basic Training of Pavlo Hummel* (1971), *Sticks and Bones* (1971), *The Orphan* (1973), *In the Boom Boom Room* (1974) and *Streamers* (1975). Joseph Papp became an early champion of Rabe's work in the 1970s, and produced (and in one case directed) all five plays.

The Basic Training of Pavlo Hummel premiered at the Joseph Papp Public Theater, as part of the New York Shakespeare Festival, in 1971. Jeff Bleckner won an Obie for Distinguished Direction, and the production starred William Atherton as Pavlo. Critical and audience response were positive, with Clive Barnes of the *New York Times* calling Rabe a 'new and authentic voice of our theatre'.[1] A later Broadway production in 1977 was directed by David Wheeler and starred Al Pacino as Pavlo.

Rabe wrote the first version of *Sticks and Bones* while doing graduate work at Villanova after returning from Vietnam. The play was first staged at Villanova in 1969, then, following the success of *Pavlo Hummel*, was produced Off-Broadway at the Joseph Papp Public Theater (directed by Jeff Bleckner) in 1971, where it ran for 121 performances. The cast for this performance included David Selby as David and Tom Aldredge as Ozzie. There followed a Broadway production at the John Golden Theatre in 1972, which ran for 246 performances, with the same cast but for the replacement of David Selby by Drew Snyder. Critical and audience response for the Papp and Broadway productions were generally positive. The play earned the 1972 Tony Awards for Best Play and Best Performance by a Featured Actress in a Play (Elizabeth Wilson as Harriett), as well as Drama Desk Awards for Outstanding Director (Jeff Bleckner), Outstanding Actor (Tom Aldredge) and set design, in addition to the Outer Critics Circle Award for Best Play. Bleckner and Aldridge were also nominated for Tonys (Best Director and Best Performance by a Leading Actor, respectively).

Streamers debuted at the Long Wharf Theatre in New Haven, Connecticut, in 1975. A Broadway production followed in 1976, at the Mitzi E. Newhouse Theatre at Lincoln Center, produced again by Papp, directed by Mike Nichols and starring a young Paul Rudd in the role of Billy (replaced in later productions by Mark Metcalf). This production ran for 478 performances and earned a Tony nomination for Best Play and a Drama Desk Award for Outstanding New Play, as well as Drama Desk nominations for Outstanding Actor in a Play (Peter Evans) and Outstanding Director of a Play (Nichols). The play proved popular with critics and audiences, and is today largely considered Rabe's most important work.

The other two plays from Rabe's work in the 1970s are not generally considered as important as his Vietnam plays. Based on an earlier, shorter version of the play that debuted at Villanova, *The Orphan* opened at the Papp Public Theater in 1973, directed by Bleckner and starring Tom Aldredge and Rae Allen. The production was not a critical or popular success. *In the Boom Boom Room* also saw an early production at Villanova, and then opened on Broadway at the Vivian Beaumont Theater in November 1973, directed by Joseph Papp. Papp produced the play again in 1974 at the Public Theater with Robert Hedley directing in a production that earned the Runner Up Award for Best American Play from the New York Drama Critics' Circle.

The critical discussion of Rabe's work is overwhelmingly centred on questions of genre. The dialogue in his plays tends to be mostly realistic with sudden, sometimes jarring, forays into poetic language. The sets tend to be minimalist, with a few carefully chosen and highly realistic details. In 1978, Robert Brustein named Rabe as one of the few American playwrights to escape what he saw as an unfortunate allegiance to a strict causality that, according to Brustein, made no sense in the modern 'age of Einstein'.[2] William Demastes and Michael Vanden Heuvel see Rabe (and his contemporary Shepard) as part of a line of American playwrights taking realist (and naturalist) theatre, forms originally derived from a positivist, rationalist, Newtonian, mechanistic view of the world, and adapting them to a contemporary view that accommodates the uncertainty principle and chaos theory. They write that Rabe's 'theatre presents a hybrid form, something that gravitates between the strict causality of naturalism and the utter randomness of absurdism', and identify in plays like *Streamers* a kind of 'unpredictable determinism': 'While straightforward naturalism may lead audiences to expect a single line of causality to determine ultimate outcomes, something akin to a butterfly effect intrudes into the events of a play like *Streamers* to produce determined, yet unpredictable, behavior.'[3]

This blending of realism with non-realist elements has led Toby Silverman Zinman to note what she calls the 'puzzling and powerful distantiation' of the Rabe play,[4] where all seems at once real and unreal, where characters 'do not take their own humanity quite seriously' and tend to 'quote' their actions in the manner of a comic strip.[5] This seems on one level like something akin to the Brechtian 'alienation effect', and the influence of Brecht on Rabe's work has probably been underappreciated.[6] Another and perhaps more useful term for describing what is happening in Rabe's plays is *the uncanny*, the English translation of Heidegger's *'unheimlich'*, referring to that which seems to reveal something even as it conceals it. Freud further developed this idea, defining the uncanny as 'on the one hand ... that which is familiar and congenial, and on the other, that which is concealed and kept out of sight'.[7] It is also 'that class of the terrifying which leads back to something long known to us, once very familiar'.[8] In this way the uncanny is, according to Freud, a kind of 'testing' of reality.[9]

Reality and its relation to language, and to signs generally, is, I would argue, *the* major issue in Rabe's work, and his treatment of this issue is inextricably bound up with questions of genre. Rabe's plays of the 1970s show him simultaneously steeped in dialogue with the traditions of American realism and naturalism. Walter Benn Michaels has drawn fruitful connections between literary naturalism – and especially American literary naturalism – and an anxiety over issues of material reality and representation. Specifically, Benn Michaels looks at the way issues related to the nineteenth-century 'gold standard' debates inform the work of American naturalist writers like Stephen Crane and Frank Norris, identifying in the fear of an 'insubstantial' paper currency and fetishization of precious metals a cultural logic based on the repression of money as free-floating signifier, which expresses itself in various attempts at 'escape' from the money economy. An aesthetic expression of both the desire for and the seeming impossibility of this escape, naturalism obsesses over the ontological and epistemological questions raised by money, becoming, in Benn Michaels' analysis, 'the working out of a set of conflicts between pretty things and curious ones, material and representation, hard money and soft, beast and soul'.[10] Drawing a homology between economies of money and economies of signs, this view sees naturalism as animated by an anxiety over the unbridgeable gap between, in psychoanalytical terms, the real and the symbolic. Characters in naturalist works attempt to deny this gap by insisting on 'hard' distinctions between the symbolic and the real, dividing the world into hard, essential substance (naturalism's 'beast within', usually) and empty, untrustworthy or even threatening signs. What this view fears and denies, ultimately, is the unavoidable involvement of the symbolic in the real.

The anxiety over economic life and signification more generally that played so large a role in American naturalist fiction has been a major animating force in American realist drama. This should not be surprising, since many of the foundational writers of the American realist theatrical tradition did their most important work during or in the first couple of decades after the Great Depression. Miller described the Depression as 'only incidentally a matter of money. Rather it was a moral catastrophe, a violent revelation of the hypocrisies behind the façade of American society.'[11] In fact, Miller's work is especially important for understanding Rabe. In important ways, Miller's 1949 masterpiece *Death of a Salesman* brought American anxieties about economic life and the relation of the symbolic to the real into the modern age, and the play's exploration of distinctions such as 'talk' and action, seeming and being, and technology and nature has had an undeniable influence on the work of American playwrights of the 1970s such as Rabe and Mamet. Miller's seminal play examined the ways in which the 'hypocrisies' exposed by the Depression had become both deeper and more widespread as the post-war industrial boom and the explosion of the advertising and public relations industries worked to create the commodified, hyper-mediated world we live in today – one in which the ubiquity of 'business' values and the superseding of all values by economic ones have contributed to a difficulty to think of oneself other than as a commodity. This difficulty certainly is a major theme of Rabe's 1970s output.

Economic events of the 1970s only deepened Americans' anxiety over the seeming lack of 'hard' value in money, in signs and in ourselves. In 1975, President Nixon signed an order allowing gold, that old American fetish of substantial value, to be traded freely on the market like any other commodity. The oil crises of 1973 and 1979, with their resultant 'price shocks', were likened in both their economic and psychological impact to the Great Depression. In fact, perhaps even more powerfully than the Depression, the oil crises made notions of an essential American 'character' increasingly difficult to maintain in the face of what was emerging as the vulnerability of American currency – and American values – to international events. America's involvement in Vietnam, which escalated in the early 1960s and sparked a revolutionary counter-culture movement that lasted beyond the official end of America's military involvement in 1975, was a further, and even greater, shock. If its involvement in the Second World War left America able to think of itself as the great saviour of the world, atrocities like the My Lai massacre made this view increasingly difficult to hold. These economic and historical events haunt Rabe's plays of the 1970s, and they do this most powerfully in the three plays that make up what critics refer to as his 'Vietnam Trilogy'.

The Basic Training of Pavlo Hummel begins with a young 'everyman' soldier picking up a grenade tossed into a Vietnamese brothel by a fellow American soldier, and dying from the blast. It then goes back to tell the story of Pavlo's experiences in basic training: his constant stealing; his failed attempts at connection with his fellow soldiers, his mother and a lover back home in New York; and his suicidal insistence on being transferred to the infantry from a relatively safe position as a medic. *Sticks and Bones*, the second part of the Vietnam trilogy, makes use of characters from the well-known television sit-com *The Adventures of Ozzie and Harriet* (which ran from 1952 to 1966) by having the eldest son of the family, David, return home blind and traumatized from Vietnam, having abandoned a young Vietnamese woman with whom he'd become romantically involved. David confronts parents and a younger brother who seem to embody the very mid-century-American, middle-class values his war experience has taught him to reject. *Streamers*, the third play in the trilogy, is set in 1965 and focuses on three young soldiers about to be deployed in Vietnam: Richie, a young New Yorker struggling with his sexual orientation; Roger, a middle-class African-American; and Billy, a seemingly straightforward but ultimately deeply repressed young man from Wisconsin. Violence erupts near the play's end, when the 'vagrant' Carlyle fatally stabs both Billy and the drunken, battle-hardened Sgt Rooney.

In these plays, characters explore the distinction between the symbolic and the real – expressed most often as a distinction between 'talk' and action. The plays ultimately reject this distinction, moving toward something closer to a Postmodern notion of an intergenerative relationship between the symbolic and the real. However, whereas Postmodernism is generally seen as celebrating or at least playing with this relation of symbolic to real, Rabe's work seems to view that relation as a tragedy. In a 1990 interview, David Rabe notes that in his plays, 'It seems that I like to have a world in which a particular lingo or argot exists that people are restrained by – an idiom that is a kind of vision of the world.'[12] This notion of language defining one's 'vision of the world' – another way of saying that language is always intensely ideological – is explored relentlessly in Rabe's 1970s output. In Rabe's plays, characters tell stories in an attempt to construct new identities and to slough off old ones. But in each case this attempt at identity construction through narrative is a tragic failure. Characters are repeatedly seen to struggle against the prisons of other people's narratives, usually by spinning their own stories, but ultimately they are shown to have at their disposal only that very language and ideology that imprisons them. However, in their struggles to articulate something that the limits of their American language forbid, the characters attain a kind of heroism. [13]

The Basic Training of Pavlo Hummel

Like most Rabe characters, Pavlo Hummel establishes himself early on as a storyteller – or what his brother Mickey calls 'a mythmaker'.[14] The play opens in a bar in Vietnam with Pavlo telling stories, first about a man he bested in a fight (by the play's end we will learn this is Sgt Wall, who in a moment will throw the grenade that kills Pavlo), then about an old lover who rejected him. The stories demonstrate both the depth of Pavlo's need to construct identities for himself and also the impossibility of Pavlo's escaping certain toxic cultural narratives – the very narratives that seem to lead inexorably to his death.

Like characters in other plays of the American realist-naturalist tradition that makes up a major part of Rabe's literary inheritance, those peopling *The Basic Training of Pavlo Hummel* embody a paradoxical attitude toward the relation of the symbolic to the real, language to material reality, 'talk' to 'action'. On one level, Pavlo seems to understand, in a sense, an interrelated relationship between symbolic and real. This is Pavlo the 'myth maker'. He tells his fellow recruits stories about daring feats he almost surely never accomplished, such as the one about his stealing twenty-three cars. When it is suggested he is lying, Pavlo responds 'I wasn't lyin', it was storytelling' (20). At one point, Pavlo tells a story about an uncle in San Quentin. Then later in the play, in conversation with his brother Mickey while he's on leave in New York, he refers to his fellow trainee Kress as having an uncle in San Quentin, ascribing to Kress a life detail he once claimed for his own story. Conversely, his brother Mickey espouses a view of signification as totally unrelated to reality. When Pavlo tells Mickey he's in the army, Mickey responds, 'How do I know?' Pavlo thinks his word is enough, despite his constant and obvious lying: 'I'm tellin' you.' Mickey remains in doubt, and when Pavlo tells him he is going to Vietnam, Mickey even claims, 'Vietnam don't even exist', reducing what has been referred to as 'the first televised war' to an empty signifier and nothing else (56).

While Pavlo tries, and fails, to use 'talk' to construct an identity, he simultaneously displays a naiveté regarding the relation of talk to action, the symbolic to the real. Near the end of Act One, Pavlo passes his exam to complete his training. When it is learned that his fellow trainee Kress flunked his exam, Pavlo needlessly taunts him, which leads to Kress violently attacking Pavlo. Afterwards, Pavlo is indignant and insists, 'He had no call to hit me like that. I was just talkin' (45). Pavlo's naiveté concerning the practical, physical effects of his 'talk' plays a major role in the character's death by a grenade thrown by a soldier just after Pavlo verbally humiliated him in a dispute over a prostitute. Once again, and for the last time, Pavlo is 'just talking' and pays a real price for it.

These disputes – with Kress and with Sgt Wall – display Pavlo ultimately not as mythmaker, but as someone helpless to resist living out certain American myths regarding war, heroism and gender. Rabe emphasizes the role of media, and specifically film, in purveying these myths through the words of Pavlo's mother. Like male characters in Rabe's other Vietnam plays, Pavlo does not know who his father is. When he questions his mother concerning his father's identity, she responds in a way that implicates certain American myths of masculinity in Pavlo's self-destructive behaviour:

[Y]ou had many fathers, many men, movie men, filmdom's great – all of them, those grand old men of yesteryear, they were your father. The Fighting 76th, do you remember, oh, I remember, little Jimmy, what a tough little mite he was, and how he leaped upon that grenade, did you see, my God what a glory, what a glorious thing with his little tin hat. (63)

Pavlo of course meets his end by leaping on a grenade, though one thrown by an American army sergeant in a bar/brothel, not by a foreign combatant on the field of battle. When Ardell, who seems to be a sometimes encouraging, sometimes mocking projection of Pavlo's mind, asks the dead Pavlo what he was thinking picking up the grenade, Pavlo answers that he was going to throw it, in imitation of another male hero, the pitcher for a softball team he saw play as a child who 'could do anything with a softball underhand that most big leaguers can do with a hardball overhand. He was fantastic' (7).

Pavlo's storytelling and his need to self-create is played out against a background of an American army whose logic reduces Pavlo to a faceless tool and commodity. After the grenade blast that kills Pavlo, Ardell brings up what develops as a major theme in Rabe's Vietnam plays: the valuing of things (and commodities) over human life. '[T]hat the way it happen sometimes,' explains Ardell: 'Everybody hit, everybody hurtin', but the radio ain't been touched, the dog didn't feel a thing; the engine's good as new but all the people dead' (5). In fact, Hummel's army training would erase the distinction between people and machines, as Pavlo and his fellow trainees are conditioned by Sgt Tower to adapt the most basic biological processes to a strict mechanical regularity. 'You are gonna fall out. By platoon,' explains Tower early in the play, '[w]hich is how you gonna be doin' most everything from now on – by platoon and by the numbers – includin' takin' a shit. Somebody say to you, ONE, you down; TWO, you doin' it; THREE, you wipin' and you ain't finished, you cuttin' it off' (12).

It is here, where everyone is reduced to a moving part of the American war machine, that Pavlo seeks to somehow carve out an identity. Even his name is an attempt at self-creation: he tells Ardell – though we learn quickly not to place too much trust in his stories – that his real name is Michael, but he had it changed to Pavlo. Ardell responds in a way that emphasizes Pavlo's *lack* of a coherent self: 'You black on the inside. In there where you live, you that awful hurtin' black so you can't see yourself no way. Not up or down or in or out'(38).

The trade-off Pavlo is offered for adapting his mind and body to the mechanical rhythms of the American war machine is a degree of self-reliance in a world that becomes manageable and navigable (figuratively and metaphorically), and this idea is embodied by Sgt Tower. Repeatedly throughout the play, Tower is shown offering advice for successful navigation of the most fraught, even seemingly doomed situations: how to navigate by the stars at night; how to kill with a gun, a knife and one's bare hands; how to 'seal ... off' an open chest wound (59). But this view of life (and war) as survivable if one would only learn how to live by one's wits is repeatedly undercut by the speech of other characters in the play. In response to Sgt Tower's lesson on navigation by the North Star and constellations, Ardell asks Pavlo, 'You ever seen any North Star in your life?' Pavlo says he 'seen a lot of people pointin'' and Ardell states that '[t]hey a bunch of fools pointin' in the air' (82). This need to reduce a threatening and unknowable world to a kind of machine likewise plays a part in male characters' views of women. Pavlo, whose fear of rejection by women is always close to the surface, describes one woman who rejected him as a sort of machine: 'a little bit a guinea-wop made outa all the pins and sticks all bitches are made a' (4). Similarly, one of Pavlo's fellow recruits describes Vietnamese women as having 'no nature' and moving too mechanically during sex (6).

Ultimately, it is not Tower's narrative of self-created individuals navigating a tamed and understandable (and survivable) world that the play endorses, but an opposite view given voice by the limbless, suicidal war victim Brisbey, for whom Pavlo cares in his career as a medic before asking to be transferred to battle duty. Brisbey's defining myth paints life not as rational and knowable but as terrifyingly absurd. He tells Pavlo a story of another navigator, 'ole Magellan, sailin' round the world', who drops anchor as deeply as he can (200 feet) to try to find the bottom of the ocean, and when he doesn't find bottom, 'thinks because all the rope he's got can't touch bottom, he's over the deepest part of the ocean. He doesn't know the real question. How far beyond all the rope you got is the bottom?' (73).

It is Brisbey's view, not Tower's, that characterizes the closest thing Pavlo has to an epiphany, near the play's end. He recalls a moment from his childhood when he dived into the Hudson River at night and became disoriented: he reaches out toward stars, but they are really reflections of stars in the water, and he dives in and, as he tells it, 'I was twisted in all that water, fighting to get up ... and I was going down, fighting to get down. I was all confused, you see, fighting to get down, thinking it was up. I hit sand. I pounded. I pounded the bottom. I thought the bottom was the top. Black. No air' (85).

Sticks and Bones

As if to transition from the earlier play's military setting to the present play's domestic one, *Sticks and Bones* contains an early scene worthy of its predecessor in its depiction of the American war machine's need to treat human beings as things – and, more specifically, as commodities. An army sergeant major drops off the blind, traumatized David, and speaks of David and the other war wounded as packaged commodities: 'Who's gonna sign this for me, mister?' he asks Ozzie. 'It's a shipping receipt. I got to have somebody's signature to show you got him. I got to have somebody's name on the paper.'[15] The sergeant major explains that he has 'deliveries to make all across this country' (107). If David and his fellow 'deliveries' found military life to be an inhuman machine-world where human lives are reduced to tools and commodities, *Sticks and Bones* makes clear that they won't find their situation much more pleasant at home.

The theme of the unreliability of 'talk' (and ultimately of all signs) that began in *Pavlo Hummel* continues into *Sticks and Bones*, where we encounter unreliable narratives from the first lines of the play. Ozzie receives the call that David will return home from Vietnam, specifically noting that he spoke not to David but to 'some clerk'. Yet Harriet just a few lines later tells Ricky, 'Your father talked to him [David]' (100). Just a bit later, it's Ozzie's turn to lie, when he tells a story of once beating Hank Grenweller (who seems to represent all the 'wholesome' middle-class ideals that he and Harriet want to embody) in a footrace, though Harriet says, 'You know that's not true' (102). Later in the second act, Harriet says of aspirin that it makes your stomach bleed. Ozzie responds, 'That's not true. None of that. You made all that up' (137). Throughout the play we are repeatedly given reason to doubt the words of the play's apparently wholesome, honest, middle-class American characters. Like characters in the plays of Pinter and Mamet, Rabe's characters use words not to convey information but to create an effect in the listener or to create some new reality for the speaker – they are always making what J. L. Austin called 'speech acts', verbal utterances meant not to *say* something but to *do* something. In this environment, not only can no one's words be trusted, but arguments over such seemingly irrelevant things as the gastric effects of aspirin become heated, even paranoid, arguments over the nature of reality. This play's characters would spin narratives to place themselves in the best light and cause pain or (often) severe existential angst in others. Acts of signification, therefore, become deeply threatening to the play's characters.[16]

In fact, perhaps nowhere is the bad faith of the play's characters more evident than in Ozzie's ostensibly honest, soul-searching, autobiographical monologues. We are tipped off to the performance Ozzie is giving in these sections by being told repeatedly that he addresses the audience. The stories Ozzie tells are meant to explain, even to excuse, his middle-class American life, and those stories are full of ridiculous clichés: 'soot in my fingers, riding the rails. A bum, a hobo' (140). Not only does this past seem incredibly unlikely given the present Ozzie we see in the play, but it is also riven with clichés, many from films. Moreover, the fictional and ideological nature of Ozzie's narrative is highlighted by the surreal, almost mythic turns the story takes. One moment he is bumming a ride on a freight train, the next a brakeman first embraces him, then throws him from the train where, says Ozzie, 'I fall, I roll. All in the air, then slam down breathless, raw from the cinders ... bruised and dizzy on the outskirts of this town. I'm here.' This sounds more like a creation narrative than an even partially true story of Ozzie's life, and the 'fall' he describes is, like the biblical one, a fall from innocence into economies of signs and sex: 'We point young girls out in the street. I start thinking about them; I start having dreams of horses and breasts and crotches.' Then Ozzie decides to get back from whence he came, but upon returning to where he was thrown from the train he discovers that trains 'no longer come that way; they all go some other way'. Then Harriet appears as both Eve and the Serpent: 'I turn to see Harriet, young and lovely, weaving among the weeds. I feel the wonder of her body moving toward me. She's the thing I'll enter to find my future, I think.' Of course Harriet is 'the thing' to the narcissistic, deeply misogynistic Ozzie, who will at one point in the play suggest she have her reproductive organs torn out of her. She is also simply an object that only derives meaning as part of *his* life story: '"Yes," I yell. "Sonofabitch! Bring her here! C'mon! Bring her on! It's my life! I can do it!" Swollen with pride, screaming and yelling, I stand there: "I'm ready. I'm ready ... I'm ready"' (141). In *The Basic Training of Pavlo Hummel*, Pavlo is called by his brother 'a mythmaker'. The characters of *Sticks and Bones* are all either mythmakers or (failed) myth destroyers. And as we see Pavlo's failed self-creation through repetition of certain American myths he's imbibed, here similarly we see Ozzie, the would-be mid-century American 'self-made' middle-class man, telling stories that only point out the way he is doomed to live out the same poisonous myths.

Another factor in the general slipperiness of signs in *Sticks and Bones* is the fact that the highly commodified signifiers that fill its world are always to be suspected precisely because they are commodified. The play directly implicates the commodification of speech as a factor in the unreliability of signs through its characters occasionally lapsing into advertisements for products, just as the real Ozzie and Harriet did during commercial breaks. Harriet responds to one of David's outbursts by suggesting that Ozzie 'Get him some Easy Sleep' pills, which, she says, will 'give you the sleep you need, Dave; the sleep you remember' (110). Later, Ozzie goes into similar commercial-speak about his brand of cigarette: 'I light up – I feel like I'm on a ship at sea. Isn't that one hell of a good-tasting cigarette?' (121). In fact, the Nelsons' living room itself takes on the disturbing aura of an advertisement: Rabe describes the room as '*an American home, very modern*', with '*a sense of space and, oddly, a sense that this room, these stairs belong in the gloss of an advertisement*' (98). In fact one of the most powerful and disturbing aspects of the play is its meditation on the near-total commodification of life in post-Second World War American culture. The Nelsons even seem to live solely on modern, unwholesome junk food such as fudge and soda.

If words cannot be trusted in this play, visual signs seem even more fraught. Through its very appropriation of the Nelson TV characters as well as its featuring a TV set facing upstage throughout the play '*glowing, murmuring*', Sticks and Bones implicates television and advertising in what David comes to see as a 'fraud'.[17] Interestingly, however, the play goes further to critique visual culture as a whole. Repeatedly in the play, speech is contrasted with visual images, and the latter are shown to be even slipperier signs than the former. Ozzie complains to Harriet that the family television, that omnipresent symbol of artificiality, has a picture but no sound (112). This makes it a sort of opposite of the film David shows the family, which has no images but only sound, in the form of David's terrifying narration of Vietnamese men and women hanging in trees, one of the women pregnant. Ozzie, horrified, describes David's film as '[j]ust all those words and that film with no picture' (134). Then there is the most insidiously vapid character, Ricky, who throughout the play is repeatedly seen snapping photos of the other family members with his camera, often at the most grotesquely inopportune moments. Finally, the visual is also associated with a kind of sick prurience and control, as Harriet and Ozzie ask David if they can look behind his dark glasses and see his damaged eyes (117).

Sticks and Bones premiered just three years after the My Lai Massacre, in which between 347 and 504 unarmed Vietnamese civilians – men, women, children and infants – were killed, at least some of the women gang raped and their bodies mutilated. David's narration of his blank film contains several details that resemble accounts of the massacre. In this context, the other characters' need to censor David calls to mind the now well-known attempts to cover up this especially shameful episode in America's Vietnam involvement. Ozzie, Harriet and Ricky's need to control signs (even as those signs continually slip out of their control) means they must try to silence David. The things that 'haunt' David 'would mean nothing at all', declares Harriet, they 'would be of no consequence at all – if only you didn't speak' (117). David does speak, but he (and we as readers or audience) finds that his speaking, in a sense, 'truth to power' – his telling the rest of the family of the horrors of the war in Vietnam, and in particular of the violence inflicted on innocents by Americans – is inadequate to convince them that, as he says, 'we live by fraud'. More importantly, David's speech is inadequate to free *him* from the very ideologies he would violently reject. Those ideologies are dominated by his family's racism and fear of miscegenation. Ozzie's outburst at the end of Act Two lays this cultural logic bare: 'LITTLE BITTY CHINKY KIDS YOU WANTED TO HAVE! LITTLE BITTY CHINKY YELLOW KIDS! DIDN'T YOU! FOR OUR GRANDCHILDREN!' (146). This is the thinking David would have had to reject if he were to take his Vietnamese lover Zung back with him as he'd promised, and tragically, like other Rabe protagonists, David is unable to transcend this thinking. He recalls the dilemma he faced and his own inability to think outside his parents', his culture's racism:

> 'She's the thing most possibly of value in my life,' I said. 'She is garbage and filth and I must get back to her if I wish to live. Sickness, I must cherish her.' Zung, there were old voices inside of me I had trusted all my life as if they were my own. I didn't know I shouldn't hear them. So reasonable and calm they seemed a source of wisdom. 'She's all of everything impossible made possible, cast her down,' they said. And I did as they told. (147)

One such 'reasonable' voice is that of Father Donald, the family priest, who refers to Zung as 'That whore. That yellow whore', and justifies his racism by appealing to the authority of a magazine article: 'It's all here – right here – in these pages. It was demonstrated beyond any possible doubt that people – soldiers – who are compelled for some reason not even they themselves – to establish personal-sexual relationships with whores are inferior to those who don't' (147).

Ultimately *Sticks and Bones* documents not only David's failure to think past a certain cultural logic, but America's failure to do the same. David's cultural heritage taught him to think of Zung as '[s]ickness', and repeatedly in the play ideas beyond the cultural horizon of characters are labelled as sickness. In this vein, Ozzie insists that Vietnamese women carry some sort of essential sickness within them – 'An actual rot alive in them' (124) – and eventually ascribes a kind of sickness to all women, as becomes clear in his outburst at Harriet near the end of Act Two: 'YOU! Your internal organs – your internal female organs – you've got some kind of poison in them. They're backing up some kind of rot into the world. I think you ought to have them cut out of you' (146). If sickness, in this play, is the label for what a culture cannot or will not think, then Rabe's view, at least in 1971, of American culture's ability to think past this limit is not an optimistic one. Each of the play's two acts opens in the future, with a voice, presumably Ricky's, narrating a slide show he presents to his own wife and children. When a slide appears showing David's face at the moment he slices his wrists (with Ricky's help), Ricky simply says it is a picture of 'somebody sick' (97). In this way, the play depicts the narrative of David's life and (in a larger sense) of Americans' experience in the South-East Asian conflict as ultimately transformed into another of Ricky's images – one for which *he* will ultimately provide a narrative.

Streamers

A failed struggle to write one's own story and transcend the limiting narratives of one's culture likewise characterizes the third play in Rabe's 'Vietnam Trilogy', *Streamers*. The play opens with Richie, a gay upper-class Manhattanite, trying to help another character, Martin, who has cut one of his wrists in an attempt to get out of the army. The first lines of the play highlight a failure of language. Exasperated with Martin, Richie laments, 'Honest to God, Martin, I don't know what to say anymore. I don't know what to tell you.' Then just a few lines later Richie sees language as the solution: 'We've got to make up a story.'[18] The rest of the play is on one level a meditation on language, storytelling and make-believe and their relation to the real. In fact, the major characters of *Streamers* can be seen as embodying different notions of the uses of speech and the relation of the symbolic to the real.

Of the men who make up the cast of the play, Roger, a middle-class African-American, would make the hardest distinction between the symbolic and the real, 'talk' and action. Roger is the most physically active of the characters: upon first entering the stage, he does push-ups, then suggests they mop the floor; later he prods Billy into playing basketball with him. Moreover, Roger demonstrates little patience for what he sees as idle talk. When Billy does not want to accompany him and Carlyle on a night of boozing and whoring, Roger accuses Billy of 'always talkin' how you don't do nothin' – you just talk. Let's do it tonight – stop talkin'' (210). For Roger, talk always *takes the place of* action and so is a waste of time. Near the end of the play, after Billy has been killed by Carlyle, Roger, to Richie's horror, starts mopping up the blood, as if it were better to do something – anything – than reflect on what just happened. He then attacks Richie for both wasting his time with talk and for not talking to him about his homosexuality: 'How come you made me waste all that time talkin' shit to you, Richie? All my time talkin' shit, and all the time you was a faggot, man; you really was. You shoulda jus' tole ole Roger. He don't care. All you gotta do is tell me.' Richie, who throughout the play has repeatedly let his actions speak and acted like exactly who he was – a gay man – insists 'I've been telling you.' But Roger's simplistic divide between talk and action cannot recognize this and he insists what Billy says is 'jive' (233).

Unlike Roger, Richie understands talk as instrumental – that is, he seems to understand signs not as taking the place of the real or even simply reflective of the real, but as part of the way the real is constructed. He would make up a story that would characterize Martin's cut wrist not as a suicide attempt but as something else. Accordingly, Richie sees early on that Carlyle is dangerous, despite the latter's insistence that no one should 'mind the shit I say' since 'I just talk bad, is all I do; I don't do bad' (206). Richie also understands Billy's story of someone he knew back home who was once heterosexual but 'turned' gay as more than just a story told to kill time: Richie sees that Billy may very likely be talking about himself in a roundabout way, or at the very least be expressing his own anxieties about the possibility of his being gay, or at least of being attracted to Richie. Richie responds by calling Billy 'a storyteller'. When Roger asks what he means, Richie repeats that Billy is 'a storyteller, all right; he tells stories, all right' (191). Recall that Richie's earlier use of 'story' was in reference to a fiction he would create to change the understanding of Martin's slit wrist. Here, similarly, Richie understand Billy's story as a kind of fiction, in this case as a story that both elides and admits his (Richie's) doubts about his own sexuality.

In fact Billy's storytelling goes beyond this one incident. In the course of the play, it becomes apparent that in important ways Billy's whole life is a kind of storytelling, a kind of performance. Compared to Roger and Richie, the middle-class white Midwesterner Billy seems on one level a more straightforward character – he first enters whistling and carrying a slice of pie (155) – but in reality he is nothing of the sort. Richie, unsurprisingly, is onto Billy's performance from very early in the play. When Billy breaks the pattern of the simple, white working-class idiom he's been using in the first few lines of the play to use the word 'obliterate', Richie responds, 'Oh, Billy, you better say "shit," "ain't," and "motherfucker" real quick now, or we'll all know just how far beyond the fourth grade you went' (161). In fact, Billy seems to lie about his education in the course of the play, at one point saying he dropped out of college and then was drafted, and later calling himself a college graduate and even an 'intellectual goddamn scholar type' (221). Later in Act Two, Richie again catches Billy adopting a performatively uneducated idiom, in this case the speech pattern of the black characters Roger and Carlyle: '"Where we was," he says. Listen to him. "Where we was." And he's got more school, Carlyle, than you have fingers and ... toes. It's this pseudo-earthy quality he feigns – but inside he's all cashmere' (214).

Since Billy is involved in a kind of continuous performance, it is no surprise that he is aware of and deeply troubled by what he perceives as a gap between surface and reality. Act Two opens with Billy telling a story about people back home in Wisconsin: 'All those clear-eyed people sayin "Hello" and lookin' you straight in the eye. Everybody's good, you think, and happy and honest. And then there's all of a sudden a neighbor who goes mad as a hatter.' Billy goes on to tell the story of one such neighbour who one day attacked moving cars with axes. Billy explains that people back home thought he 'overcomplicated everything', but that he always felt he 'was seein' complications that were there but nobody else saw' (195–6). Billy recognizes and fears these 'complications' in people, but he is never able to accommodate himself to them. Instead, in a familiar Rabian pattern, he labels that which he abhors in others and fears in himself a kind of sickness. In Act Two, when Richie asks if the story Billy told about the man turning gay was really about himself, Billy explodes: 'You are really sick. You know that? Your brain is really, truly rancid! Do you know there's a theory now it's genetic? That it's all a matter of genes and shit like that?' (208).

Ultimately, *Streamers* rejects the hard line characters would draw between the symbolic and the real, surface and depth, talk and action, and it does so in two ways. The first is through the violence that erupts near the play's end, when Carlyle murders first

Billy and then the inebriated Sgt Rooney. Carlyle, whose anger at Billy's refusal to let him have sex with Richie in the barracks the men share has been building, ultimately stabs Billy as a result of words – specifically Billy's racist outburst: 'you are your own goddamn fault, SAMBO! SAMBO!' Carlyle, who earlier says that he 'talks' bad but doesn't 'do' bad, stabs Billy because he cannot let 'nobody talk that weird shit to me', demonstrating in tragic fashion the complicated relationship between the symbolic and the real (222).

Another way the play demonstrates this relationship is through its meditation on games and make-believe and their relation to real violence. The play begins with Richie saying they have to make up a story, and ends with the extremely drunk Sgt Cokes, recently returned from Vietnam, telling of his war experiences in Korea in a way that demonstrates his own inability to clearly separate fact and make-believe – and, as in the first two plays, media (specifically film) plays a large role here. Cokes describes an encounter he had with a Korean soldier as 'like a goddamn Charlie Chaplin movie, everybody fallin' down and clumsy ... And he was Charlie Chaplin. I don't know who I was. And then he blew up' (238). A few lines later, Roger even suggests, 'Sergeant ... maybe you was Charlie Chaplin, too' (239). In fact, throughout the play, repeatedly we see the men alternately speaking of war as if it were a game or telling stories of their 'playing war' as children. Billy, early in Act One, talks about playing war as a young man: 'I started crawlin' around the floor a this house where I was stayin' cause I'd dropped outa school, and I was goin' "Bang, bang," pretendin' Jesus' (159). Roger twice refers to Vietnam as 'Disneyland' (158, 175). And Sgt Rooney, somewhat ridiculously, calls out 'No fair. No fair!' when he is stabbed by Carlyle (227). Ultimately, despite characters' attempts to draw hard lines between 'talk' and action, play and 'real life', the games, the narratives, the fictions of these men are both reflective of and productive of the American war machine, and the last sound we hear in the play is the dangerous man-child Sgt Cokes making *'the soft, whispering sound of a child imitating an explosion'* (240).

Minor works and conclusion

Despite Rabe's insistence that it (and not *Streamers*) represents the true third part of his Vietnam trilogy, his 1973 play *The Orphan* has proven relatively unpopular with audiences and critics and has been largely ignored by scholars. A retelling of the *Oresteia* of Aeschylus, the play draws parallels between the conflict in Vietnam and the Trojan War, as well as between Orestes' killing of Clytemnestra and the violence of the Manson family. As do the Vietnam plays, *The Orphan* plays with time and identity: Clytemnestra is divided into Clytemnestra One and Clytemnestra Two, the same character at two different points in time on stage simultaneously. Characters gain knowledge of their future actions and long to change identities: knowing Aegisthus will kill him, Agamemnon wishes to be Aegisthus. Robert Andreach writes that by '[d]issolving causal, sequential relationships into simultaneous, circular motion and individual identities into shifting role-appropriations, the action is the undifferentiated flux before self-differentiation'.[19] And like characters in other Rabe plays, those in *The Orphan* come up with seemingly rational explanations for what the play ultimately portrays as mindless, brutal violence. A character called 'The Speaker' even 'advances scientific explanations such as electrical "impulses leaping to the brain"'.[20] In an Afterword to the published edition of the play, Rabe relates his treatment of irrational violence to the play's somewhat chaotic structure, and ultimately to issues of genre: 'Violence is not rational. It is not mechanical. The well-made play reflects the Newtonian clockwork universe. What I was after is more like nuclear fission in which the explosion of something miniscule unlooses catastrophic, ungovernable devastation.'[21]

Ultimately, it is the exploration of the tangled relationship between narrative and material reality, between the symbolic and the real, in the thinking of (for the most part) American men that is David Rabe's enduring legacy from his plays of the 1970s. I say 'American men' because if critics have identified a failure of imagination in these works – and in Rabe's works to the present day – it is what some see as a tendency to present women as more or less significant only insofar as they reveal the tragic limitations of men. Women are spoken of by these men as machines (as in *The*

Basic Training of Pavlo Hummel), as nature embodied (in *Sticks and Bones*, David describes Vietnamese women as 'the color of the earth' [135]) and as commodities (note the prevalence of prostitutes in these plays). Still, some see Rabe's 1973 play *In the Boom Boom Room* as the author giving a female protagonist her due, though this story of a naïve, idealistic dancer named Chrissy, reduced to working at a strip club in Philadelphia, dreaming of getting to New York and trying to come to terms with vague memories of sexual abuse by her father, is at the very least problematic in terms of its portrayal of female agency. Unlike the protagonists of the Vietnam plays, Chrissy does at least endure (and survive), but the play's final image of Chrissy performing an erotic dance, bare-breasted and with her face masked, at a go-go club in New York raises serious questions about a play whose apparent aim is to argue against male hegemony. Les Wade notes that 'authorial intent aside, the very serious question arises as to whether or not Rabe's work reproduces the oppression it repudiates', and he proposes that this 'final image gives us theatre at its most basic (a naked body in an empty space) and thus invites the most basic of questioning: how is the body (the female body) empowered or enslaved upon the stage?'[22] Wade sees the final image of the nude body as one in which 'the actor and character separate', creating a powerful instance of Brechtian alienation and implicating the audience in Chrissy's subjection.[23]

Stephen Watt sees *In the Boom Boom Room* as an investigation into the 'postmodern subject', an investigation that anticipates the concerns of Rabe's major play of the following decade, *Hurlyburly*. Watt notes that in the later play, the 'most frightening scenes' are ones in which 'characters demonstrate their inability to apprehend others as anything but images'.[24] Within the limitations of her existence as an 'image-commodity', Watt reads the final scene of *In the Boom Boom Room* not as one of total 'abjection': 'On the one hand, the final moments of *Boom Boom Room* might indeed reconfirm Chrissy's further victimization by men,' he writes. 'On the other hand, her move to New York also represents a move away from Philadelphia, the site of her past exploitation, and the advancement of one more step in her dancing career.' Chrissy is 'developing a new dance, realizing one of the several performing selves dancing "in her head all the time"; she has attained a new level of freedom, even if we are quite justifiably cynical about her new refuge'.[25]

In defending his female characters, Rabe does seem to have difficulty imagining them as other than embodiments of something valuable in the male characters. In a 1990 interview, he defends himself against his 'reputation with the feminists' by noting that 'In *Sticks and Bones*, the fact that the girl [Zung] is killed in the living room of this nice middle class house has a feminist component to it – what I would take to be one – because what is being killed with her is that intuitive, feeling, resonant part of that house, the vet, all of them, of life itself, or that potential. In order that they can be permanently false.'[26] If, as some critics claim, Rabe's treatment of his women characters lacks the depth of his investigations into American masculinity, it cannot be denied that his work, and particularly his Vietnam trilogy, depicts in powerful fashion the existential horror of what he calls being 'permanently false'. Rabe's explorations of the intergenerative nature of narrative and material reality, of a kind of tyranny of the visual in American life and of the reduction of human beings to machines/commodities and simultaneous elevation of things to the status of living reality both develop and complicate the American realist/naturalist and anticipate many of the concerns of the theatre of successive generations of playwrights.

4

Sam Shepard: *Curse of the Starving Class* (1977), *Buried Child* (1978) and *True West* (1980)

Mike Vanden Heuvel

Introduction

Sam Shepard's meteoric rise to prominence in the 1960s and 1970s, followed by a more gradual ascent to celebrity in the 1980s – as a Pulitzer Prize-winning playwright, moderately successful screenwriter and bankable film actor – makes for one of the enduring tales of success in the American theatre. Notably, his was not the rages-to-riches myth culminating in Broadway acclaim: he belongs, in Stanley Kauffmann's phrase, to a 'post-Broadway' generation of playwrights for which Shepard is the archetype.[1] Arriving fresh from California in 1963 at the age of nineteen, Shepard disembarked at the centre of the vortex that formed when the Off-Off-Broadway phenomenon that established close links with the counterculture movements exploded across Greenwich Village. Shepard became the most prolific playwright of this scene, and, by the close of the 1960s, had established himself with its coterie audiences and the few drama critics willing to follow the *Village Voice* to view the plays.² Perhaps to return the favour, Shepard was absent from Broadway itself for many years: his first Broadway show was a revival of *Buried Child* in 1996, seventeen years after it won the Pulitzer Prize and more than three decades since his plays first appeared in New York.

With the famed Off-Off-Broadway companies at Theatre Genesis and Café La MaMa, Shepard established a house style that strongly shaped his later work. His influences include the Continental Theatre of the Absurd, Artaud's seductive shamanism and radical experiments with aesthetic form and politics in work ranging from Allan Kaprow's Happenings to the Living Theatre and Joe Chaikin's Open Theater.³ Shepard himself claims his early inspirations also included the paintings of Jackson Pollock, the jazz he heard while working at the Village Gate and rock music of the early British School (the Who and the Rolling Stones). What brings together all these formative influences is a common focus on authenticity, and this would remain a touchstone for Shepard's art.

In general, the early plays are characterized by concatenating scenes shaped more by rising and falling emotional intensities than by a coherent narrative, created through a potlatch of disassociated images drawn from comic books and pulp novels, B-films (mostly westerns) and rock legends, all filtered through the rhapsodic consciousness of characters momentarily inhabiting mythic identities. 'By myth,' Shepard said, 'I mean a sense of mystery and not necessarily a traditional formula,'⁴ expressing pithily the connection he would explore between the function of myth and the dramatic formulae that might convey mysteries at their deepest level. He sought such new forms through a carnivalesque overflow of verbal images and ever-shifting lines of plot and character arc, which conveyed some of the qualities of the street games and drug-induced flights Shepard experienced while living in the East Village. These voyages of liberated consciousness are sometimes launched in long, solo linguistic flights that aspire to incantation, referred to as 'arias' by early reviewers to convey the emphasis on rhythm and expressive tone over discursive meaning. These are not, as Herbert Blau pointed out, the brooding confessions of an O'Neill, but rather 'the Whitmanian flecks and flashes of a performing self, the body leaping through a sluice of disjunct images to some other dimension, going with the flux of words, a long jazz-riff of images reaching for an identity'.[5]

During the 1960s, after a string of Obies, productions that moved from Off-Off- up to Off-Broadway houses, and even (in 1970) a disastrous show at Lincoln Center, Shepard appeared poised to follow the hallowed path to conquer Broadway. However, in 1971 he moved abruptly to London, purportedly to pursue a career as a rock musician but also to escape the celebrity and drug scenes in New York. After seeing several of his plays produced in the UK, including the world premiere of *The Tooth of Crime* (1972), *Geography of a Horse Dreamer* (Shepard's first crack at directing, 1974) and *Action* (1974),[6] Shepard returned to America but not to New York. Instead, he opted to settle in Mill Valley, California, and to premiere many of his plays thereafter at the intimate Magic Theatre in San Francisco.

Thus, the 1970s marked for Shepard both a return and a rebirth as a specifically 'American' dramatist. Critics have pointed to the coincidence of a series of more realistic and conventionally plotted and structured plays following his return to the US, some even suggesting that Shepard's encounter with British classical acting and its *belle lettres* tradition of dramatic writing influenced this turn. And, indeed, after premiering a series of works in San Francisco and New York after 1974, his best-known plays arrive between 1977 and 1980 to form the retroactively-named 'family trilogy', recognized as much by their common setting – a naturalistic box set representing a family home – as by their more linear plotting, fuller casts of developed characters and shared theme of families in crisis. Quite naturally, reviewers and some scholars writing during the period announced that Shepard had 'matured' into more 'serious' writing by marking, as Thomas P. Adler says, 'a turning point to a more realistic, perhaps somewhat O'Neillian dramaturgy'.[7]

However, despite the prominence of these plays in this chapter and in Shepard criticism more generally, the appearance of the trilogy does not mark an absolute departure from his earlier style nor an abandonment of recognizably alternative forms of theatre writing. Coincident with the family plays, Shepard continued to write highly experimental texts that incorporated movement (*Jacaranda*, 1979), live musicians (*Inacoma*, 1977) and dialogue co-authored by Shepard's long-time collaborator Joe Chaikin and delivered with accompanying percussion or music (*Tongues*, 1978; *Savage/Love*, 1979). The signature edition of Shepard's selected works (*Sam Shepard: Seven Plays*, 1981) remains a standard text in part because it recognized the variety of the playwright's work as his fame began to grow, and thoughtfully combined the more realist family plays (*Curse of the Starving Class*, *Buried Child*, *True West*) with instances of his earlier styles (*La Turista* and *the Tooth of Crime*) and his truly experimental work (*Tongues*, *Savage/Love*).

Over time, then, critics have seen the realist work in wider context, and determined that Shepard's family trilogy marks not so much a consistent turn toward realism as a side project devoted, in part, to its unmaking. By blending realism's fundamental tenets with strategic infusions of the more anarchic, elliptical and opaque dramaturgy of his Off-Off-Broadway phase, the playwright revised the form for a more complex age. Shepard did not pursue modifying realism in a vacuum, of course: in *Beyond Naturalism*, William Demastes recounts how Shepard, as well as David Mamet, Marsha Norman and other contemporaries modified realism during the 1970s and 1980s in order to confront new and more complex forms of causality (see also Jon Dietrick's chapter on David Rabe in this book). Various nomenclatures have been suggested to delineate this style, from 'new realism' (Demastes); 'metarealism' (Laura Graham); 'nova-realism' (John Glore); 'neo-' and 'deconstructed' realism (Thomas Adler); 'suprarealism' (DeRose); 'performance theatre' (Vanden Heuvel); 'super realism' (Toby Zinman); and an amalgam of realism and avant-garde styles such as expressionism and surrealism (Bonnie Marranca and others).

That Shepard should turn to a form familiar to generations of American spectators and readers (through dramatic predecessors like Saroyan, O'Neill, Miller, Inge and Williams, but also through the classic realism of popular film and even television serials) only to deconstruct both the form and its manner of structuring meaning seems very much in keeping with the mood of 1970s America.[8] In the wake of Watergate and the Pentagon Papers, the omnipresence of 'Tricky Dick' Nixon on the airwaves covering up scandals while also revealing secret negotiations to end the Vietnam war caused Americans to develop a natural suspicion for the conventional narrative and a general distrust of authority.[9] Just as importantly, these sanctioned chronicles of the time often mapped neatly onto America's mythic heritage in order to confirm the nation's image of itself in history, 'articulat[ing] salient patterns that we see in our past and hold us to our present value and purpose'.[10] As the country struggled with its defeat in Vietnam, the time was ripe for an evaluation of its sustaining myths: of the frontier, of individualism, of American identity based on notions of exceptionalism and power. Exacerbated by the energy crisis and the general drift into economic and cultural malaise, the need to understand how the nation had deviated from its original trajectories and moral high ground seemed pressing. On the other end of the spectrum, the various counterculture alternatives to American bourgeois values had foundered, and utopian initiatives like the commune movement began to dwindle or, worse, descend into 'helter-skelter' (as with the cult of Charles Manson). Or, like EST and rolfing, alternative lifestyles were absorbed into the middle-class mainstream of the 'Me Decade'. More distressingly, as the civil rights movement was perceived to have faltered, counter-movements evolved (the Black Panthers and American Indian Movement for instance, on the Left, and the Klan and the American Independent Party from the Right) that utilized ferocious rhetoric and espoused violent means to achieve change or to conserve the status quo. In the lean years of the early 1970s, Americans and American artists alike felt the collapse of certain verities, and Shepard was among the most effective at creating a dramaturgy that both elicited nostalgia for recognizable structures of meaning and assurance before – sometimes violently – wrenching these away and revealing what might lie amid the rubble of their collapse.[11] Blau, again, places Shepard in the fraught moment:

> By the time of *The Tooth of Crime* (1972), he was listening more nervously, still with admiration, but put off, frightened by something ominous in the sound. What he heard was a sound dispossessed of history, savagely, distorting the rituals of liberation by which the sixties were possessed. There was a rock-bottom violence in the high-tech sound, and it didn't sound liberating at all. At the dead end of the sixties, there was rage mixed in with the disenchantments. After the Love-Ins and the Be-Ins and the instant gratifications – in the movement from the festival at Woodstock through the Velvet Underground to the festival at Altamont – the Rolling Stones embraced the Hell's Angels and there was bloody murder in the LSD. No mere image

of violence, no fiction, no pleasurable lie, but the real sordid indescribable thing – the fucked-up vision of an empty myth.[12]

In response, Shepard's family trilogy is characterized by a shift in dramatic form and in the function of the mythic dimension of the plays. What was startling was the new concentration of theme, the tighter focus on causality and the resulting shift in emphasis from a theatre with ritual pretentions to one exploring a particular understanding of myth. The issue of genre, then, is closely aligned to the treatment of myth, and by subverting the former Shepard could similarly disrupt the function of the latter. This turn also necessitated a movement away from character as performative and improvisational to one bound by history, blood and circumstance. Thus, to better understand Shepard's turn toward a modified realism in the 1970s, one must comprehend first the forms and ideas in which his career as a playwright began.

When Shepard started out in the 1960s, influenced by the versions of Artaud's ideas as filtered through groups like the Living Theatre as well as experiments in minimalist art and John Cage's explorations of temporality, theatrical time could be explored as coincident with the time of the spectator: as in ritual, the action taking place, even when narrating past events, was meant to transform the experience of the spectator as a present event. Like listening to jazz, the important thing was to be in the moment, keen to the improvisations and the unexpected vistas that might open up. Understood thus, the unmotivated actions and linguistic *non sequiturs* that pervade Shepard's early work could help spectators achieve, as DeRose says, 'a string of perpetual presents'.[13] Christopher Bigsby mitigates Shepard's relation to the theatre experiments in 1960s New York, pointing out that from the beginning he positioned himself ironically in relation to groups like the Living Theatre regarding the 'solemnizing [of] the body as a sign of transcendent truth'.[14] But even as he distanced himself from the more utopian agendas of the human potential movement, Shepard was keen to explore modes of liberating – if not the transcendent body then at least the individual consciousness – from socially imposed conformity. He participated in the Open Theater's seminal transformational acting workshops, where he found resonances with his notion of character as a malleable state open to transformation in the time of the performance (again, in the manner of a jazz improvisation) rather than a fixed and determined subjectivity. In a state of liberated flux, the individual still, Shepard hoped, could tap into deep and resonant mythic patterns to inhabit them and thus penetrate to a more profound or even archetypal level of consciousness. Such transformations are effected not by well-structured plot or discursive dialogue, but through game-playing, syncopated rhythms of speech, movement and action, and the disruptive monologues that leap into being unmotivated by the action, without predicate logic but – as in the case of Boy's astonishing apostrophe on rough sex near the end of *The Rock Garden* (1964) – deeply expressive of the need to assert alterity on the path to liberation.

In Shepard's early one-acts of the 1960s, characters often conjure remarkable stories about themselves and perform outrageous acts of momentary recreation so as to embody, if only temporarily, some mythic impulse or identity: two notions, identity and myth, that remain conjoined in Shepard's work of the 1970s. As he told Carol Rosen in a 1993 interview, 'the ancient meaning of myth is that it served a purpose in our life. The purpose had to do with being able to trace ourselves back in time and follow our emotional self. Myth served as a story in which people could connect themselves in time to the past. And thereby connect themselves to the present and the future.'[15] The ritual elements of performance that infuse his early work, then – what Shepard goes on to describe as 'dance, music, all of those forms that lead people into a river of myth',[16] and which also encompasses language in its incantatory form – were means to an emancipating end.

In the family trilogy, conversely, Shepard's focus turns from the present-ness of consciousness and its possible sources of freedom to the seemingly contrary (yet deeply imbricated) need for rootedness. To explore the characteristics and consequences of identity grounded by something essential, the focus turned to the past and how it impinged on the present, the retrospective narrative of events now utilizing myth in ways at once more capacious and yet more deterministic. As Rosen points out, by the time he returned from Britain, 'Shepard's idea of myth becomes more complex than it was in his early plays, where myth simply meant a conjuring image, a prop or figure that resonated on stage. Now myth is connected to an expansive view of characters and archetypal emotions.'[17] By the late 1970s, Shepard brings to the forefront an anxiety present, but much abated, in his earlier plays: that myth as a wellspring of emotional truth and growth has dried up, or perhaps never existed in the first place.

> Myth in its truest form has now been demolished. It doesn't exist anymore. All we have is fantasies about it. Or ideas that don't speak to our inner self at all, they just speak to some lame notions about the past. But they don't connect with anything anymore. We've lost touch with the essence of myth.[18]

In the family trilogy, Shepard explores the failure to connect with the essence of myth, and the repercussions of finding oneself seduced instead by its fantasies, cut off from renewal and bereft of authentic individuality. Myth, debased and deadened, leads not to freeing consciousness but rather forecloses all escape routes by restricting vision to narrow cycles of repetition. Shepard's emerging understanding of the operations of myth in the family trilogy, then, questions it as a source of transformation and transcendence. Instead, he re-visions myth as a kind of archetypal fate that determines the trajectories and limits the freedom of sons and daughters, mothers and fathers, brothers and sisters: 'Every day I can see it coming,' says Ella in *Curse of the Starving Class*: 'And it always comes. Repeats itself. It comes even when you do everything to stop it from coming. Even when you try to change it. And it goes back. Deep.'[19]

Curse of the Starving Class

Whereas Shepard's early plays seemed to arrive fully clothed from a parallel but distinct dimension, the first play of the family trilogy was marked by recognizable, even familiar, trappings. There were first a number of autobiographical elements, which would characterize the trilogy and lead to Shepard's increasing output of autobiographical non-fiction writing, culminating in *The Motel Chronicles* (1982).[20] Second, the structure of *Curse of the Starving Class* and its sustained evocation of the traditional myths associated with the American family – of patrimony, of generations succeeding one another while improving the family legacy, and of the alignment of family succession with the rhythms of nature – resonated strongly and familiarly with audiences. Here one sees, by virtue of Shepard's willingness to write a story about elements of his own past and to frame it artfully within a linear dramatic narrative, both how the play marks a new relationship to realism and also a different relationship to myth. Now, rather than myth acting as a transformational source of deepened experience, it functions, instead, by virtue of being shaped by the deterministic structure of the realist play, to provide the stories that bind characters, families and histories to a 'cursed' cycle of decline. Figures like Wesley in *Curse of the Starving Class* find themselves incorporated into pre-existing identities and behaviours from which they struggle, unsuccessfully, to escape.

That the new encounter with realism also involves the subject of the family would seem to mark a growing maturity on Shepard's part, a willingness to address subjects with more scope and amplitude than his earlier small-cast, one-act plays could attain. It was even suggested that Shepard might be aiming for a kind of crossover mainstream acceptance by making his plays increasingly accessible and familiar. However, critical responses to the trilogy have recognized that Shepard's explorations of family were shaped strongly by the tumultuous cultural context of American life in the 1970s. As Stephen J. Bottoms argues:

> Certainly these pieces have many elements in common with their famous predecessors. Yet even as the subject of family is embraced in an apparent search for a sense of rooted, stable identity, these are distinctly postmodern dramas, characterized by discontinuity, pastiche and a sense of insoluble tension in both family structure and dramatic form. Shepard, far from making some belated bid for mainstream respectability, was bringing his sense of experiential crisis home to roost.[21]

This simultaneity of the recognizable themes and structure of the play and its discontinuous elements, carried over from his earlier style, proved difficult for initial audiences and critics, first in London (1977) and then New York the following year. Cultural conservatives in the UK like Benedict Nightingale found it clichéd as a realist piece of family drama, while radicals like Charles Marowitz were taken aback by its conventionality.[22] In New York,

Harold Clurman, for many years critical of Shepard's undisciplined writing, saw in the semblance of a realist family drama a foundation against which to improvise and wrote, 'its faults are part of its virtues'.[23] Others found the blend of realism and myth less convincing, leading to confusion or, for Martin Duberman, 'unacknowledged sentimentality'.[24] After the initial short run, the play was revived successfully at New York's Promenade Theater in 1985 and has since become a staple in regional and university theatre seasons, and in part, as James Crank notes, '[b]ecause of its sparse set and small cast, it has been one of Shepard's most easily produced plays'.[25]

The plot falls between what the play's initial American director, Robert Woodruff, called 'The Great American Melodrama' ('I got the deed! No you don't! I got the money! Here come the cops! And the guy with the black moustache comes on at the end twirling it')[26] and a contemporary retelling of Chekhov's *The Cherry Orchard*. Weston Tate, the drunken and often-absent family patriarch, is in debt owing to gambling and land speculation. He seeks escape from both family and financial responsibilities, and dreams of hightailing it to Mexico. Meanwhile, his estranged wife, Ella, schemes to sell the property to Taylor, a local businessman interested in destroying the farm in the name of urban progress. Neither of the two children, Wesley or Emma (the nearly anagrammatic resemblance to the parents' names foreshadows, in Michael Taav's view, how family roles have become 'unfixed and interchangeable'),[27] shows any interest in either scenario. Wesley wants to retain the family home and improve it, while Emma constantly dreams of escaping the toxic environment. None of these plans come to fruition, however, and the action of the play traces the consequent unravelling of the already tenuous family structure and the failure to escape the family 'curse'. Weston, after a failed ritual of rebirth, flees to Mexico and thereby inadvertently causes his daughter's death. Wesley, virtually reborn in his father's image and wearing his tattered clothes by the final scene, recounts with Ella a story Weston used to tell about a tomcat plucked from the ground by a screaming eagle, and how they tore at one another in midair until 'they came crashing down to earth. Both of them come crashing down. Like one whole thing' (201).

The action follows the mortgage plot only so far as to highlight the sense of dispossession that infects the family. Shepard deploys some brilliant staging and consonant imagery to bring home the point. Often, this takes the form of enacted rituals that intrude upon and destabilize the coherence offered by the familiar realist framework. A refrigerator becomes a kind of oracle, with family members obsessively peering into it, Tantalus-like, and seeing their own spiritual and material scarcity reflected back (the usual comment is 'Nothing!'). Emma even converses with it, filling it with the illusory sustenance of the American myth of promise ('It's all right. You don't have to be ashamed ... You'll get some company before you know it. You'll get some little eggs tucked in to your sides,' 150–1). Weston's typical quick fix is to fill it with desert artichokes bought on the cheap on his way back from a bender, creating the illusion that he's the family breadwinner: 'MR. SLAVE LABOR HIMSELF COME HOME TO REPLENISH THE EMPTY LARDER!' (158). Later, Weston describes to Wesley his reawakening and rebirth, a transformation he sanctifies with 'a big old breakfast of ham and eggs ... Somebody left a whole mess a' groceries in the ice box. Surprised the hell out of me. Just like Christmas. Just like somebody knew I was gonna be reborn this morning or something.' He tells Wesley that his rebirth culminated in a new understanding that family 'wasn't just a social thing. It was an animal thing ... And I started feeling glad about it. I started feeling full of hope' (187). But Wesley, bleeding from an encounter with Ellis, the man to whom Weston has promised the property, turns not to the redeemed father but instead to the refrigerator, and says only, 'I'm starving' (187).

The ritual acting out of scarcity and hunger confronts the American myth of the New Eden, while others serve to undermine Christian myth and symbology. The live lamb, brought on stage in the first act to be treated for an infestation of maggots, is eventually cured by Weston at the beginning of Act Three. Adler writes that '[t]he biblical echoes are many' but concludes that Shepard alludes to all of them ironically to show how Wesley, who eventually slaughters the lamb for food, projects himself into the Christ-like role of saviour only to discover that such redemption will fail to transubstantiate the family's condition: 'The sacrifice was not efficacious; and what should have been a sacrament of communion became instead a grotesque offering that did not satisfy spiritual hunger.'[28] Just as the realist plot structure does not resolve the pressing tensions of the play – Who will own the property? Will

Wesley receive the family patrimony? What ultimately will happen to Weston? – so the mythic patterns are interrupted and rendered impotent, revealed as mere fantasy.

Throughout, references are made to moments of latent individual nourishment and transformation, but unlike the potential for conversion in Shepard's earlier plays, each of these is thwarted or mocked. Emma rebelliously tells her mother that cooperating is 'deadly. It leads to dying' (148). She is headstrong and eager for escape. Angry with her brother for urinating on her 4-H project, she threatens to run away and gets as far as the paddock before being thrown from her horse. She returns to the house and tells her mother 'I was down there in the mud being dragged along ... Suddenly everything changed, I wasn't the same person anymore. I was just a hunk of meat tied to a big animal. Being pulled.' On the threshold of escape – 'I had the whole trip planned in my head. I was going to head for Baja California ... I was going to work on fishing boats. Deep sea fishing' – Emma first imaginatively, like a character from Shepard's earlier one-acts, projects a transformation in identity, possibly even her gender. After the fall, however, she reverts to 'being pulled' and seems no longer in control of her destiny: as with her initial menstrual cycle, she has the curse.

The third act, somewhat jarringly, lifts the action from the naturalistic to the elemental by all but dispensing with the social and economic themes and focusing almost exclusively on the mythic patterns of renewal. Weston opens with a long, rambling monologue recalling a time as a boy when he could viably link his life to something larger, retroactively constructing a connection to nature in the days when he tended to his flock. The speech ends with his vivid recollection of how, as he castrated lambs, an eagle would swoop down to fetch the testes, thrilling him with its single-minded and violent hunger: 'I had to stand up on that one. Somethin' brought me straight up off the ground and I started yellin' my head off. I don't know why it was comin' outa' me but I was standing there with this icy feeling up my backbone and just yellin' my fool head off. Cheerin' for that eagle, I'd never felt like that since the first day I went up in a B-49' (184).

Linking his wartime experience as a pilot ('I was in the war. I know how to kill ... It's no big deal' [171]) with this image of rapacious animal survival, the memory bookends the experiences that distort Weston's understanding of masculinity. The placement of the monologue is significant because it arrives *after* his self-devised ritual of regeneration that, he believes, has restored his connection to his family. He recalls the experience for Wesley: after walking through the orchards and then naked through his own house to initiate his rebirth, Weston took alternating hot and cold baths. He tells Wesley that this ritual renews him, evidence of which is the discovery of nourishing food in the refrigerator (placed there earlier by Ella, so in no sense a miracle) and the joy he takes in doing the family laundry. His epiphany that 'family is an animal thing' returns us to the eagle and reminds the spectator that his entire conversion is mitigated by the opening monologue because it's only after the redemptive rituals that Weston is healing the lamb. Even in that state of suspect self-imagined grace, Weston's recollection of the rapacious bird can only conjure for him, again, the curse of the starving class: to be always famished and needing more sustenance, like the eagle chasing the testes even if it means destroying the very source of origin.

Weston's later petulant cries when he learns from Wesley that he's still being pursued by enforcers – 'It's not working because I don't have to pay for my past now! Not now! Not after this morning! All that's behind me now! YOU UNDERSTAND ME? IT'S ALL OVER WITH BECAUSE I'VE BEEN REBORN! I'M A WHOLE NEW PERSON NOW!' (193) – confirm the willed and inauthentic nature of his conversion. Unlike the moments of actual transformation Shepard pursued in his earlier work, Weston's attempt fails abjectly. Despite his protests, he's forced to flee to Mexico where his past will continue to haunt him: as Emma says when she learns of his departure, 'He won't last a day down there. They'll find him easy. Stupid to go to Mexico. That's the first place they'll look' (196).

Moreover, Weston cannot flee the effect his 'poison' has had on Wesley, who in his final scene with his father stands before him wearing the filthy, urine-stained clothing thrown aside when Weston envisioned himself reborn in freshly laundered clothes. In addition, Wesley evidently has absorbed Weston's understanding of masculine survival as connected to violence and a never-satiated hunger, for he slaughters the lamb Weston claims he has saved from its infestation. Despite the heaviness of the Christian imagery, the act clearly conveys that Wesley has assumed the role of violent patriarch and that Weston's feeble attempt at redemption and regeneration has failed to lift the family curse. The starvation, the 'savage hunger at the bottom of the need to belong among people',[29] finds stark expression when Wesley then deposits the contents of the refrigerator on the floor and begins 'eating it ravenously' (193).

Despite the unevenness of the dramaturgy and the uncertain relationship of the archetypal themes to the mortgage melodrama, *Curse of the Starving Class* initiated Shepard's new relationship with the American public. Appearing at the same time as his first full-length film, *Days of Heaven* (directed by Terence Malik), in which he played the laconic (and iconic) American frontier farmer, the play became evidence that Shepard – like his film persona – represented a quality of 'Americanness' that would henceforth be attached to him.[30] As he became increasingly identified with the ensuing plays of the trilogy, Shepard was no longer the *enfant terrible* of the New York avant-garde or the returned expat hippie playwright of the west coast, but rather the shining example of a home-grown original seeking a way back to America's lost roots. These myths of American exceptionalism, and the view of Shepard as their vehicle, like those he would evoke and subvert in the following plays of the trilogy, would prove both enabling but, in the end, a kind of trap.

Buried Child

By accepting Weston's unintended inheritance, Wesley seemingly closes off any hope that the family curse will be broken: a notion Shepard returns to in *Buried Child*. The second play of the trilogy is both bleaker than *Curse* but also more ambiguous regarding the possibility for redemption or enlightenment. The themes of sin and expiation, too, are clearer in *Buried Child* because there is no pretence that what curses the family lies without, in class or economic sources: here, the infestation clearly lies within. As well, the play's structure is made coherent by a seemingly strict application of the techniques of classic realism. In Lynda Hart's description, these include the revelation

> of a fatal secret deeply hidden beneath the surface of a mundane domestic scene [that] is gradually revealed through dialogue

and action, the revelation resulting in a profound conflict that threatens the permanent disruption of the normality and tranquility of the domestic life of the family. As the catastrophe approaches, weighty significance is retrospectively attached to words and behavior that originally appeared without import ... In this familiar dramatic form, the structure of the plot is essentially a puzzle with each character in custody of clues that are part of the total picture, a picture that begins fragmented but will cohere as the action unfolds, forming a conceptually satisfying unity.[31]

In maintaining the link between dramatic structure and the function of myth, the play also hangs together by the working through of several overtly familiar mythic plots: the Arthurian Fisher King (by way of Eliot's 'The Wasteland'), the vegetation myth of the Corn King, the biblical Prodigal Son and even the Holy Grail.[32] But these once-potent narratives have declined into cliché, and the deconstruction of the realist form makes clear that Shepard intends to subvert the myths as well.

The play certainly shows substantially greater structural coherence than *Curse*, possibly owing to its obvious references to forebears like Ibsen (especially *Ghosts*), Pinter (*The Homecoming* and *Old Times*) and the O'Neill of *Long Day's Journey into Night* and *Desire Under the Elms*. In a dilapidated Midwest farmhouse, a disturbing family, fixated on keeping past wounds hidden, spends a rainy day opening up new ones among themselves. Dodge, the patriarch, and his wife Halie are estranged and bitter, and the unexpected arrival of their troubled eldest son, Tilden, has only increased the anxiety. The fact that he brings in corn and carrots from fields long fallow does little to allay their concern. Amid their mutual recriminations, a terrible secret involving a dead son is touched upon, then covered up in silence. Another son, Bradley, appears, a violent bully with a missing leg whose actions are in contradistinction to Tilden's, who seems more orphaned than dangerous ('*Something about him is profoundly burned out and displaced*'). Later that evening, with Dodge alone for the moment, grandson Vince arrives with girlfriend Shelley as they travel cross-country. Amazingly, first Dodge and then his own father, Tilden, fail to recognize him. Perplexed, he departs to buy liquor, leaving Shelley with the family. She connects with the shy Tilden, but suffers abuse from Dodge and eventually, at the hands of Bradley, endures an unnerving symbolic rape. The next morning, with Vince still missing, Shelley turns the tables and emasculates Bradley by holding hostage his prosthetic leg, and entices Dodge to confess the family secret. The dying patriarch spits out a story of incest and social disgrace that culminates in him drowning Halie's illegitimate child, most likely by Tilden, and burying him in the back yard. In an ironic rebirth following this revelation, Vince suddenly returns, drunk and disorderly, and begins to assert a violent authority over the family. Dodge, expiring on the floor, bequeaths the house and his possessions to Vince, who in turn stretches out on the paternal couch to assume his new place in the family line. As Vince stares at the ceiling, Tilden re-enters unseen carrying the bones of the buried child upstairs toward Halie.

The play seemingly brings to resolution (one almost wants to say fruition) not only the realist structure's demand for the retrospective unravelling of the mystery of the buried child, its origins and its murder by Dodge, but the various mythic strands as well. Yet, as before, the setting up of expectations that characters with explicable motives will resolve plot trajectories, and that moral positions will be clearly staked out, quickly reveals itself as a ruse. A series of strange stage actions and exchanges create an uncanny friction with the realist presentation. Tilden inexplicably covers his father's sleeping body with sheaves of freshly-husked corn near the end of the first act. Later, Bradley brutally shears his father's hair while he sleeps, drawing skin and blood. Subsequently, when he first encounters Shelley in the final scene of the second act, Bradley chillingly tells her to open her mouth and when she does, he silently inserts his fingers. He then goes to his prostrate father and drops Shelley's rabbit fur coat over his sleeping head. When Vince returns, intoxicated and still in the grip of the vision of his family line he encountered while driving through the night, he violently enters the door by cutting through the screen and tumbling into the room. As Hart argues, 'the realistic surface of the drama has been irreparably cracked'.[33]

While none of these events lies beyond causal or psychological explanation, they evoke deeper, elemental meanings that we might expect to be contained by the mythic plots. And indeed the Prodigal Son is forgiven, the Dying King is displaced by the Rising Son/Sun and the patriarchal order is seemingly maintained. Yet studies of

Shepard's use of allegorical motifs in the play almost uniformly find that these, too, are not used straightforwardly. Tucker Orbison believes that the *mythos* of the Corn King (the fertility myth) is sustained, while that of the Holy Grail (the myth of the ascent of the new King) is subverted: thus, '[t]he vision of *Buried Child* is characterized by a bitter irony: while the natural world is renewed, the human world is not'.[34] Others go further still, arguing that 'all the mythic patterns' have been 'twisted to prevent regeneration'.[35] Once again, the subversion of the realist structure goes hand in hand with the sabotage of the conventional function of myth, and the result cannot be simple regeneration but more complex shapes of meaning and extremely ambiguous dimensions of affect.

The family haunts its own home. From the opening curtain, the setting, with the decrepit Dodge holding centre stage on a deteriorating couch and wrapped in a symbolic – but nevertheless tawdry – blanket, suggests a charnel house.[36] We seem to be below ground (and Dodge refers to himself as 'a corpse'), with a set of stairs leading nowhere and a spectral light emanating from the front porch behind the couch mirrored by the 'flickering blue light' coming from the omnipresent television (63). While the environment seems, in the tradition of naturalism, a causal agent of the inner state of the dilapidated souls who inhabit the space, it soon becomes clear that in fact the locale is an exteriorization of the moral state of a family bound not by love, history or shared joy but by a collective sin that binds them in a communal hell over which Dodge presides.

With his cantankerous, sneering dialogue and helplessness, Dodge (whose ability to avoid and deflect responsibility makes him worthy of the name) is the first buried child we encounter – but certainly not the last. As we meet his progeny, all evince forms of childish behaviour. Tilden, who Taav calls 'the most consistently childlike of the three', is either a half-wit or so traumatized by the mysterious event that got him thrown out of New Mexico that he has forsaken his maturity.[37] He conveys 'disassociation' and ineptitude but also a sense of innocence. His discovery of the corn and carrots (and eventually the buried child) suggests a visionary capacity for the miraculous. He connects immediately with Shelley and, unlike Dodge, eagerly talks about the family past. By first bringing up the dead child with Shelley, Tilden initiates the process by which the mystery is unravelled and thus clarifies his role as the likely father. Bradley, on the other hand, violently represses any sign of helplessness by bullying everyone to assert power as the younger son. His veneer of bluster, however, is bared whenever his prosthetic is taken from him, thus exposing the source of his castration anxieties and foreshadowing his regression to a puling child in the final act. Even Vince, the next generation, initially exhibits a charming boyishness. In the face of his father's and grandfather's inability or unwillingness to acknowledge him, Vince's first response is to play silly games with them, like drumming his teeth, to jog their recollections.

While the tale of the buried child eventually is revealed to be Dodge's murder of the infant likely born of incest between Halie and Tilden, the revelation comes early in the final act and thereby weakens its dramatic weight. The truly significant moment arrives when Vince returns, smashing empty whisky bottles against the house and raving drunkenly while singing the 'masculine' Marine battle hymn. In this degenerate state Halie can finally recognize him, and, like Weston in *Curse of the Starving Class*, he violently crosses the threshold of the home by cutting his way through the screen door and tumbling into the main room. An unsettling image of self-birth, the gesture resonates strongly with the earlier dialogue about the murder and secret burial of the child. Seemingly, only violence confirms one's identity and position in the family, and Vince reveals his patrimony by threatening to usurp the 'territory' and take control of the family homestead by force.

Buried Child is saturated with the burden of the past and the manner by which memory both buries history and reanimates it. When Tilden re-enters in the final action of the play, bearing the bones of the murdered child, the image communicates both despair and hope. Within the conventions of realism, Vince might be expected to play the role of the external agent whose arrival instigates the process of a revelation that he, himself, might culminate. Vince is the only family member who seemingly has no prior knowledge of the dark secret of the child, nor does he see it when Tilden carries the remains up the stairs toward Halie. Vince's monologue describing the vision of his family legacy encountered while attempting to escape toward the Iowa border is the major statement of self-identification and family continuity in the entire play, and so if anyone should succeed in establishing a new, transformed order in the family line it should be him. But that vision concludes with '[e]verything dissolved'(130), and Vince abolishes his origins rather than penetrating to the heart of the myth of family. Reminiscent of Weston's false rebirth in *Curse of the Starving Class*, Vince fails to effect any healing change. He might have escaped the cycle of guilt and anomie that followed the murder and led the next generation of the family forward, but instead Vince assumes his place on Dodge's couch, covered in the cape of the returned Prodigal Son and positioned physically much like the deceased Dodge on the floor. Like Wesley garbed in Weston's filthy and infested garments, Vince has failed to resurrect the buried child within himself to restore equilibrium to the family.

One interpretation of the image, then, suggests a hereditary poison, similar to the one invoked in *Curse of the Starving Class*, which will continue to course through the family bloodlines: Vince, literally, cannot get 'out of Dodge'. The appearance of the dead child, then, merely confirms, as Les Wade argues, 'the full revelation of familial guilt and corruption'.[38] However, as he goes on to say, 'The final image of *Buried Child* challenges the viewer, for it allows no closure of easy understanding of what has preceded.'[39] Balancing Vince's horizontal position on the couch alongside the dead father is the upright figure of Tilden carrying the murdered child, his legs '*dripping mud from the knees down*' (132). Throughout the play, Tilden has been associated with the earth, discovering the miraculous vegetables, 'gently' covering Dodge with corn sheaves, communicating openly with Shelley and beginning the process of exorcising the guilt of the murdered child by confiding in her. His alterity builds from the moment we encounter him through his exchanges with Shelley and finally to the moment when Dodge reveals that the child is likely Tilden's by incest. As such, unlike Vince, who is reinscribed into the family narrative, Tilden is suggestive of an alternative order to both the Oedipal and patriarchal structures imbued in the traditional myths and which have damned the family to its heritage of despair. As Taav notes, with regard to the Oedipal conflicts in early plays like *The Tooth of Crime* and *The Holy Ghostly*, 'the son's victory was achieved through the death of the father, who, being of some power, needed to be overcome by force; whereas in *Buried Child* it is achieved sexually via the seduction of the mother'.[40] In the final scene, we are scenically provided with a split screen of possible outcomes. This leads some critics to see the arrival of the buried child as the final, ironic reunion (albeit one we do not see completed) in a play in which family members fail to reunite or even recognize one another. As Tilden returns the bones to the offstage mother, Halie looks out of the upstairs bedroom window and finally is granted vision to see the crops growing outside: 'Maybe it's the sun. Maybe that's it. Maybe it's the sun' (132).

This superimposition of very different fates allows us to remain suspended, then, between a strict realist structure and one that allows room for the fantastic and the grotesque to render its smooth surfaces rough and lumpy, fractal rather than regular in its dimensions.[41] At the same time, Shepard seems less intent than in *Curse of the Starving Class* at foreclosing all hopes of an escape from the cycle of familial violence and deceit. What seems clear is that such liberation cannot occur if cherished myths are not also exposed, interrupted by difference and redirected.

In its production history, the play brought to the surface latent issues with regard to Shepard's blending of realism and his earlier gestalt style. When the play premiered at the Magic Theatre in San Francisco in 1978, directed by Robert Woodruff, audiences were by now better prepared for the mix of realism and the fantastic, and the production succeeded so well that it transferred quickly to New York. After a short run at the Theatre for the New City in 1979, *Buried Child* opened at the Theatre de Lys in Shepard's old stomping grounds of Greenwich Village and ran for another four months: a solid but hardly spectacular production run.

However, despite earning Shepard his Pulitzer Prize and after nearly 20 years of successful productions in regional and university theatres, in 1996 Chicago's Steppenwolf Theatre (whose influence on *True West* is recounted below) revived the play and unexpectedly began receiving rewrites of key scenes from Shepard. The ensuing version of the play was a massive success and eventually became Shepard's first play to move up to Broadway, arriving for an abbreviated run at the Brooks Atkinson Theatre in April 1996. The revised text of the play, published in 1997, aroused substantial critical debate about whether the new version rendered the unsettling elements of the original (such as Tilden's patrimony of the dead child) too pat and obvious.[42] This, in turn, called into question Shepard's 'turn' toward realism and greater clarity, suggesting to some that he may have been seeking greater popularity at the expense of the raw power with which he imbued the first version of the play. However, the double-coding of realism and mythic elements remained, leaving even the revised text to convey 'the impression of something at once disconcertingly familiar and inexplicably strange'.[43]

True West

With a Pulitzer behind him, Shepard embarked on what turned out to be his most popular play, yet one that caused him great effort to produce, having gone through 13 drafts before being realized as the third entry in the family trilogy. *True West* carries over many themes from the earlier plays, but here they find expression explicitly in the comic and ironic modes (though touched by moments of real terror). The family bond that harnesses the two brothers, Lee and Austin, seems less fateful since the father figure is never present (though often evoked). The trophy for the victor in the sibling struggle, as well, is diminished: rather than fighting for something elemental, such as patrimony or identity, the brothers wrangle over a Hollywood screenplay. Finally, as James Crank says, '[T]he conflict between the brothers creates outrageous situations that, at times, border on farce and parody, and the action reminds the audience of a situation comedy on television ... Shepard channels Neil Simon's *The Odd Couple*.'[44] For these and other reasons, the split between the two brothers can be understood quite explicitly as the absurd divisions that rend families and individual personalities alike into warring factions, both of which desperately need the other to survive.

Don Shewey provides a succinct summary of the play's action:

> Clean-cut screenwriter Austin is holed up at his mother's house in Southern California (she's on vacation in Alaska), finishing a project he's pitching to a Hollywood producer. He is being distracted by his older brother Lee, a slovenly drifter and cat burglar who takes after his father, now living 'out in the desert', drunk and broke. While the producer meets with Austin, Lee butts in, claiming that he has a good idea for a Western. Something happens over a game of golf ... and he decides to drop Austin's story and do Lee's. The brothers switch roles,

but Lee can't spell, let alone type, and Austin's idea of crime is stealing all the toasters he can from the neighborhood. Mom arrives home from Alaska (the new Western frontier?), takes one look at her ravaged bungalow and her drunken brawling boys, and decides to check into a motel. Moonlight settles on the two brothers circling each other silently, in deadly combat.[45]

The tone Shewey adopts in reviewing the 1980 New York production (after premiering with a different cast at the Magic Theatre earlier that year) captures some of the pace, humour and insouciance of Shepard's text. Unfortunately, a heavy-handed production by Joe Papp could not channel the comedy, and the play originally flopped.[46] To the rescue, in 1982, came Chicago's Steppenwolf Theatre, whose seminal production not only revived the flagging reputation of the play but also introduced John Malkovich (as Lee) to the theatregoing public (Gary Sinise played Austin and directed). The successful production, based on Steppenwolf's trademark physicalization of character and fearless exploration of the slapstick comedy in even the heavier moments of the play, transferred quickly to the Off-Broadway Cherry Lane Theatre in New York where it continued its successful run.[47] The PBS film of that production, by which many students and spectators are first introduced to Shepard's drama, still captures some of the manic physicality and absurd comedy of the text.

Although the play rounds out the family trilogy and Shepard's work of the 1970s rather neatly, the play in no sense resolves the tensions that first drew him to the family theme. In fact, Shepard returns to the issue of family explicitly in three later plays (*Fool for Love*, *Lie of the Mind* and *The Late Henry Moss*) and touches upon it in much of his fiction and non-fiction writing after the 1970s. But *True West* makes explicit, and to some degree brings to completion, Shepard's exploration of the creative tensions that arise when seemingly antithetical structures of meaning are superimposed. The play literally casts opposing epistemologies by investing Austin (staying in his mother's home) with the character of the successful urban artist who cranks out well-shaped screenplays that, while they remain familiar and recognizable, never plumb the depths of the archetypal or mythic. Lee, on the other hand, by maintaining contact with the chaotic and primal by virtue of his life in the desert (and close to the father), can vaguely sense the movement of the mythic, but is utterly lacking the power to articulate it in narrative. Their struggle – over the car keys, the toasters and typewriter, but also over the authentic memory of their father and of course over the story that will be optioned by the producer, Saul Kimmer – forces the opposing principles to interact dynamically; and the result, even with the comic touches, is an odd hybrid of meaning and affect.

Shepard follows up the tentative exploration in *Buried Child* of breaking free of the black hole of hereditary gravity by giving us, in *True West,* the comic version of that impulse. Austin seemingly escaped the cycle of inbred family isolation and dependency that the father has bequeathed to his family. The antithesis of Tilden, Austin escapes by seemingly living a stable family life and enjoying a successful professional career. He looks and acts the role of healthy, self-possessed autonomy, and initially conveys unimpeachable confidence. Yet, having witnessed attempts by characters like Weston and Dodge to repress their respective pasts and be reborn guiltless and free, we are not surprised that when the lights come up in the first scene, this avatar of sane existence is being shadowed by his *doppelganger,* brother Lee, and struggling to maintain his veneer of self-possession. Indeed, critics have remarked on how the opening dialogue, in which Lee claims to have himself been an artist, one whose work was 'ahead of its time', suggests an uncanny scene in which the young Sam Shepard of Off-Off-Broadway ('a rock-and-roll Jesus with a cowboy mouth') is visiting his more successful, mainstream self in the act of crafting a well-structured piece of fiction that is very much 'of' its time.[48]

If Austin is the travesty version of Shepard as a realist playwright, content to pound out work with familiar themes and trajectories ('a worthwhile story' [14]), Lee is delineated in strokes just as broad to evoke the artist as dangerous shaman mumbling prophecies, a stereotype often applied to the young Shepard. He is the perfect foil to Austin's desires for rootedness and home, the coyote to the younger brother's dog. His connection with the desert makes explicit the contrast Shepard draws between the traditional myth of the frontier and the more contemporary myth of the 'new west' that would be revived, without Shepard's corrosive irony, in neoliberal terms by Reagan (Hollywood's progeny) just a year following *True West.* Austin lives in northern California, and stays in the urban sprawl of Los Angeles when he visits the southern part of the state. Lee won't travel north to stay with Austin's family, finding his roots in the desert south. As Wade says, the 'sense of familial bifurcation informs the play's geographical imagery'.[49]

But these and other borders are permeable, and as the polarities shift with Lee attempting to establish a foothold in Hollywood and Austin yearning to escape to the desert, it becomes clear that each sibling defines and creates himself only in relation to the other. This in turn shapes the dynamic between the realist structure of the play and its evocation of the frontier myth, put into motion when Lee convinces Saul to set aside Austin's project and instead pick up the option for his own screenplay, 'a true-to-life Western' (19). While Lee is able only to synopsize the story for Saul, his dictation that closes Scene Four has the cadences of one of Shepard's early arias:

> So they take after each other straight into an endless black prairie. The sun is just comin' down and they can feel the night on their backs. What they don't know is that each of 'em is afraid, see. Each one separately things that he's the only one that's afraid. And they keep ridin' like that straight into the night. Not knowing. And the one who's chasin' doesn't know where the other one is taking him. And the one who's being chased doesn't know where he's going. (27)

This stark revision of the frontier myth, now with sinners fleeing into the West without direction and driven by fear, becomes a mirror because for all its hackneyed stereotypes it reflects exactly the struggle Austin and Lee enact. Typecast in a drama of their own making, the brothers then set out to shape this unpromising throb of mythic energy into a screenplay that, like *True West*, can't contain it because it inherently lacks resolution. The limitation of the form, however, creates the dynamic out of which authenticity can emerge: the 'true West' is the one that lies too deep for words and must be communicated otherwise. The essence of the tale remains ungraspable for Lee, and not just because he can neither spell nor type. To fulfil the terms of the 'project' with Saul, the story must be expressed in language, and the dreaming world simply doesn't speak in that tongue. Lee's thrashing of the typewriter with the 9-iron late in the play makes the mechanical source of words literally explode and scatters language and denotative meaning across the stage. Yet, like the kitchen itself, language is not destroyed utterly but strewn about in a kind of order incomprehensible by rational structures of signification, much like the mysterious grammar of myth.

The manifest content of the story, which Austin rightfully mocks, is incoherent as a well-shaped story but powerful in its suggestiveness of a latent pulse of deeper meanings. Lee is able to clutch momentarily the rhythms of the essential myth, but words betray him, especially as he collaborates with his brother to shape the tale in accord with Hollywood expectations. Here, myth is translated into mere fantasy by the vitiated forms, like realism, that make it palatable and repeatable while diminishing its essence. Austin is powerless to help him, as his connection to language has been shaped by the screenwriter's need to give the people what they want: 'What's he know about what people wanna see on the screen! I drive on the freeway every day. I swallow the smog. I watch the news in color. I shop in the Safeway. I'm the one who's in touch! Not him!' (35).

Like the siblings, myth and artistic form are co-dependent, locked into a relationship that can never be fulfilled or annulled. When one accepts that the form truly captures the spirit of myth, however, responses to the play perforce become limited, as when critics argue that two brothers are symbolically re-enacting the struggles between the Old West and New West (William Kleb); Cain and Abel (Jeffrey D. Hoeper); Shepard's conflicted attitudes toward his father (Henry I. Schvey); or the Jungian 'first self' and its shadow (Tucker Orbison). These interpretations expect that a realist structure will be competent to resolve such binaries. Yet this means responding to the struggle between Austin and Lee only in absolute terms, and dictates that the realist structure of the play will, in fact, deliver a judgement on whether the conflict has been resolved successfully or not. Orbison, for instance, thus must argue (Austin playing ego to Lee's shadow) that 'Austin cannot achieve a total psychic integration', and, therefore, at play's end 'Austin and Lee continue their night journey on "an endless black prairie"'.[50] In the realist form, integration can only be successful or unsuccessful.

But despite the rigidly linear plot, the balanced polarities between the brothers (that reverse but remain stable) and the smooth rising action, the play never fully submits to the structures of meaning associated with classical realism. There are, finally, no firm outcomes that provide examples of what constitutes true masculinity or the real West, and even the MacGuffin of the screenplay is left unresolved. Instead, the play ends with the theatrical coup of the final tableau: '*a single coyote heard in the distance, lights fade softly into moonlight, the figures of the brothers now appear to be caught in a vast, desert-like landscape, they are very still but watchful for the next move*' (59–60). Antipodal to the resolution required by the realist structure (one cannot imagine Austin coming up with this scenario), the scene also fails to image forth the crux of myth because it is a tired cliché (so one certainly can imagine Lee including it). Thus, rather than (only) suggesting an eternal standoff of the opposing forces, the tableau's effect becomes 'absurd' in the sense of the mathematical surd: the square root that can't be simplified; irreducible, spinning off infinite decimals that don't repeat and thus remain irrational and therefore (like the frozen characters of the tableau) 'inaudible'. The scene, finally, cannot speak in the language of realism because its message is imperceptible through that structure of meaning.

But of course the final stage picture isn't silent. We should recall that Shepard took pains in the first stage direction to differentiate the '*distinct yapping*' of the '*Coyote of Southern California*' by likening it to a hyena. The tableau is thus accompanied by manic, if not hysterical, laughter. Furthermore, we should remember how stage time operates, and not immediately forsake the doubling of space that occurs here. The vast desert landscape is coexistent with the kitchen, and even if by some trick of lighting the real space of the home has seemingly been eliminated, it remains as an after-image on the eye, ghosting our reading of the space. That once-tidy space is teeming with beer cans, dying plants, burnt and crumpled drafts of the screenplay, whiskey bottles, golf clubs, the shattered typewriter and the infamous toasters. The penultimate and final stage images conflate, therefore, not just the desert junkyard of the father (collapsing differences between desert and urban environments) but also, uncannily, the dual structures of meaning explored in the play. The tidy, enclosed kitchen limned in realistic details seems easily interpretable, like the artificial grass; and the chaotic and chthonic debris dredged out of the deepest levels of the siblings' unconscious appears as a disorder teeming with multiple possible meanings. Each has its own way of signifying, but only when they are jarringly brought together, as Shepard has done, does real complexity emerge.

Conclusion

After the release of the film *The Right Stuff* in 1983 (based on the 1979 non-fiction bestseller of the same title by Tom Wolfe), in which Shepard gave an Oscar-nominated performance as the rough-and-tumble pilot Chuck Yaeger, the playwright came to occupy a contradictory position in American culture. Not surprisingly, it was one caught up in American mythology. Wolfe's book provided a nostalgic look back to when post-Second World War avatars of the original pioneers (the test pilots seeking to break the sound barrier in the late 1940s) recreated a Wild West atmosphere whose success embodied American technological and moral exceptionalism. This carried over into the early years of NASA and led to the stunning Apollo achievements that culminated in the first Moon landing in 1969, America's pinnacle of global technological and ideological eminence. The Apollo programme, however, was curtailed after the return of Apollo 17 in 1972 when budget cuts forced the cancellation of future lunar landings. The demise of an active space exploration programme (and its replacement by Skylab, a 'mere' research facility carrying little of the romance of the Moon landings) was often offered as evidence of America's declining power and daring.

Ronald Reagan, elected in 1980 and re-elected in 1984 with the declaration that it was, once again, 'Morning in America', was conflated with Wolfe's book and eventually the film. His presidency was widely received as the 'right stuff' to cure the malaise of the Carter years and a hyper-masculine turn away from Hollywood's 'Vietnam Syndrome' and its attendant attitude of defeat and guilt. Many hailed the return of the heroic mode and a new frontier spirit, and no one embodied this more dramatically in the film than Shepard. Coupled with his Pulitzer for *Buried Child* (1979), all evidence pointed to him assuming the mantle of the revitalized American hero, the 'American Original' trumpeted in a 1984 *Playboy* interview. This was despite the fact that *Buried Child* and the other plays of the trilogy had presented a bleak analysis of the American family and American myths. But a deeply conservative vein runs through Shepard's family trilogy, and as Wade points out, '[h]is works castigate the shortcomings of the present and stir longing for a bucolic American past, free from government intrusion and the ills of modernity', and this certainly found resonance with the anti-government conservatism of the Reagan years and beyond.[51] As Wade remarks, 'It is perhaps one of the great ironies of the contemporary American theatre that the wild-boy renegade of the Greenwich Village counterculture should be catapulted to the pinnacle of his acclaim during the height of right-wing conservatism.'[52]

Shepard ended the 1970s having thoroughly investigated the state of the American family and having perfected a hybrid dramatic form that allowed him both to express nostalgia for the decay of the nation's founding myths while also exposing their corrupting influence on contemporary models of masculinity, identity and patrimony. His expansion of what realism could communicate theatrically remains a key development in the history of American drama. Shepard caught the pulse of mainstream American life as the country staggered out of the eventful 1960s and found itself in a state of volatile transition. His plays, especially the family trilogy that arrived as the 1970s were waning, captured some of the key contradictions that would define the next decade and beyond: the loss of home bartered away for the rootless existence of late capitalism; the sense of decline accompanied by the nation's 'single superpower' status after the fall of the Soviet Union; and most of all, the prospect that, in O'Neill's words, America had become the tragic tale of possessors self-dispossessed.

Shepard's dramatic output after 1985 dropped considerably. In his 'late phase', he continues to delve into issues of traumatic memory, authenticity and masculinity in a variety of styles and media.[53] While his period of celebrity had passed and his position at the centre of American theatre had diminished, the sum total of his work makes a strong case for Shepard as the most important dramatist the country has produced since Tennessee Williams.

5

Ntozake Shange: *For colored girls who have considered suicide/when the rainbow is enuf* (1975), *spell #7* (1979) and *boogie woogie landscapes* (1979)

Neal A. Lester

Introduction

A prolific and ground-breaking poet-playwright of the 1970s, Ntozake Shange has penned over a dozen pieces for the stage, pieces which convey her distinct creative aesthetic and her definitive poetic sensibility: *for colored girls who have considered suicide/when the rainbow is enuf* (1975) – nominated for a Tony Award, Grammy Award and Emmy Award; *A Photograph: Lovers-in-Motion* (1977) – produced Off-Broadway at the Public Theater; *Where the Mississippi Meets the Amazon* (1977); *A Photograph:*

A Study of Cruelty (1977); *boogie woogie landscapes* (1979) – first produced at Frank Silvera's Writers' Workshop in New York, then on Broadway at the Symphony Space Theatre; *spell #7: geechee jibara quik magic trance manual for technologically stressed third world people* (1979) – produced Off-Broadway at Joseph Papp's New York Shakespeare Festival Public Theater; *Black and White Two Dimensional Planes* (1979); *Mother Courage and Her Children* (1980) – produced Off-Broadway at the Public Theater and winner of a 1981 Obie Award; *Three for a Full Moon* (1982); *Bocas* (1982) – first produced at the Mark Taper Forum in Los Angeles; *From Okra to Greens/A Different Kinda Love Story* (1983); *Educating Rita* (1983), an American adaptation of British playwright Willy Russell's comedy – premiered at the Alliance Studio Theatre (Atlanta); *Three Views of Mt. Fuji* (1987) – first produced in San Francisco at the Lorraine Hansberry Theatre and first produced in New York at the New Dramatists; *Daddy Says* (1989); *Betsey Brown: The Musical* (1989) – based on Shange's novel of the same title and premiering at the American Music Theater Festival (Philadelphia); and *Whitewash* (1994), a *Teaching Tolerance* film animation produced and directed by Michael Sporn based on Shange's picture book of the same title. Shange's *Hydraulics Phat Like Mean* (1998), based on Shakespeare's Sonnet 128, is part of a collection – *Lover's Fire* – of seven playwrights responding to seven Shakespearean sonnets.

In all of these published and performed works, Shange approaches the stage as a poet with a very specific cultural focus and aesthetic:

> as a poet in American theater / i find most activity that takes place on our stages overwhelmingly shallow / stilted & imitative. that is probably one of the reasons i insist on calling myself a poet or writer / rather than a playwright / i am interested solely in the poetry of a moment / the emotional & aesthetic impact of a character or a line. for too long now afro-americans in theater have been duped by the same artificial aesthetics that plague our white counterparts / 'the perfect play,'... / a truly european framework for european psychology / cannot function efficiently for those of us from this hemisphere.[1]

With cultural nuance missing from representations of black lives on the commercial American stage and with punctuations violating the artificial and often nonsensical rules of 'Standard English' on the page, Shange establishes in her work what she terms a 'colloquial universal' – a universe with different vital and sustained standards of operation. This 'alternative' universe creates and promotes community and legitimizes and documents lived experiences absent from or marginalized in mainstream America. Shange's poems, whether as independent performance or staged production, embody a characteristic boldness aesthetically and politically, never more symbolized than in her 1970 self-naming: 'ntozake', meaning 'she who comes with her own things', and 'shange', meaning 'she who walks like a lion'.[2] Her politics and her aesthetic converge in her self-definition as a 'war correspondent': 'I am a war correspondent after all because I'm involved in a war of cultural and esthetic aggression. The front lines aren't always what you think they are.'[3]

Shange's identity as a poet foregrounds her work and cultural influence, declaring in an interview with Henry Blackwell, 'Poetry is my life.'[4] Raw and honest emotion informs her work and engages her readers and audiences without alienating, demonstrating that intellect can separate in ways that emotion can unite: 'quite simply a poem shd fill you up with something/cd make you swoon, stop you in yr tracks, change yr mind, or make it up. a poem shd happen to you like cold water or a kiss.'[5] About the raw emotion in *for colored girls*, editor Margaret B. Wilkerson (1984) summarizes: 'Powerful. Gripping. Moving. Intense. Bitter. Shattering. These are only some of the adjectives used to describe the play that propelled Ntozake Shange into theatrical fame.'[6] Shange's use of emotionalism serves as a catalyst for social awareness, personal awakening and personal actions toward some personal or social injustice. For instance, Beau Willie's dropping his two children from a high-rise apartment window is not the final moment of *for colored girls* even though this moment is the most remembered in the choreopoem. While other moments in the piece are equally and differently emotional – a young female's willing initiation into womanhood on her graduation night, an abortion from an accidental pregnancy, a male partner's infidelity, acquaintance rape, vengeful and futile sexual intimacy, unrequited affections, vulnerability and disappointment – this unparalleled emotional moment in American theatre underscored the still-problematic way in which males' actions are more important to audiences – past and present – than the complicated circumstances that bring both Crystal and Beau Willie to this ultimate moment of self-destruction: a place where they are both suffocating literally and figuratively in a system that denies them human dignity and offers no compassion. While systems of inequity are critiqued, these two African-American adult characters are not without personal responsibility for choices they each make in their own lives and in the lives of their two innocent children. Connecting her subject and content to performance, Shange clarifies how her stage work challenges actors: 'My work is difficult for actors to perform because I demand all kinds of emotional commitment that they don't necessarily have to give other playwrights.'[7] Mirroring in her work the rawness of everyday experiences and elevating everyday speech to poetry is then Shange's contribution to the stage and to literature.

The sentiments of female and black struggle and triumph have kept Shange's poems and poetry-related staged pieces alive and introduced generations to a feminist expression birthed in women's poetry bars in California and taking form on stages across the USA and beyond – Australia and England, for example. To know the impact and influence of Shange is to look at the ways that her work has been memorized, performed, memorialized and revised, evidencing the social and political relevance of her body of work. The aesthetic innovation of the choreopoem form continues to attract and liberate generations of poets, performers, students, scholars and artists paying homage to Shange's writing for the stage.

for colored girls who have considered suicide/ when the rainbow is enuf

The poems that constitute *for colored girls* are both monologues and dialogues about these major issues: female sexual agency, domestic abuse, acquaintance rape, abortion from an unplanned pregnancy, heteronormative relations between persons of colour, self-love and sisterly bonding for women of colour. While Shange's choreopoem form – arguably her most important innovation in American theatre – resonated with some as powerful and new, mostly white male critics deemed it unsophisticated, its thematic focus on the rainbow trope pedestrian. Especially critical in his review of the Broadway production was *The New Leader*'s John Simon (1976):

> Is this poetry? Drama? Or simply tripe? Can you imagine this being published in a serious poetry journal? Would it have been staged if written by a white? ... The sad thing about *for colored girls* is that it is no more theater than it is poetry; indeed, these random snatches of writing were not even intended for the stage.[8]

Intended or not, the poems were performative, and bringing the twenty poems together as a whole and then dividing them among seven speakers was indeed innovative and new. Giving the actors freedom to move outside prescriptive stage directions was also liberating and intimidating for actors used to traditional roles and character interactions. It was equally disconcerting for some audiences who expected a choreographed consistency that would not be found in productions of *for colored girls* as actors had creative license to move as the poems' performances moved them individually. Clive Barnes (2001), however, wrote differently about the play: 'This is true folk poetry. It springs from the earth with the voice of people talking with the peculiarly precise clumsiness of life. It is the gaucheness of love. It is the jaggedness of actuality.'[9] About Shange's writing more broadly, the poet Ishmael Reed contends, 'No contemporary writer has Ms. Shange's uncanny gift for immersing herself within the situations and points of view of so many different types of women.'[10]

The choreopoem form has not been nearly as off-putting for critics and audiences today as for the work's first wave of critics who neither understood nor embraced the narrative's non-linearity, the lack of traditional characters to analyse or the way the independent poems could be divided into multiple connected and connecting voices. That Shange puts the stage piece together to express some of the good, bad and unpretty realities of being a 'colored girl' in a vernacular format linguistically and aesthetically – punctuated by physical movement that is not artificially choreographed and stagnant – was pioneering and impactful. That form is also very connected with African traditions that imagine and document the world more holistically through movement, dance, music and song that is not traditional musical theatre. Poet and performance artist Jessica Hagedorn (1990), frequent collaborator with Shange, articulates a shared stage expression for the lives of people of colour:

> The current trend towards 'multicultural' theater may come out of mainstream theater having been inhospitable, confusing and predictable. There has always been a need for any audience, especially one that has been deprived of seeing any recognizable form of its own experiences, to demand something more – something that speaks to them and is inclusive, not exclusive. As long as mainstream theater and arts remains unchallenged by both artists and audiences, then we will continue to have what is lovingly known as 'universal' theater (read: white, Western, male-dominated), with the occasional marginal ethnic theater thrown in for added 'color' and funding purposes ... Low-brow to some, maybe too lofty for some others – performance is definitely a riskier and demanding experience that involves the audience in a more direct way than traditional theater.[11]

Not only are the experiences of people of colour generally and of women of colour specifically manifested in a 'non-traditional' form that is narratively looser, some of the poems in *for colored girls* can be rearranged without weakening the message bracketed between female sexual awakening on its own terms in the first moments and the Beau Willie/Crystal emotionally-climactic moment near the end. Shange's sense of character and characterization as a poet in American theatre explains why doing character analyses forces a form that will not fit. Paul Carter Harrison (1989) contextualizes that how she writes and creates characters who do not fit traditional representations explains the seven women in *for colored girls*:

> Black theater, too, when aesthetically uncluttered by realism, is testamental. The inclination to testimony is the direct outgrowth of blacks attempting to overcome the rifts of consciousness created by regionalism and elitism so as to identity the tracings of a collective ethos, a sense of common purpose. Thus archetypal characters are more vital for public testimony than individuated characters pursuing their personal assessment of reality. Like the blues singer, archetypes provide potent communal references that illuminate the social landscape.[12]

The Lady in Brown's plea, for instance, at the opening of *for colored girls*, announces this blues piece. Her challenge to the audience and by extension to other artists in the theatre is also an explanation of the piece Shange creates in the choreopoem proper: the answer to her own question about what is deeply missing in staged expressions of black women's lives on the stage. Literally and figuratively then, for these women and any women assuming these roles of the seven women, their singing is about rawness, honesty, unpretentiousness, vulnerability, personal and social validation, pain, triumph and a cultural realness:

> somebody/anybody
> sing a black girl's song
> bring her out
> to know herself
> to know you
> but sing her rhythms
> carin/struggle/hard times
> sing her song of life
> she's been dead so long
> closed in silence so long
> she doesn't know the sound
> of her own voice
> her infinite beauty
> she's half-notes scattered
> without rhythm/no tune
> sing her sighs
> sing the song of her possibilities
> sing a righteous gospel
> let her be born
> let her be born
> & handled warmly.[13]

That Shange's work is unapologetically female-centric and about people of colour is also a hallmark of her contribution to the stage and to literature:

> I am a [poet] playwright. But I am a woman first. I am not a generic playwright. I am a woman playwright. And I would hope that my choice of words and my choice of characters and

situations reflect my experience as a woman on the planet. I don't have anything that I can add to the masculine perception of the world. What I can add has to be from what I've experienced. And my perceptions and my syntax, my colloquialisms, my preoccupations, are founded in race and gender.[14]

Shange follows a tradition of early black feminists giving voice to black people and black women silenced every day. Even as the very title of *for colored girls* alludes to suicide and then maps circumstances wherein 'colored girls' have considered or might consider suicide, attention to mental illness typically goes to Beau Willie Brown and his presumably PTSD-related behaviour; he has returned from the Vietnam War with no psychological or social services to integrate him back into civilian life. Few focus on mental illness and suicide among African-American women as Diana Martha Louis (2013) does, who contends that 'The relationship between sanity and social contexts in which such myths – ['angry black woman', 'sapphire', 'jezebel', 'mammy'] – are pervasive is at the heart of Shange's depiction of Black female experiences in *For Colored Girls*. The play encourages a rejection of the language and accompanying hegemonic social pressures that deem Black women "crazy bitches".'[15] The eventual triumph of these 'colored girls' through heightened self-awareness and sisterhood continues to ignite audience imaginations.

spell #7

Focus on black arts, black performance, conscious blackness and political black consciousness, black stereotypes in white minds and blacks' internalized self-hatred is at the centre of *spell #7* (1979), arguably Shange's second most popular theatre piece. Like *for colored girls*, *spell #7* is a series of vignettes that resume the choreopoem form with poems divided among multiple speakers to become one voice. Just as poems in *for colored girls* come together from Shange's independent poetry readings in women's bars, much of the material in this play exists as poems in her poetry volume *Nappy Edges*, itself a celebration of black culture and black aesthetics via the trope of black people's unchemically touched hair. One section of *spell #7* – the story of the girl with a lot of big hair that she obsessively brushes, and invoking rhythm and blues icon Chaka Kahn rather than Rapunzel – appeared earlier as a short story in *The Black Scholar* (1978). Like *for colored girls*, the stage is full of unchoreographed physical movement and rhythm with music and song. Unlike *for colored girls*, however, this theatre piece is divided into two acts with an intermission, and has more traditional characters with names and identities, and a set with props. Like *for colored girls*, the narratives offer a state of black experience both on and off the commercial stage. Like *for colored girls*, the format of the choreopoem, even with its more traditional stage elements, left some critics wanting a more structured and linear piece despite the fact that the piece is indeed structured with a beginning, middle and end modelled after the American minstrel shows. Production review headlines speak to the lukewarm critical reception.[16]

A self-referential and consciousness-raising piece, *spell #7* exposes the unconscious psychological attitudes that sabotage blacks' best sense of themselves ethnically, racially and creatively. Finding within the stage setting the safe space of a racially segregated bar, a community of unemployed black male and female actors lament and act out their frustrations with commercial American theatre and the limited and limiting stage roles created for and presented to them. These black female and male actors see the history of American racism embodied in the oversized black minstrel mask that looms over the set and punctuates the production at the beginning, during the intermission and at the end. These black actors support each other in their individual and communal struggles to be psychologically and emotionally healthy in twentieth-century America.

In one of the early rehearsals of *spell #7*, Shange recalls that white stage hands left the stage. She interprets their departure as being upset about what the piece communicates about white people. In fact, the choreopoem does invert racial stereotypes and indicts white America's continual dehumanizing, boxing in and otherwise invalidating of black creativity and black life. Whites on Shange's stage are background even though they are the source, Shange would maintain, of black stereotypes that prevent and stifle black human creativity and accomplishment. *spell #7* redefines the contours of black self-awareness and psychological survival through song, music, stories and dance. The 'magic' of the piece comes not in a single linear plot per se, but rather in challenging others' definitions of oneself as less than another and embracing one's black identity as power and possibility beyond the racially-biased stereotypes Sterling A. Brown identifies in the writings by early white American authors: the contented slave, the wretched freeman, the comic Negro, the brute Negro, the tragic mulatto, the local colour Negro and the exotic primitive.[17]

An American history lesson of sorts, *spell #7* unfolds as a piece structured visually and in terms of the action, format and the giant minstrel mask that grabs the audience's attention when the play opens and closes and is foregrounded during the intermission. Structured as a minstrel show, a popular late eighteenth- and early nineteenth-century American entertainment wherein white male actors blackened their faces with soot or burnt cork and pretended to be blacks in the most nonsensical and unflattering ways, *spell #7* includes the narrative prelude, action and message via skits and monologues and epilogue wherein the various parts of the traditional minstrel show are re-enacted not so much around whites in blackface doing cooning and buffooning, but rather as a black magician asked to do the impossible – make a young black female child white. Here, a little black girl wants to be white because everything around her paints whiteness as a universal ideal of physical beauty, moral goodness, desirability and allegedly all that is right in and with the world. The dilemma for any black American magician – the reality itself of a black magician is rare for those in the USA who know only the likes of Criss Angel, David Copperfield, Siegfried and Roy, Penn and Teller, David Blaine and others – is this: why does a young black female child want to be another race? From this problematic political and personal premise, Shange works her 'magic' to show that blackness is not about limitations on the mind and spirit even when limitations and restrictions exist externally in twentieth-century North America. To interrogate this dilemma, the actors transform the bar into a safe space – not unlike the safe and sacred space of the barbershop or beauty shop, past and present, in black communities across the country – a place where dreams and fears can be articulated to build support among those connected through the same struggles for cultural legitimacy and validation.

As a feminist who is also an artist, Shange takes her stage magic beyond race to tease at the nuances of gender within imposed black limitations. And if the very notion of a black magician is rare in America, the idea of a black female magician is even rarer. Hence, Shange as poet and writer challenges historical American representations and misrepresentations of black people. Karen Cronacher (1992) acknowledges that as an artist, Shange adopts the traditional male form of American minstrelsy to advance her feminist and womanist messaging: 'Shange's play addresses the absence of a subject position for African American women by reclaiming and rewriting the legacy of minstrelsy, writing herself back into a history in which she was excluded by virtue of her sex and implicated by virtue of her race.'[18] She demonstrates the dangers of self-effacement and of settling for less than what is spiritually and psychologically satisfying as practising actors and as artists of colour. More didactic than *for colored girls* and with psychologically less urgency than thoughts of suicide literally or metaphorically, *spell #7*, because of its focus on historical patterns of racial representation and misrepresentation, does not reach the same level of 'universal', commercial or mainstream applicability that many witness in *for colored girls*, with its focus on women generally and on women of colour specifically. The message of *spell #7* is targeted and specific – to reshape blacks' self-destructive thinking about themselves. The fact that the black actors are in blackface as the piece opens and then shed their blackface to reveal themselves and their vulnerabilities, frustrations and disappointments as the choreopoem unfolds, concretizes the magic and personal exorcism that the play facilitates for these actors and Shange's audience.

In two acts, *spell #7* critiques the limited and limiting stage roles for trained actors of colour. As the black ensemble of friends demonstrates community in their shared disillusionment about the commercial stage, they actively engage in conversations about the popular racist stereotypes that continue to subsume them professionally. Unsurprisingly, the emphasis of these fantasy creations acted out and pantomimed is on the kinds of complex roles these women actors, in this instance, long to see created for them – roles that showcase their creative range emotionally and that do not present them as inauthentic in the language, cultural rhythms, experiences, values and desires. They, in other words, long for roles that white female actors get, not the racist stereotypes of prostitutes and other morally loose characters. Thus, the different scenarios the actors self-consciously create represent the complexity of black women's experiences, both lived and imagined.

The story of Fay, for instance, imagines a black woman who is both a mother and a female exercising her sexual agency and challenging popular notions about black women as morally and sexually loose. While this perspective is not one that plagues males in precisely the same way, the piece does not question Fay's integrity as a mother or as a black woman worthy of respect no matter how she dresses, flirts with men or otherwise presents herself in public. Motherhood is important to Fay, but motherhood is neither Fay's single identity nor her sole identity. The sketch challenges intersecting notions about blacks, women and black women as Fay is neither a loose woman nor a negligent mother. In Fay's story, Shange challenges the respectability politics within black communities and the perception that motherhood, in Fay's case, has to be an all-consuming identity. Such a role that allows a black female actor a range of experience also challenges both racist and sexist assumptions on the American commercial stage and in the American psyche. As Viola Davis, the first African-American female to win an Emmy for Outstanding Lead Actress in a Drama Series, stated in her 2015 acceptance speech, 'The only thing that separates women of color from anyone else is opportunity. You cannot win an Emmy for roles that are simply not there.'

In contrast to Fay's, Sue-Jean's story is one of careless desperation and futility: a tale of warning about identity based on motherhood. In it, Sue-Jean creates herself by orchestrating a pregnancy that leaves her psychologically and physically empty when the reality that a child's dependence on its mother as a source of its livelihood is not without its limitations. In other words, as long as Sue-Jean is pregnant, her unborn is hers to control; she controls its nourishment, nutrition and its safety. However, when the child emerges from its mother's womb, it immediately takes on an independence not necessarily tied exclusively to any individual, including Sue-Jean, its mother. When that child begins to explore the world as all healthy babies will do, an independence decentres the child's mother, a mother whose identity has been created by that very child's existence. Unlike Fay's celebratory and liberatory message, Sue-Jean's is a story of tragedy wherein she is unable to control her infant, significantly named 'Myself'. A baby, Shange argues, cannot create an identity for a woman who is spiritually and emotionally needy. Such futility of creating one's self through validation from any external entity is the warning here. Sue-Jean's scenario likewise transfers to the choreopoem's focus on commercial stage roles defining actors themselves.

While the roles for actors of colour are often limited to popular stereotypes and caricatures on the American stage, the reality of needing work to sustain one's livelihood is also real and immediate. In contrast, a plethora of diverse roles for white actors, male and female, exist, with some white actors even playing roles written as characters of colour. Shange's commitment to her craft as a poet, as a female poet, as a female poet of colour even within the arena of a racist, sexist and classist commercial American stage that cannot always pigeonhole her work into neat genres or categories, is voiced thus through Eli:

> ... i am a poet / i write poems
> i make words cartwheel & somersault down pages
> outta my mouth come visions distilled like bootleg
> whiskey / i am a radio but i am a channel of my own
> i keep sayin i write poems / & people keep askin me
> what do i do / what in the hell is going on?
> ... I am a poet/.[19]

Since roles that white American female actors get are more plentiful and have greater range, Natalie creates a fantasy about being a white woman, at least the stereotypical white woman with whom the media, film and television continue to have a love affair. Her alleged definitive beauty becomes the measure of other women's worth, and for black women, the worth is of little value in the open market: 'so many men like white girls/ white men/ black men/ latin men/ jewish men/ asians/ everybody. so I thought if i waz a white girl for a day i might understand this better' (48).

This game of pretending to be a white girl takes place in two parts of Act One, both parts critiquing the ways in which white women are just as limited by sexist notions of a woman's life and worth. Still, stereotypes of white women's empty and purposeless existence and the social fascination with white and blonde female beauty, from the fictitious Rapunzel to Marilyn

Monroe and Farrah Fawcett, aligns Shange's efforts here with feminist attacks on white patriarchal limitations on white male agency and the misrepresentations of their lives as well. Some production reviewers took issue with what they saw as Shange's philosophical inconsistencies by calling for a liberation of black creative thought and expression allegedly at the expense of white stereotyping.[20] Shange is not an integrationist; she is writing on her own terms a 'race play' that testifies to the psychological unhealthiness of whites' stereotypes of blacks as they filter through blacks' unproductive thinking about each other and themselves.

Punctuating these pantomimes are monologues that Shange again divides into multiple voices – characteristic of the choreopoem form – so that other characters speak. The poems are accompanied by group dance and popular songs as celebration of black American identity. A critique of commercial stage roles for black actors, black female actors and even for white females, the play also indicts white men who control too many aspects of commercial theatre, whether as writers or directors. These white men embody their own problematic stereotypes as they create and perpetuate stereotypes and deny true talent and creativity.

spell #7 ends as it begins, calling the ensemble of black actors and friends to attention and acknowledging that the American past of misrepresentations need not be the future. *spell #7* is Shange's self-reflexive answer to her own artistic challenge – creating and formatting productions that allow the full range of black talent and creative genius. What has happened between the opening of the play and the close of the play – and even during the intermission – is a kind of magical exorcism meant to prompt a rethinking of how black people and black actors see themselves in an American theatre world that may or may not fully understand the gravity of these limitations. With the play's bold focus on blackness, it is easy to see how this piece may not have experienced the tremendous commercial success of *for colored girls*. The problem of the twenty-first century, to borrow from W. E. B. DuBois' *The Souls of Black Folks* (1903) and what Shange's play would offer for today's audience, is still the problem of the colour line, both on and off the American commercial stage.

boogie woogie landscapes

boogie woogie landscapes continues Shange's creative and political use of the choreopoem format. Integrating aspects of both *colored girls* and *spell #7* but significantly different from both, *boogie* explores the psychological interiority, the unconscious memories and the imaginings of a young 'all-American colored girl' as she sleeps on a given night.[21] Using the motif of dream sequencing, the piece exposes Layla's social and political consciousness as she interacts with six 'night-life companions' – three males and three females. During her dream – the duration of this production – Layla invokes her innermost fears that meet at the intersection of her being black in America and being female in a white American patriarchal society that devalues her person and her perspectives on the world. Far from being a piece about victimization, *boogie* is a study in self-empowerment through self-awareness. As the night-life companions re-enact scenes with and for Layla, Shange establishes and validates a 'colloquial universal' that characterizes the landscapes of any and every 'colored' daughter's geography, a geography that demands combating sexism and racism while simultaneously embracing life's challenges through music, song and dance that do not constitute a Broadway revue.

Layla's session of memories and imaginings underscores the vitality and power of music, song and dance to create community and to sustain an individual's spirit of triumph. As the night-life companions move back and forth through the walls of Layla's bedroom, Shange demonstrates the centrality of music, song and dance to Layla's full existence, thus Layla's opening and closing sentiments of the choreopoem:

> dontcha wanna be music/ dontcha wanna be music/ dontcha wanna be daybreak & ease into fog a cosmic event like sound/ & rain[22]

As Layla's existence takes on cosmic proportions, the expressionist technique puts the focus on memory and dream structural fluidity. Affirming the lives of women generally and of black women in particular, *boogie* is Layla's story of self-saving and self-preservation.

Layla's dream journey through this night takes on a stream-of-consciousness that affords a loose linearity. In her childhood, Layla is challenged to accept her blackness in a world that disparages blackness. Described as existing in a two-dimensional life in 'black and white' without colour and 'without shadows', Layla inhabits a black childhood full of confusion, contradictions and strained family relations. Deeply desiring the passion of colour beyond black and white, Layla encounters a spiritual dimension that opens her world. Her encounter with Jesus goes beyond the radio evangelist and a religious church experience in much the same way that the seven women finding god in themselves in *for colored girls* is less about finding something external to themselves to validate themselves. Instead, in both *for colored girls* and *boogie*, rebirth comes from within. Layla's move from childhood into womanhood, however, means that she has now to be more aware of the local and global threats to and attacks on her livelihood and her survival physically, emotionally and psychologically.

Men as seducers and manipulators in *boogie* will surely draw attention again to Shange's presentations of men in her body of work. Here, males are 'companions' – actors – in Layla's dream sequence. Their flattery and manipulation occasion Shange's protest against rampant rape culture and the global devaluing of females. Her protest takes the form of a treatise that outlines what is necessary to address the perpetrators of sexual violence. In short, Shange contends that rape culture and the mutilation of women's bodies will cease only when males cease using violence against women to define and demonstrate an illusory masculinist power.

Shange's protest against racial, class and gender bias also involves a critique of American media as embodied in the global and domestic social and political reverence accorded the *New York Times*. Clearly, the *New York Times* is not centrally focused on the lives of people of colour or those not in the middle class who are marginalized, if present at all, in the public policy and political decisions that define this country. Her challenge then to mainstream America is to value each and every human life on the planet:

> the ny times has never asked me what i think abt a goddamn thing.
> ...

no / the ny times has never helped in times of need
or offered his eat to a pregnant woman on the irt
...
still i wd like to get the ny times out of my social life
the next time someone asks me if i have seen the paper /
i'll say / i've seen more news than is fit to print (125)

As Shange critiques American mainstream media that values some lives over others, she comments on global race relations as the subject worthy of American media attention. America, by way of the *New York Times*, is personified as a self-serving white male without conscience or concern about lives beyond himself, a characterization that applies to male perpetrators of all forms of violence against women across the globe.

Shange weaves into *boogie* moments of her own autobiography to underscore her personal movement into adolescence; these rites of passage for females coming of age are also warnings about others bent on denying female agency on the basis of gender and race. About this autobiographical dimension of the work, Shange acknowledges that *boogie* is about 'the secrets and traumas of an Afro-American childhood, a *double entendre* about myself, the many different places I have lived, and their varying psychological topography'.[23] Adolescence, for girls then, is both a cause for celebration and for alarm not because of anything females do or do not do, but rather because a patriarchal society allows assaults and violations to occur with little or no consequence to the typically male perpetrators.

While the dream and the subconscious dictate the structure of *boogie* – Shange's 'most experimental play'[24] – this story of Layla met with a mixed critical reception.[25] What resonates with many as appropriate for the cultural contexts Shange creates and celebrates is precisely what leaves others wanting more structure and, in this case, more Western theatre of the white male-centric tradition. The character of Layla shows up again in Shange's 2005 production *Lavender Lizards and Lilac Landmines: Layla's Dream*. Still using the choreopoem form to embody Layla's new story, Shange presents Layla LaPierre, a black woman in her 20s 'aspiring to be a writer ... [and] having trouble breaking up with her manipulative boyfriend, Yves. She is visited by several spirits – people from her life and characters from her dreams – that challenge her to explore her own needs and desires.'²⁶ An earlier production of *Layla's Dream* in Chicago left reviewers and audiences once again perplexed and unsatisfied, Scott C. Morgan (2005) commenting that the piece at Congo Square Theatre was 'head-scratching and disjointedly ponderous', 'ellipsis-inducing', 'contrived and pretentious', 'overstuffed', ' a mixed bag' with a 'shaky framework' and an 'odd scattershot approach'.²⁷ *boogie* is boldly painted with Shange's aesthetic brush strokes that continue to move beyond the boundaries of critical and social expectation.

Conclusion

As a body of work that continues to have an impact on generations, Ntozake Shange's writings for the stage challenge the traditional parameters of American theatre by defining, redefining and documenting American culture and cultural aesthetics from a non-Western perspective. Harkening to a tradition of African storytelling, Shange uses music, song and dance to embody the lives of people of colour and women never before embodied in quite this way on the commercial American stage. She creates a space for herself further through her use of black vernacular, phonetic spellings and punctuations that connect more with poetry than prose, revealing a 'colloquial universal' to combat some of the cultural and aesthetic constraints and restraints of sexism, racism and classism.²⁸ Beyond the aesthetics of the choreopoem form and what the words of her (choreo) poems look like on a page, award-winning young adult author Rita Williams-Garcia (2011) says that Shange's work gave her a model of excellence:

> [W]hen I saw the production of Shange's work on the stage and read the text in a published book, I wanted to study *For Colored Girls* ... from every possible angle. Shange has answered questions I struggled with about writing for 'everyday use' ... and writing in pursuit of literary excellence. I was always an avid reader and read widely, but it was from reading *For Colored Girls* ... that literature and the spectrum of humanity in characters opened up for me. It added fearlessness, ugliness, and beauty to my grasp of writing.²⁹

Indeed, the impact and influence of Ntozake Shange's work is unquestioned. Frequently anthologized as an important American woman playwright, Shange through her work continues to inspire and to have an impact on generations across the broad spectrum of cultures and experiences. The accessibility of anthologies means more exposure of others to her work.[30]

Shange's works are also often included in monologue volumes for women such as *Women: The Contemporary Monologue* (1995) edited by Michael Earley and Philippa Keil, which includes 'Serial Monogamy', from Shange's volume *The Love Space Demands*. The editors explain this particular selection for inclusion in the volume, highlighting the characteristic performative nature of Shange's poetry:

> This poem demands to be performed. But like any poem spoken aloud it should not sound like verse but normal speech. It begins like a lecture and then transforms into a flashy surreal performance piece ... The sections of 'I say' and 'he say' turn into a duet, allowing you to control the fantasy notion of jade flying in every direction.[31]

Selections from *spell #7* are included in *Moving Parts: Monologues from Contemporary Plays* (1992), edited by Nina Shengold and Eric Lane. *spell #7* also appears in the volume *SOLO! The Best Monologues of the 80's* (1994), edited by Michael Earley and Philippa Keil, and is described thus: 'This collection of 75 solo speeches and performances pieces for actors has been selected from the finest material being written today for theater in America and England.'[32] Inclusion in such volumes further evidences that Shange's words continue to resonate with and to have an impact on generations of actors, performers and audiences. For instance, the choreopoem form of performative poetry has inspired a generation of young artists using hip-hop and spoken word on the stage. Says artist and writer Will Power (2007) about this influence and impact:

> What we in the hip-hop theatre and spoken word movements owe her is both enormous and obvious: Shange is one of the supreme pioneers of her generation in terms of presenting verse on the stage; in terms of actors melding speech, song and

movement to create character and story; in terms of performers using various extensions of their spirit to share an experience on stage. From our vantage point, she's the matriarch of the whole thing.[33]

Shange's work has been critiqued, parodied and imitated as authors, artists and activists continue to find in her work a liberation from restrictive forms and reductive thinking about the world and about their lives. Still others have mocked her work, as in the case of George C. Wolfe, whose *The Colored Museum* (1987) challenges the notions of 'sacred cows' and the 'legacy of suffering' in black American theatre – Lorraine Hansberry's *A Raisin in the Sun* and Shange's *for colored girls*, both of them much commercially celebrated. Specifically, Wolfe's 'Lady in Plaid', from the exhibit 'The Last Mama-on-the-Couch Play', speaks in an exaggerated black dialect that mocks Shange's homage to ancient African rituals – particularly the Sechita monologue – suggesting that the poetry and allusions in *for colored girls* are pretentious and culturally disingenuous. Wolfe combines Shange's female-centred expression with Hansberry's black male-centric play to have Walter-Lee-Beau-Willie-Jones dropping his brown rag doll children from the high-rise apartment window. Wolfe's parody seems to question the fact that these two female playwrights of colour received such Broadway acclaim for what he sees as a limited view of black experience. Granted, one of the central critiques of *for colored girls* is Shange's preoccupation with heteronormativity as well as her presentation of black men. In response to what he perceives as limited views, Wolfe created his *Colored Museum* to comment on various aspects of black American experience beyond black feminism and racism. In this case, Wolfe could only do what he does because Hansberry and Shange did what they did. Perhaps his use of 'colored' in his title gains additional signification by reference to hers.

Another mark of Shange's influence is the fact that she is a character in Anna Deavere Smith's *Fires in the Mirror: Crown Heights and Other Identities* (1993). Not only does Smith adopt the vignette/monologue format that also blurs the genre line between prose and poetry, but she opens *Fires in the Mirror* with her portrayal of Shange from Shange's own words in a phone interview she had with Shange about identity. Smith constructs Shange speaking about identity and place in 'Ntozake Shange:

The Desert'. This clarity about self is central to Shange's work and why Smith finds it so important to infuse her work with artistic creations – this sense that community is not stagnant and that all individuals are members of multiple communities simultaneously. In her Acknowledgments to *Fires in the Mirror*, Smith thanks Shange: 'For inspiration ... Ntozake Shange for what her presence has done to redefine the position of Black women in American theatre.'[34]

Creative responses to Shange's work have been many, some meant to challenge the alleged anti-black male sentiment many identify with *for colored girls*.[35] Perhaps the most significant milestone in measuring the mainstream impact of Shange's work overall and of *for colored girls* in particular is the fact that filmmaker Tyler Perry brought the choreopoem to the big screen in 2010, exposing Shange's work to a new and different audience generationally and multiculturally. While the choreopoem is a staple in women and gender studies classes from high school to college, the film tries to a very questionable degree to bridge Shange's literary world with Perry's popular culture world. What was produced provoked mixed critical reviews and not a little audience confusion when characters were noticeably talking in poetry true to Shange's text. Roger Ebert (2010), for instance, offers this common response to the film rendition:

> Many in the audience will have seen it onstage, and that will be an advantage; they'll understand what Perry is attempting. Ordinary moviegoers, accustomed to Perry's mainline films, are likely to be thrown off by the unconventional approach here. Perry tries to be faithful to the play and also to his own boldly and simply told stories, and the two styles don't fit together ...[36]

Kirk Honeycutt (2010), of the *Hollywood Reporter*, agrees:

> For once, Tyler Perry doesn't put his name above the title, but perhaps he should with *For Colored Girls* to distinguish this train wreck of a movie from the stunning theater piece of 36 years ago by Ntozake Shange.
>
> Hers was a tragic and sensuous hybrid of poetry, dance, drama and feminist theology – it even has been called the most important work about black female identity ever ... [H]is style

is too crude and stagy for Shange's transformative evocation of black female life, and his moralizing strikes exactly the wrong notes to express the pain and longing that cries out from her heated poetry.[37]

The film is most effective when characters deliver Shange's hallmark monologue poems. Adding a Whoopi Goldberg character who physically fights with her young daughter seems a major mistake and cheapens the film's aesthetic. The film does, however, represent Shange's updates to her original text – references to the US–Iraq war, HIV/AIDS and a new heterosexual black couple where the male is allegedly on the Down Low and sleeping with other men.[38]

Perry's is the only existing big screen version, but the play was actually presented on Public Broadcasting Service's *American Playhouse* (Thirteen/WNET New York, 1982) with little critical enthusiasm. Shange herself appears in that version, and one of the actors, Laurie Carlos, revealed in a phone conversation with me in August 1986 that the cast still sees that as an unsuccessful effort:

> The television production was perfectly awful. Here, take my copy. I use it as a doorstop. The television version doesn't work. The production was a case of black artists being afraid to claim what is their own. Zaki and Oz Scott [director] felt they could do more with a form that wasn't so limited ... The television production made the piece more palatable, thus losing some of the impact of the piece. Lines connecting each scene were missing.[39]

What also makes the television version of *for colored girls'* eighteen poems not work is the fact that what Shange creates so poignantly in words and images is often dramatized. Males are present and distracting in scenes that are monologues being acted out on the stage, and the barrenness of the choreopoem's original stage and the monochromatic costumes typically worn in live productions and that become visually and figuratively symbolic of the title's 'rainbow' that saves these women is missing altogether. In both the film and television versions, the visual aesthetic of colours associated with characters is lost in realism and personality. In both versions, only the poignancy of Shange's unadorned monologues works to capture the raw honesty of the original staged choreopoem.

That Shange's choreopoem was a pioneering format for cultural documentation and relevance, especially as demonstrated in *for colored girls*, *spell #7* and *boogie woogie landscapes*, is her legacy in American theatre. Performed in part or whole on college campuses and community theatres, or read in book clubs, her work has nourished and nurtured generations of women who see themselves in her words and who find their renewed spirits in her characters' honesty and vulnerability.[40] Indeed, Shange's work has also taught males about women's realities and given artists, poets, writers and scholars new models for creative self-expression. She has legitimized lives and birthed new ways of imagining what we can expect on the American stage. The occasion of the fortieth anniversary of *for colored girls* spawned celebrations across the USA. For instance, New York's Schomburg Center for Research in Black Culture has created an exhibition entitled 'I found god in myself', and is described as follows by the *New York Times*:

> Opening on September 19, 2014 and running through January 3, 2015 the fresh look at Ms. Shange's self-described choreopoem, or spoken-word drama, will be represented through 20 commissioned pieces that correspond to 20 poems in the text. The work, by artists who include Margaret Rose Vendryes, Kimberly Mayhorn and Renee Cox, is meant to interpret issues faced by the women in *Colored Girls*, whose challenges included rape and slain children. The exhibition also includes archival material, like Ms. Shange's papers, and the playbill and photos from the original Broadway production.[41]

Such a tribute to Shange, and this work in particular, highlights a legacy of impact across cultures and generations: 'The exhibit is a fitting tribute for a text that has so powerfully influenced feminism, African American literature, theatre, and dance. Undoubtedly, Shange's *for colored girls* will continue to resonate for readers and theater goers for generations to come.'[42]

A headline by Jai Tiggett for *Shadow and Act: On Cinema of the African Diaspora* (about the lack of diversity in Hollywood's 2014 Oscar nominations) further signals the impact of Shange's work within and beyond the academy and in the context of current popular culture: 'For White TV Writers Who Have Considered Racism When "Ethnic" Diversity Is Too Much'.[43] Tiggett challenges modes of culturally biased creative expression that have not always legitimized the complexity of the lives and experiences of women and people of colour in mainstream America. As long as there is racism, sexism, linguicism and violence against women and children, Shange's work will be relevant and will surely resonate with those who are socially conscious.

6

Richard Foreman: *Sophia = (Wisdom) Part 3: The Cliffs* (1972), *Pandering to the Masses: A Misrepresentation* (1975) and *Rhoda in Potatoland (Her Fall-Starts)* (1975)

Geoffrey King and Craig Werner

Introduction: Cogito ergo boom – Richard Foreman's Ontological-Hysteric Theatre

(Editor's note: Given the peculiar nature of Foreman's creative process and his mode of scenographic writing, the structure of this chapter will differ somewhat from the other three case studies. The reader will benefit from the authors' close contextualization of Foreman's thought and training through a longer introduction. To clarify relationships between the playwright's influences and theatrical practice, a number of subheadings are provided.)

Although Richard Foreman has created and produced his own work on a nearly annual basis since the late 1960s, the Ontological-Hysteric Theatre is not well known outside the worlds of the New York and European avant-garde. As with numerous other epochal American theatre-makers of the 1970s – Robert Wilson, the Wooster Group, Mabou Mines and Squat Theatre – Foreman's primary audience has been either in New York City, south of 14th Street, or in Europe, where his productions attracted enthusiastic responses in Berlin, Rome, Stockholm, Japan and, above all, Paris. A polymath seemingly conversant with every book that appeared on the new arrivals shelves of the St. Mark's Bookshop during the 1960s and 1970s, Foreman has placed himself in conversation with French post-structuralist theory and Bertolt Brecht's sense of 'alienation', the most frequently cited touchstone for critical responses to his work. From the beginning, some critics contended that Foreman was incapable of crafting a coherent narrative; that his plays were too long; that his non-professional actors were 'wooden'; that his sense of proportion was problematic or non-existent.

Very few, however, have doubted Foreman's extraordinary ability to activate a theatrical space. Observing that he expanded his work to fill every area of the theatre because he couldn't imagine why any theatregoer would accept a territory more circumscribed, Foreman described the core of his creative process:

> I write – usually at the beginning of the day, from one half to three pages of dialogue. There is no indication of who is speaking – just raw dialogue. From day to day, there is no connection between the pages, each day is a total 'start from scratch' with no necessary reference to material from a previous day's work. (Though it sometimes – infrequently – happens that there is a thematic carryover.)[1]

The idiosyncrasy of this approach can make it difficult to know which are the right questions to ask when engaging his productions. Are they pre-eminently psychological and/or autobiographical, a reflection of Foreman's personal obsessions? Are they philosophical – staged versions of Derrida, Lacan or Kristeva – or a series of moments manifesting an elusive existential 'now'? Are they purely aesthetic events that resist reduction to vocabularies other than the multilayered layers of the theatre space? What, if any, political vision does Foreman project?

One thing is certain: Foreman's work requires an audience that will come out and meet the performance, one that is drawn to the lure of the circus, one organized around three frenetically kinetic rings. There is nearly always more than one area of focus; the viewer's attention roams the stage, first here, then there and then back again. But contrary to popular rumour – a rumour rife among those who have only read or heard about Foreman's work – it is not necessary for spectators to immerse themselves in hermeneutics, post-structuralist theory or, for that matter, Nietzsche, to appreciate the Ontological-Hysteric Theatre. Even in *Bad Boy Nietzsche!* (1999), Foreman invoked only a handful of lines from *The Gay Science*. For those spectators who do wish to wax academic about Foreman's aesthetic, the more profitable approach might well be through Wittgenstein and Gilbert Ryle, perhaps the most famous representatives of what was once called 'ordinary language philosophy'.

But, however many references, echoes and citations Foreman embeds in his texts, it's not necessary to be steeped in shamanism, Orphism, Gnosticism or Hermeticism to engage in his work. After experiencing some forty years of his theatre work, even the most experienced viewer would be hard put to venture a guess as to what he is for or against; his theatrical rhetoric is both aggressive and fleeting, offering and withholding interpretive frameworks, often defused among various figures – 'characters' in anything like a conventional sense often feel like an imposed vocabulary. The moment and the viewer's relationship to the object in the present moment is the primary, frequently the only, consideration. There are no intermissions in Foreman's work after 1973, and no one is admitted after the play begins (there is no proscenium curtain and only rarely a proscenium stage): *be here now* is a dialectical pact that the audience makes with Foreman's work, like it or not. Audiences that come out to meet the work rarely attempt to leave prematurely. What's crucial is that they be open to the notion that reality is richer than any circumscribing idea.

Six-time winner of the Obie Award and recipient of a McArthur Award in 1995, Foreman has been honoured by the National Endowment for the Arts for a career that has spanned over 45 years. He has written, designed and directed works in America and Europe. He has written, designed and directed seven musicals in collaboration with composer Stanley Silver; directed Poe's *The Fall of the House of Usher* (1992) and an opera by Arthur Yorinks and Philip Glass, as well as writing, designing and directing *Astronome: A Night at the Opera*, with music by John Zorn in 2009. When not directing his own work, Foreman has designed and directed work by Brecht, Büchner, Mozart, Molière, Gertrude Stein, Botho Strauss, Kathy Acker, Vaclav Havel and Arthur Kopit. He has designed and directed films and videos, including *Out of the Body Travel* (1975), *City Archives* (1977), *Strong Medicine* (1979), *Radio Rick in Heaven and Radio Richard in Hell* (1987) and *Total Rain* (1990).

Born in 1937 in Scarsdale, a suburb of New York City, Foreman focused his energy on a career in theatre and film from his undergraduate days at Brown University. After earning an MFA from the Yale Drama School in 1962, he spent a number of frustrating years attempting to break into the commercial theatre. By 1967, Foreman, whose trade name in print would eventually morph into 'R. Foreman', had decided that there was no future for him in that direction. Seeking alternatives, he immersed himself in New York's burgeoning downtown culture in the middle and late 1960s: Happenings, the performance art of the Fluxus group, the continuing influence of the Living Theatre and the increasing importance of new café theatres such as Caffe Cino and La MaMa. Off-Off-Broadway was being born, and most spectators and participants in downtown Manhattan embraced the idea that the exciting new forms were never intended to move uptown. It wasn't the equivalent of an out-of-town tryout and the work wasn't auditioning for Broadway. It was right where it belonged, primarily below 14th Street in Manhattan, and it had an eager audience, much of it composed of fellow artists.

Foreman recalled the creative possibilities offered by that aggressively alternative scene:

> [I] delighted in my ability to not-so-much write as REWRITE plays so they would 'work' on stage (i.e. so the actors would find the kind of material with which they – and the director – could

manipulate the audience through a desired sequence of emotions and emerge at the end with a nice, not too simple but not-too-subtle, 'meaning').[2]

In 1968 the Ontological-Hysteric Theatre – less a specific group or theatrical space than an aesthetic event written, produced, designed and directed by Foreman – was born and would remain a constant presence in the avant-garde scene for more than 40 years.

A cross between a (white) college professor and an acrobat

Meditating on his own work, Foreman phrased one of the crucial questions as 'what are the limits of academic art?'. A key moment in his evolution came when he left Yale in 1962 and came to New York where he encountered 'the underground cinema people ... [who] were interested in contemporary American literature, which, up until then, I had denigrated completely'.[3] He was already aware of the Europe-centred intellectual, aesthetic and critical landscape of the 1950s and 1960s, but his early days in New York focused his attention on his Big Three influences: Brecht, Gertrude Stein and – less surprising in a world where C. G. Jung was a major presence – alchemy, a triumvirate that would define the structural determinates of his work for the next 40 years. Foreman valued Stein because of her attempt 'to write in the continual present'; Brecht for his alienation effect, 'the desire for nonempathic theatre'; and alchemy as a metaphor for the transmutation of the raw material of experience into idiosyncratic aesthetic gold.[4]

As he began to hone his own approach, questions of language emerged as the unifying concern. From the 1960s on, language would occupy the centre of gravity in Foreman's work, a source of propulsion and frustration with which Foreman aims to underscore, divert and subvert the viewer's hopes and fears about what is being said – right here and now. Structurally, Foreman developed a continuing commitment to working at the most local of perceptual levels, a level he refers to as 'the cell'. The dramatic matrix where a particular 'impulse' first appears, the cell is emphatically not material for subsequent development, especially any type that suggests a teleology.

'I invariably choose to express how I feel about the preceding moment of generated text,' he observed. 'Mostly, how I feel about the energy that generated that preceding moment.'[5] The centre not only doesn't hold, it doesn't exist; it is at the never-fixed periphery where the revelations resonate, at the periphery where the audience may discover 'the shape of the now-moment ... So it becomes a matter of forms, more than a matter of structure' (173). Like many of his contemporaries in downtown theatre, Foreman had displaced any notions of an Aristotelian dramatic arc, opting for a 'meaningless' event in a field of experience (172).

The Ontological-Hysteric Theatre's work is always experienced in a specific and fixed stage site, but from the 1970s, Foreman has aimed to discourage the spectator from assuming the imaginary, transparent 'fourth wall' of much traditional theatre. The action take place within the three walls of the stage, but Foreman often introduces a railing, some string or a wall of Plexiglas between the front row of the audience and the playing field in an attempt to 'reinforce aesthetic distance'. The spectator is encouraged to keep an aesthetic distance, and to resist any semblance of empathy. Any erosion of these physical barriers risks luring the spectator onto the stage, inviting identification with this or that character, thereby collapsing the divisions fundamental to Foreman's work. Throughout his career, he would hold fast to one of the fundamentals of alienation: 'I hate seeing people onstage reaching across the footlights, asking for love.'[6]

How to activate a space (at a distance)

Theatre is a public meeting; it is a ritual.

RICHARD FOREMAN[7]

The concrete sign-systems of the theatre include bodies, props, light, sound and words. Foreman places tremendous pressure on all of these elements; their relationship is a curious mixture of complexity and simplicity. While he almost always writes the dialogue first, the ritualistic, ceremonial nature of the theatre rests on the interaction of every aspect of the production: the set must be protean, capable of turning on a dime without significant technological demands or elaborate lighting pyrotechnics. Cues and set-ups are intricate, timings complex, but high-tech stage mechanics and traditional lighting techniques – elaborate hue, value and chroma designs, dramatic spots, the most obvious dimming effects – are anathema. On-off is the basic organizational principle: the lighting is generally overhead, varying its degrees of intensity to highlight different areas of the stage, and he will very slowly, imperceptibly, dim one area of the stage while simultaneously increasing, again very slowly, the lighting in another area. While often (and increasingly) filled with disorienting objects, often in the form of movable props, Foreman's sets typically refer to ordinary places where one might encounter groups of people: hotel lobbies, lecture halls, school rooms, a doctor's office or a courtroom.

The Ontological-Hysteric Theatre's staging has never involved either audience participation (e.g. the Living Theatre) or aleatory elements (John Cage); every movement, of people and objects, is precisely choreographed and timed. His rehearsals, which often required eight-hour shifts for two months, are both rigorous and exhausting. As Foreman has remarked, the only improvising is on his part as the director during the rehearsals. In the early days, he made models of the set in advance, but gradually shifted to mapping out his blocking ideas only at the rehearsals in the actual performance space.

That approach means that a given production is intimately tied to the performance space. Over the decades, he has mounted productions in proscenium stages such as Houston Opera and the Public Theatre in New York, and small spaces like St. Mark's Theatre in New York. Each space serves as a structural determinate in his 'scenic writing'; scenographic space is never a given and every performance constituted a site work.

From 1975 through to 1979, Foreman performed his work in his own theatre loft downtown at 491 Broadway in New York City, and its features were distinct, maybe singular:

> Consisting of a narrow room, the stage and audience area are both only 14 feet wide. While seven rows of audience seating measure about 16 feet in depth, the stage itself is a full 75 feet deep. The first 20 feet of that is at floor level, but the entire stage width from then on is built at steep rake running the next 30 feet of depth, finally leveling off at about a six foot height for the remaining depth. During the performance people and objects

often roll down that 30 foot rake, and sliding walls would enter from the side of the stage, creating a series of quickly changing spaces which varied from 12 to full 75 feet in depth.[8]

The plays produced in this theatre would be impossible to recreate anywhere else. Foreman's interest in circuses and carnival shows conditioned his approach to pieces performed in what became known as the shooting gallery. The list of shooting gallery productions includes the plays that established Foreman's reputation: *Pandering to the Masses: A Misrepresentation* (1975), *Rhoda in Potatoland* (1976), *Book of Splendors: Part II* (1977) and *Blvd de Paris: I've Got the Shakes* (1977).

In each, Foreman manipulated the actors and the sets to focus the spectator's attention on the stark fact of the space itself. Sometimes he would use it as a long, deep space, and at other times, a wall (flat) would slide in to foreshorten the perspective:

> I like to assume that the spectator is watching the entire stage at all moments of the play, so I try to make a stage picture in which every inch of the stage dynamically participates in the moment-by-moment composition of the piece. I might carefully adjust the tiniest detail, far away from what seems to be the focus of attention in a scene, because I want to maintain the compositional tension across the entire panorama of the stage.[9]

Those who witnessed his early works would express something resembling nostalgia for the shooting gallery loft. Writing in *Performance Arts Journal* in 1981, Richard Schechner, who founded the Performance Group in 1967 and was its artistic director until 1980, went so far as to date the end of the glory of American avant-garde theatre, which he traces to the Cage–Cunningham collaborations of 1952, to the sale of the Ontological-Hysteric Theatre in 1979.[10]

During his time at 491 Broadway, Foreman refined his approach to the stage as a distinctly defined and confined space, variously layered and object oriented. From the mid-1970s on, his process involved cross-referencing the text with the set, which he viewed as 'a machine'.[11] Dialogue and narration merge into the 'articulation of the entire space-object, which is the performance' (116). Targets, objects invoking alchemical instrumentation, and much more: the stripes and checkered patterns on the walls and mobile flats, Romanesque arches with alternating light- and dark-coloured brick around the arch, the obviously home-made props, clocks of every vintage and size, cooking implements, a non-working radio, mirrors, things to lean on (for which he has expressed a special fascination) and cards, lots of cards with mysterious markings. As with the rest of the set, every prop had to be protean in function, frequently disrupting and discombobulating the actor's gesture or dialogue, while eliciting an almost burlesque-like incongruity.

While Foreman never relinquished control over his stage, his approach developed in dialogue with John Cage's emphasis on process, an omnipresent aspect of the artistic world Foreman entered after leaving Yale. Most of the artists who claimed direct descent from Cage were fascinated with mathematical pattern-making, among them dancers Lucinda Childs and Trisha Brown and composers Philip Glass and Steve Reich. Varying the approach in an idiosyncratic manner, Foreman fixed on orthogonal gestures:

> To be present meant to create a simple, strong, readable grid of right-angle relationships. To this day, I usually tell the actors I do not allow diagonal crosses onstage. If they have to get from upstage right to downstage left, they must do it by walking straight down and then making a right turn, rather than making the simpler diagonal cross.[12]

That approach generated one of the Ontological-Hysteric Theatre's signature gestures: 'the string thing'. Beginning with *Hotel China* (1975), Foreman's productions invariably incorporated strings running at various angles across the front of the stage. Although Foreman contends that at first the strings were functional, even diagrammatic, they soon took on a life and legend of their own, evolving into something more than merely symbolic props. Much as a painter would add layers of paint and texture to set off or render askew the subject matter, Foreman's strings initially accentuated his scenography in ways that recall the Renaissance painter Giotto's use of horizon lines and diagonal lines (often in the form of heavenly beams) to draw attention to the main idea of the fresco, such as in *The Stigmatization of St. Francis*. In *Hotel China*, strings were attached to the sides of the stage in a widening gyre, which targeted a point on the performer's brow, and objects the performer desired were hung from the strings. As Foreman's string theory evolved, it became clear that his goal was not simply to achieve a kind of visual control echoing cinematic close-ups but to add 'compositional intensity' to the set by crisscrossing it with lines that could be used for multiple purposes, most importantly dissecting the picture plane of the fourth wall, the window through which the audience views the performance. While the strings altered the spectator's view of the performers, they served less to control the visual than to deepen and intensify the perspective for the audience. In *Pandering to the Masses: A Misrepresentation*, Foreman placed dots of black paint on some of the strings, creating dotted black lines that floated in the front of the audience's eyes and merged with the objects onstage.

Manheim as muse: The Lillian Gish of the avant-garde

For the Ontological-Hysteric Theatre's first decade, Foreman avoided using trained actors, although many of the people in the plays were skilled performers in other venues. Nothing in his approach to directing invites actors to pursue emotional identification with or from the audience. His description of his approach reflects a pervasive distrust of anything resembling naturalistic acting: 'The actors are placed in positions that put the body in a state of tension.'[13] His instructions (Foreman, 1992: 41–2) to cast members are even more explicit, among them: 'Be hostile toward the audience, don't make them love you'; 'Always believe that when you have a line, you are saying the most intelligent thing in the world but that only a few people in the audience are going to get it.'[14] Combined, these principles distance the Ontological-Hysteric Theatre from both realism and the 'star' system operating in both commercial and Off-Broadway cultures. Very rarely do audiences who remember a Foreman production recall individual roles.

The important exception is Kate Manheim, whose association with Foreman's work began with his first work, *Angelface* (1968), and continued through to *Film is Evil: Radio is Good* (1987). There were Rhodas before Kate Manheim, but there would be no more Rhodas after her; Kate's first appearances as Rhoda came in *Sophia = (Wisdom) Part 3: The Cliffs*, thereby joining a repertoire of characters who would reappear in subsequent Foreman plays: Ben, Leo, Sophia, Max, Hannah.

To imagine that period of Foreman's work without Kate Manheim as Rhoda would be to conjure Godard's early career without Ann Karina. No follower of Foreman's work doubts the fact that Manheim has been Foreman's primary muse; she has been, as well, his partner in life for the past forty years. She performed her last Rhoda in the film *Strong Medicine* (1979), although she was to perform in four other productions: *Penguin Touquet* (1981), *Egyptology* (1983), *The Cure* (1986) and *Film is Evil: Radio is Good*, in which her character's name in the film role is 'Kate' and is paired with Foreman as 'Richard'.

Foreman never replaced Manheim as the woman in the centre of his dramas: women would continue to play key roles, but from the late 1980s on many of the memorable leads – admittedly an odd attribution in a Foreman play – would be males (John Patrick Kelly, Will Patton, Seth Allen, Henry Stram, Willem Dafoe, Ron Vawter, among others). He would continue to produce strong female roles: Lily Taylor in *What Did He See* (1988), Kyle deKamp in *Lava* (1989), Kate Valk and Peyton Smith in *Symphony of Rats* (1988) and Lola Pashalinski in *Egyptology* (1983) and *Film is Evil, Radio is Good* (1987). Only in Foreman's 'late' period, during his 1992–2010 residency at St. Mark's, did he return to plays with female leads. Even then, no female actor would assume the dominant role that Manheim held from 1971 to 1987. Foreman's women may find themselves with beards on occasion, but it is rare indeed to experience any of them in pants and, while hunchbacks appear in *Lava*, none of them are women. Women appear in varying degrees of undress in his 'early' period, notably in *Sophia* and *Pandering to the Masses*, but that uncostumed rhetoric ceased by the end of the 1970s.

Kate Manheim was something of a hybrid in Foreman's entourage. She had briefly attended the Ecole Charles-Dullin at the Théâtre National Populaire, performing scenes from classical French plays, but she 'found it very uninteresting, detached from reality, and it scared me to death'.[15] One of Mabou Mines' founders, Ruth Maleczech, herself a director and actor, worked with Kate out of friendship and in private. Although Manheim's first stage appearance as Rhoda was in *Sophia = (Wisdom) Part 3: The Cliffs*, she had performed in other Foreman works as well as having done some independent film work in France. By 1987 she was through with performance altogether and committed herself to her painting.

Manheim's departure seemed to initiate a larger shift in Foreman's approach, one that involved a much greater reliance on professional actors:

> The time came, however, when I felt I'd done all I could with nonactors. The texts began to call for skills and intensity that most untrained performers simply do not have. I must admit, however, that I'm not particularly interested in the emotional reality of the performer's psyche. I think only of how the performance will serve the text.[16]

Foreman still prefers the silent movie style of acting because it draws so much attention – some would argue to a fault – to the actor's gesture. A kind of Postmodern Lillian Gish combining a magnetic stylized presence, Manheim had the silent movie acting technique mastered – or perhaps it was inherently there? – and it is notable that this technique is considerably more difficult to pull off in theatre than in film and particularly if overt parody is not the desired result. Ironically, her acting style seems almost subdued by comparison in video and film performances, such as her Rhoda in Foreman's *Strong Medicine* (1979).

Thinking against oneself: Language

Sounding a leitmotif in his attitude toward the verbal material of his plays, Foreman wrote that, 'The text should be an open file system, so distributed in its references that all aspects of the world seem connected to it.'[17] The most innocuous, the most banal and colloquial verbal expression – layered with lighting, costumes, props and a structured dramatic rhythm, none of which are ever left to chance – creates a field in which impulses (cells) will occur and resonate. While Foreman's scripts resist the tools of traditional literary analysis, they serve as the centre of gravity around which everything else revolves.

Beginning with *Angelface*, Foreman's performance of the text was devoid of nearly all social interaction; while he is perfectly capable of writing in vernacular registers – consciously elevated diction, while not unheard of is certainly not dominant – no one will confuse a Foreman text with documentary realism. He admits to being influenced in his pursuit of 'a primitive vocabulary' by, among others, Austrian playwright Peter Handke and his *Sprechstücke*, consisting of *Offending the Audience* and *Self-Accusation* (both 1966). In his introduction to the two pieces, Handke writes:

> The speak-ins (*Sprechstücke*) are spectacles without pictures, inasmuch as they give no picture of the world. They point to the world not by way of pictures but by way of words; the words of the speak-ins don't point at the world as something lying outside the words but the world in the words themselves.[18]

Both Foreman and Handke emphasize the colloquial, the vernacular, the allegedly banal: the oral reality of how people – not actors – speak to themselves and among themselves in real life. Action is minimal, as are social gestures that connect one performer to another. There are no metaphors where none were intended. The performances are intended to document the text, not to illustrate, enhance or otherwise elaborate on it. Both playwrights insisted on seeing *people* onstage, not actors and specifically not actors acting. This is more than merely defying the traditional notion of characters; rather it is a probe, an assault, into the assumptions a traditional audience will bring to a play.

Foreman is explicit about how he writes his plays. Not only has he written on his methodology – 'How I Write My (Plays: Self)'[19] – but he offers the raw dialogue as an archive from his notebooks on his website for any other playwright to freely appropriate. He only stipulates that he be notified of the use, that he is credited in any performance or production publications and that no one may use his titles.

The approach is an outline, not a straitjacket. In 1992, Foreman conceded that 'I've never adhered one hundred percent to the writing programs I created; they were simply guidelines within which I tried to orient myself.'[20] Much like William Burroughs who defended attacks on his cut-up technique by saying 'I still had to write it!', Foreman allowed a disruption of his own rules when it served the purpose of free impulses. He was never the evangelist for his procedures that John Cage became with his chance compositional period. Rather, Foreman actively favours the notion, alluding to Barthes' comments on 'good writing', that colloquial, undisciplined or 'bad' writing can often better access first impulses and usurp the control of the overly-refined response.[21] His process was derived in part from the one Kerouac claimed (with more mythic than factual accuracy) to have followed in *On the Road* – neither writer would countenance second thoughts, rewrites or corrections. Nonetheless, Foreman does edit by eliminating lines on occasion – but rarely. Even rarer still, in the case of *Madness and Tranquility (My Head Was a Sledgehammer)* (1979), Foreman cancelled the production in the midst of rehearsals. Foreman's approach to language places him in a genealogy of artists who shared a profound suspicion of language, especially as an expression of a unified subject. The variations on the theme took radically different forms but consistently involved the questioning, and often outright rejection, of the notion of rational definition and/or control of experience: Gertrude Stein's linguistic experiments; James Joyce's plunge into the psycho-historical subconscious in *Finnegans Wake*; Jerome Rothenberg's anthologies of tribal ethnopoetics, *Technicians of the Sacred*; Kerouac's spontaneous prose; the post-structuralist political philosophers whose work would start to circulate more widely with the 1976 founding of the journal *October*. In Foreman's milieu, absolutely nothing about language could be taken as a given.

Two of the most influential figures in the challenges to conventional textuality were Burroughs and Cage. Although Burroughs is often (mis)classified as a Beat writer, the cut-up technique he developed in the Nova trilogy (*The Ticket That Exploded*, *The Soft Machine* and *Nova Express*, 1961–7) differed sharply from the intensely autobiographical writings of Kerouac and Allen Ginsberg. Seeking to undercut the 'author's coercive control over meaning' – all terms were scrutinized and ironized – Burroughs described the method: 'Take a page. Like this page. Now cut down the middle and cross the middle. You have four sections: 1 2 3 4 ... one two three four. Now rearrange the sections placing section four with section one and section two with section three. And you have a new page. Sometimes it says much the same thing.'[22] What it doesn't do is articulate a preconceived individual vision or message. In the hands of Burroughs' followers the method could be extended beyond single source texts, sometimes resulting in stunning juxtapositions, at times something resembling chaos.

Cage's repudiation of authorial control was if anything more profound. As Kay Larson has shown in *Where the Heart Beats: John Cage, Zen Buddhism, and the Inner Life of Artists*, Cage's Zen-inflected aesthetic drew the attention of a group of artists that included composers, poets, painters and performance artists, some of whom found their way to the Ontological-Hysteric Theatre. For Cage, language was less an adversary than an irrelevance, part of an illusion that interfered with apprehension of untranslatable being. It's easy to reduce Cage to bumper sticker quotes – 'I have nothing to say and I am saying it and that is poetry' – but nothing could be further from the spirit of his 1951 composition 'Music of Changes' or his 1961 book *Silence*. Both in his work and in his influence, Cage relied on chance operations that left the creation of 'meaning' or simply the experience (aesthetic or otherwise) to the audience.

Sympathetic to Burroughs' and Cage's distrust of conventional language and certainly aware of the philosophical complexities, Foreman has evinced little interest in either chance or audience participation. While he maintained an ongoing dialogue with the most important currents of the time, his practice was profoundly his own.

Politics and the dialectics of consciousness

> So now, less than five years later, you can go up on a steep hill in Las Vegas and look West, and with the right kind of eyes you can almost see the high-water mark – that place where the wave finally broke and rolled back.
>
> HUNTER S. THOMPSON, *FEAR AND LOATHING IN LAS VEGAS*

It's tempting, but inaccurate, to think of Foreman as an apolitical playwright. In comparison with the agitprop productions of the late 1960s and 1970s – Barbara Garson's *MacBird*, the San Francisco Mime Troupe's *Seize the Time*, the Yippies' showering money on the New York Stock Exchange – Foreman seems distanced from the front lines of the battles over politics and aesthetics. In fact, it's almost impossible (and pointless) to distinguish between the political arguments and those over language in which the Ontological-Hysteric Theatre played an important part.

The radical aesthetics that garnered most of the attention from contemporaries were part of a broader continuum that included conservative and conventionally liberal voices. At one extreme was an influential group of formalist academic critics, many of whom identified themselves with the 'New Criticism'. Descended from the conservative Southern agrarian movement, the formalists argued that art should transcend the concerns of everyday politics, addressing ostensibly 'universal' themes: myth, nature, identity. Although most participants in the experimental theatre scene rejected the New Critics' politics, which ranged from Goldwater conservative to Kennedy–Johnson liberal, the formalist emphasis on ambiguity and complexity permeated aesthetic debates and exerted at least an indirect effect on Foreman's treatment of politics.

Much more prominent in the milieu in which Foreman began his career, a chorus of voices from the Left insisted that playwrights, directors and performers should accept their responsibility to make a direct contribution to radical political change. One of the most powerful voices was that of black nationalist playwright Amiri Baraka (who began his career as Leroi Jones), who repudiated the intricate Modernism of his early plays (*Dutchman*, *The Toilet*) and embraced a style based on the intersection of Afrocentric ritual and what he termed 'Marx/Lenin/Mao Tse tung thought'. Similarly, the Living Theatre, guided by Judith Malina and Julian Beck, evolved from a High Modernist approach reflected in their productions of plays by T. S. Eliot and Gertrude Stein to the improvisatory *Paradise Now*, which directly incorporated the audience into productions that explicitly confronted the vacuity of a political culture that preached non-violence to demonstrators while accepting the horrors of Vietnam.

Many of the activist theatre groups cast their practice as a variation on Bertolt Brecht's political theatre, though there was nothing approaching a consensus on what 'Brechtian' meant. On a relatively abstract level, almost everyone agreed that political theatre should challenge the audience to engage the world around them directly and that performances should reflect changing conditions. One of the most incisive theorists of theatrical politics, Richard Schechner, turned from editing the influential academic journal *TDR* (*The Drama Review*) to founding the acting company that would later become the Performance Group in 1968. Schechner's essays 'Public Events for The Radical Theatre' and 'The Politics of Ecstasy' outline the theoretical approach that exploded in the Performance Group's incendiary piece, *Dionysius in '69*, which deconstructs Euripides in ways that recall Burroughs' cut-up technique and anticipate Foreman's *Sophia*.[23]

Ed Bullins, Minister of Culture of the Black Panthers and winner of three Obie Awards for Best Play during the 1970s, attempted to weave together the strands of political aesthetics in his theory of 'Black Dialectics', published in the introduction to the anthology *The New Lafayette Theatre Presents* in 1974.[24] Bullins begins by dividing political art into two currents: the 'dialectic of experience' and the 'dialectic of change'. For Bullins, effective political theatre requires an unflinching honesty about 'experience', considered in the widest possible terms. Like Foreman, Bullins believes that any conceptual framework (ideological, psycho-sexual) that interferes with the ability to receive reality creates a set of inescapable contradictions that lock individuals and groups into self-defeating cycles, call them neuroses or false consciousness. Once the playwright, director or performer attains a clear, if always partial, vision of the relevant conditions, the next step of the dialectical process consists of imagining and exploring possible paths towards change. Whether those paths offer real solutions isn't a question that can be answered within the walls of the theatre or the confines of the extra-theatrical performance space. Rather, in 'downtown Brechtian' terms, the question can only be answered in the psyches and lives of the audience.

Working in a neighbourhood where the film and theatre audiences crossed paths regularly at Film Forum, the Performing Garage, Caffe Cino and La MaMa, Foreman's work was part of a conversation that included the cinema of Michelangelo Antonioni and Jean-Luc Godard, both of whom had been exploring the juxtaposition of language, image and politics throughout the decade. Framing his project as a chronicle of 'the children of Marx and Coca-Cola', Godard developed a dialectical approach that, like Foreman's, rested on a multilayered assault of text and image. While Godard's materials and obsessions gravitated toward explicitly Pop images as ideological material, Foreman's work evinced no references – conspicuous by their absence – to anything Pop or Marxist. Foreman clearly shared Godard's distrust of traditional aesthetic virtues like verisimilitude, continuity of plot and consistency of character. The questions raised by politics couldn't be answered in the political vocabularies of the moment. For Godard and Foreman, as for Schechner, Bullins and the Living Theatre, the issue was not what positions to support, but how to think one's way through the ruins of a political culture that infected the deepest levels of the psyche.

Sophia = (Wisdom) Part 3: The Cliffs

Sophia: The Cliffs (full title: *Sophia = (Wisdom), Part 3: The Cliffs*) was presented at the Ontological-Hysteric Theatre in the winter of 1972–3. Preceded by performances of Parts 1 and 2, Part 3 is explicitly concerned with, yes, cliffs, created in wood surrounding the set and topped with little wooden houses. The two-month engagement was performed at Jonas Mekas' Film-Makers ground floor Cinematheque loft space designed by Fluxus artist George Maciunas. It is the only work of Foreman's from the 1970s commercially available on DVD.[25] Looking back on the work that first brought him serious attention from the downtown avant-garde, Foreman recalled:

> Sophia was one of my earliest works, one of a series in which the same leading characters always re-appear. My notion at the time was a theatre that at every moment confronted the audience with the sheer 'presence' of performer, text, music – as if to say 'Audience, how do you process being exposed to this concrete phenomenon.' (DVD jacket)

'The-play-was-a-success-but-the-audience-failed' bromide was something of an implicit taunt at many downtown theatre performances in the 1970s, and Foreman's relationship to his audience would change very little over the next forty years.

In *Sophia* we have the continuation of by now familiar Foreman personas: Max, Leo, Ben, Sophia, Hannah and Rhoda, who as a group constitute less a process of character development than a continuing saga of collective psychic exploration. Like Handke's *Offending the Audience* (1966), *Sophia* forces spectators to abandon their expectations concerning the roles of actors and dialogue in the traditional theatre. The people in the play were not asked to act: the gestures were wooden, determined, controlled, while the actors frequently stared straight into the audience. *Sophia*, and later *Pandering to the Masses*, constituted absolute documentation of the text nestled in frequent tableaux friezes. Minimalism was the lingua franca of New York's downtown art in the 1960s and 1970s – emphatically unelaborated and rigorous – and any embellishment was aesthetic apostasy. For Foreman, the production was a demonstration of the text, a factory tour of the play. The narrator both instructs and cues; the audience watches stagehands in business-like manner manipulate props and move the flats. The costumes are, in 1972, generic for a broad demographic sweep of white America: men in nondescript shirts and pants and shoes, women nearly always in skirts and shifts or in varying stages of undress. The exception to the rule in *Sophia* is Karl, who may be the Mountain Man who may also be the Snowman; he is elaborately costumed and wears goggles – the wild card in the costume deck. In Foreman's early work, however, costumes remained an asset that had not yet been capitalized on with the exception of the occasional use of masks. The aesthetic drive of *Sophie*, and later *Pandering*, required, with rare exceptions, that the audience not take special notice of costumes lest they be seduced into identifying the actors as traditional characters. The costumes for the most part didn't signal anything nor did they place anyone. As he moved into the 1980s, Foreman's costumes became as idiosyncratic, exaggerated and resonant as every other aspect of the set.

If costumes did not yet occupy a major place in the Ontological-Hysteric style, Foreman was paying close attention to the potential of sound, not just the voiceovers – the dialogue from the narrator and performers all emanates from the tape – but also bells, industrial-strength buzzers (loud), a metronome and music, all of which appeared not to be linked to anything like traditional scene changes. Foreman has had a particular fondness throughout his career for a kind of generic 1920s jazz band recorded with an acoustical bell that suggests childhood memories of listening to the radio, looped and at varying levels of loudness; that and nineteenth century romantic piano music.

Sophia: The Cliffs charted the major paths Foreman would pursue in his later productions, while raising fundamental questions concerning the nature of 'meaning' and 'interpretation'. Begin with the title and subtitle: During the late 1960s and early 1970s, countless writers and artists pursued variations on what T. S. Eliot called the 'mythic method' of James Joyce's *Ulysses*. Juxtaposing a classical myth and contemporary experience, the mythic method could be used either to comment on what Eliot called the 'savage parody of the insubstantial effort of degraded modern man',[26] or to reveal heroic dimensions of everyday characters. Foreman deliberately invoked what had become a familiar convention: a text appears on screen reading 'A goddess being a waitress. She keeps her identity secret.'[27] In this formulation, Sophia can be seen as an avatar of knowledge or wisdom, inviting viewers to reduce the play to, perhaps, an extended meditation on the decline of the classical search for truth in a chaotic contemporary world. The subtitle offered numerous interpretive possibilities, ranging from Greek drama to *King Lear* or perhaps Samuel Beckett's bleak land-stage-mindscapes. Did Leo's statement that 'I am no longer allowed happiness. I am no longer allowed strong feelings' (131) support an interpretation of the play as a lament for the sundering of mind and emotion in a Postmodern world? Near the end of the play, the goddess image recurred juxtaposed with the repeated line 'Oh my poor, poor feet really hurt.' Myth collapses into mundane reality.

Theoretically supportable, such an interpretation imposes an immense amount of extrinsic intellectual baggage on the present-tense experience. So would a neo-Marxist interpretation derived from the dramatic cell focusing on the 'workers' lasting for some ten minutes following intermission. We know the workers' houses are on the cliffs; we contemplate the question of whether the workers 'have inner ears'. Giving up in weariness, Rhoda says, 'Oh boy, the body should be more interesting than the workers', the cell changes and the invitation to consider the characters' alienation in Marxist terms recedes into the background along with the mythic method and a plethora of other possibilities.

Every aspect of the text and the staging resists reduction to a single interpretive framework. If any set of concerns is dominant, it's the set of psycho-sexual obsessions swirling around Rhoda's body. An object of erotic desire and fascination whose physical presence is the single most striking element of the production, Rhoda engages in a sexual tumble with a clothed male; compares her beauty with Sophia; all the while maintaining a psychic distance from the acts and words. There's no take-home message beyond Rhoda's near affect-less reflection that 'This is one of the most rigorous learning experiences I have ever had.'

That line strikes close to the heart of *Sophia*. Foreman has little or no interest in providing answers. Nor is he concerned to frame a central question or even set of questions. In *Sophia* and throughout his career, his primary concerns boil down to two lines: 'Think harder' and 'Not yet' (122). You could add the exchange between Sophia and Rhoda: 'Can you believe it?' / 'I can believe anything' (133). Or perhaps the wonderful metacommentary of 'It's very clear, all of it', 'It's been enjoyable', 'It's been wonderful because it's been so clear really' (123). Immediately afterward, they turn to the audience, saying 'Those people are still out there.' / 'What people?'

Foreman returns to that question in the play's final cell. Anticipating what would be a common practice in later Ontological-Hysteric productions, the resolution presents itself as pure overload. Echoing the image of the male thinker sitting at the back of the stage in the first cell, Rhoda holds her head, rotating awkwardly, seemingly overwhelmed by everything that has transpired. The intensity of sound increases; all of the characters, including those whose role has been limited primarily to moving props on and off stage – there is no real distinction between cast and crew – form a multilayered tableau. A voice intones the final 'message': 'The play is over. Go home. Go home. The play is over, ladies and gentlemen. Think about it if you like, but go home. Go home. Go home' (133).

It's a truly Brechtian gesture, a deferral of interpretation to the audience as they resume their lives in a world no more or less complicated and intractable than the one they've encountered on stage.

Pandering to the Masses: A Misrepresentation

Originally presented from January through to March 1975, *Pandering to the Masses: A Misrepresentation* was the first work in which Foreman seriously investigated the possibilities of sound *qua* sound; he had used tape recorders before, but now he paid particular attention to spatial placement. From this point on, sound would be a structural determinant of his burgeoning aesthetic. In his preface, Foreman explains:

> The VOICE was always my taped voice. The majority of the remaining lines were also on tape. The four principal performers ... recorded those, each separate word being spoken by a different one of those four performers in sequence, no matter who was listed in the script as the 'speaker' of a particular line. The voice of each performer was isolated on one of four loudspeakers – one at each of the four corners of the audience ... a different voice for each word, each word coming from a different place. Superimposed on this, the performers on stage hearing their own lines ... would then, softly, repeat a few key words of their speech in counterpoint to the ongoing tape.[28]

Foreman's statements reflect the influence of Cage, Karlheinz Stockhausen and Alvin Lucier, signalling his interest in the recorded voice vis-à-vis the live voice as well as the spatial placement of the acoustics – what you are hearing is inextricably bound up with how you are hearing it. In *Pandering*, Foreman for the first time made tape recorders a central aspect of the experience. His approach was typically idiosyncratic. Rarely does he employ overlapping voices in the mode of Robert Altman's films, the compositional gestures of Karlheinz Stockhausen's *Hymnen* or sound layering in the manner of Cage's *12 Radios* or Lucier's *I am sitting in a room*. Rather, he adapts the approach in ways that generate something idiosyncratic, strange:

> For a period, starting with *Pandering*, all the lines on tape were recorded by as many as four voices, alternating word by word. During the performance the tape was played back from loudspeakers located in the corners of the performance space, so each sentence of dialogue would seem to circle the audience. Since the actors would slowly and softly repeat the lines of the character they were playing in counterpoint to the tape. Since the actors onstage would speak slower rather than the tape they were cued by, it meant that they were soon overlapping each other as well as the tape. This would continue for a few lines, then a loud thud would interrupt, and a moment of silence would follow, clearing the air. Then the whole process would begin again.[29]

The taped narrator both instructs the uninitiated as to the traditional theatrical assumptions while debunking them, sometimes simultaneously. The narrator announces that what one is viewing is the Prologue, and about 24 minutes into the play announces in measured tone that the Prologue has ended and now the play 'begins'; at approximately the 60-minute mark, the ever-helpful narrator will announce a 'return to the central narration', never mind that the audience never knew they had been experiencing a narrative digression up to that point. Not to worry: the narrator will announce from time to time that the moment being viewed is 'recapitulation'. The narrator will also, from time to time, cue the actors – '*He sits down*' – and introduce a character, Max, as '*a famous writer*'.

Critics have frequently characterized the dialogue delivery in *Pandering* – aside from Rhoda's stylized vocal episodes, which incorporate a good bit of *glissandi* – as being 'natural' without ever defining what that might signify. In fact, the voices are more accurately described as uninflected or declamatory. No one speaks like that in the supermarket or the bedroom. The salient exception is Kate Manheim as Rhoda, who gives varying degrees of inflected and tonal dialogue. While the vocabulary is American vernacular – no discernible regionalisms or ethnic innuendos – the dialogue is uninflected, distancing the audience from both denotation and connotation, as well as any recognizable context. Common individual words collectively comprise sentences in call and response with the tape, delivered in, for the most part, deliberately flat announcements. The effect recalls how one might have experienced a 1930s Western Union delivery read aloud from a messenger, minus the singing.

The result is a theatrical experience embodying Foreman's idiosyncratic sense of drama: conflict preceded and followed by doubt. Crucially, Foreman feels no obligation to explicate the specifics of what precedes or follows. He provides numerous intimations, immersing his audience in an elusive and allusive world of girl fights, allusions to the secret society announced in the Prologue by the taped narrator, a stationary bicyclist pedalling furiously and then abruptly stopping. Every named character is an anonymous optimizer, an independent quester, and nearly every line of dialogue is either a question or a declamation that is in need of being questioned. In *Pandering*, as in every Ontological-Hysteric production, the question is the point.

Rhoda in Potatoland (Her Fall-Starts)

Performed from December 1975 through to February 1976, *Rhoda in Potatoland (Her Fall-Starts)* was the production that established Foreman as a serious player in avant-garde theatre and began to attract attention beyond the boundaries of downtown. The terms of that attention, however, were problematic, creating misconceptions that Foreman would struggle against for years to come. Edith Oliver's capsule short review in the *New Yorker*, a first for Ontological-Hysteric Theatre, deemed it 'a startling and startlingly original exercise in surrealism'. The problem is that neither the play, nor Foreman's work as a whole, can be accurately described as surrealism. Rather, as Richard Schechner has pointed out, Foreman's work is 'autobiographical, ironic, and *naturalistic*' in the sense that soap operas are naturalistic – 'a weave of events and reactions among a steady cast of characters'.[30] Foreman both in practice and in theory calls the surrealist bluff: 'Understand – it ALWAYS makes sense. Sense *can't* be avoided. If it first seems to be non-sense, wait: roots will reveal themselves.'[31]

The confusion over how to categorize *Rhoda* – and it's always useful to recall Foreman's profound distrust of the impulse to categorize and reduce – stems in part from Foreman's more-than-typically-opaque Prologue to the play. He writes:

> Remember. This text is – as it were – inside out. That is, its presentation – to in a sense – make it clear – insider out. Because when you see the inside outside – the inside is clear, right?[32]

Highlighting the centrality of process to his aesthetic in ways that make the challenge to the audience clear, he muses:

> Cut the text in half – you haven't seen it yet, but imagine it cut into two parts – a first part and a second part. Then in the presentation, the first part is played as the second part and vice versa. [So] what follows, precedes, and vice versa.' (207)

Many of the usual suspects appear in *Rhoda in Potatoland*. Rhoda, Leo, Max, Sophia and Hannah have been joined by Eleanor and Agatha, all of whom, it would seem, have learned to speak French following their return from Paris, where the Ontological-Hysteric

Theatre offered the only performance of *Classical Therapy or A Week Under the Influence* (in French). Building on the structural and rhythmic advances of *Pandering*, *Rhoda* suggests an accelerated dramatic rhythm and a temporal direction toward ever greater complexity and speed; the intricacy of the sets and the choreographed movements of the performers have both been stepped up accordingly. The central figure of the piece, Manheim's Rhoda, is given more lines than any single performer has ever been given in Foreman's work. *Rhoda* is approximately one hour and fifteen minutes in duration, setting the temporal benchmark for the rest of Foreman's career.

Rhoda offers experienced Ontological-Hysteric viewers a familiar set of tropisms: a jerky string of tableaux in which actors carefully place themselves and fix the audience with hypnotic stares while speaking in uninflected tones; costumes that don't place a character, save the waiter, in any place or time; the signature strings across the stage that both connect and disrupt the moment; the portentous tape-recorded voice of the narrator shouting 'cue' or commenting on the action; and the litany of Foreman sounds, from insistent buzzers and peremptory clangs to scratchy older recordings of classical and conventional 1930s jazz bands, all of which evoke aural rendezvousing with old-time radio.

The work is about potatoes in a more graphic and immediate way than, say, *Sophia = (Wisdom) Part 3: The Cliffs* was about cliffs; the potato threatens to constitute a traditional *leitmotiv*, hinting at symbolic meanings based on the awareness that potatoes must be transformed before they can be consumed. The play's world is constructed around things bound together and compared; Rhoda is seduced and cajoled and admonished and shamed into comparing her way through Potatoland in a relentless progression of relationships predicated on her physical body and words. 'Comparison will be the basis of my life,' Rhoda exclaims early in the play. 'That's how I hope to get famous' (208). For the first time, Manheim's Rhoda plays with the emotional possibilities of language, leaning in ever closer to intoning and interpreting the dialogue. Occasionally, the script demands stress, a new twist in Foreman's aesthetic:

Hannah We're ready for the race.
Rhoda I don't want to do it.

Hannah Oh Rhoda, do you think it's beneath your *dignity*.
Eleanor You and Sophia looked very *dignified* on the dinner plate. (209)

By *Rhoda*, Foreman's scripts have evolved, in the words of critic Michael Feingold, through a 'phase of prolonged defensive transactions with the public's resistance to his approach' to the point where 'now he invites them in'.[33] Rhoda is approachable, engaged and seems to have ceased referring to herself in the third person, thereby dropping a key distancing device. Before *Rhoda in Potatoland (Her Fall-Starts)* is over, she will play in an all-girl band, briefly lose herself in dance and even sing a few simple lines of a song. But despite the gestures toward a certain sort of familiarity, Rhoda remains very much a cryptic Foreman figure. Addressing the audience, she says, 'I didn't want to imagine it. I didn't want to explain it. I just wanted to experience it' (207). While disorienting, the moment, and *Rhoda* as a whole, is not surrealistic. Meaning is elusive and intensely personal, not precluded. The audience has a pretty good idea of what Rhoda means.

At this juncture, very large potatoes appear on the stage and the narrator announces, 'Now this is where the interesting part of the evening begins. Everything up to now was recognizable. It was part of one's everyday experience. Now, however, the real potatoes are amongst us. And a different kind of understanding is possible for anybody who wants a different kind of understanding' (213). Rhoda and Agatha respond by saying, 'I feel like a potato', all of which comes under the category of dramatic hyperbole, not surrealism. The audience is surprised and even disoriented – after all, that is critical to Foreman's aesthetic thrust – but such theatrical moments are not devoid of connective tissue or, more importantly, obvious efforts at pattern making. Everything is rooted; it can't be avoided.

Conclusion: Foreman since 1981 (the established avant-garde)

Foreman's 1970s work was simpatico with the minimalist aesthetic of that era, which could also be deemed the right-to-bore era; art was to be approached as something of an ordeal and that ordeal was necessary to reorient the audience both to the work itself on the most local level (cell, impulse) and to what the role of art should be. Both *Sophia* and *Pandering* are framed with that aesthetic in mind.

Beginning somewhere in the 1980s, Foreman began to show signs of softening his textual emphasis by offering to let more of the audience in: threads of yearning are evident in *Eddie Goes to Poetry City*, and *Lava* intimates an almost essayistic or long narrative shift (these terms are relative) in his work. Foreman considers himself something of a closet religious writer, but the evolution of his dialogue strategies resembles a Zen koan rather than an evangelical sermon. Foreman spent a good bit of this middle period, from 1985 to 1990, at the Performing Garage where he directed two of his pieces with the Wooster Group, *Miss Universal Happiness* (1985) and *Symphony of Rats* (1988), and two pieces without. From 1992 until 2010, Ontological-Hysteric was in residency at the theatre in St. Mark's Church-in-the Bowery, where he wrote, produced and directed 19 productions – something over a third of his lifetime theatrical output. Foreman's ability to activate a stage area in the cramped environs of the St. Mark's Theatre – the stage area, non-proscenium, is wide (38 feet), but not deep (about 13 feet), and the ceilings are low – confirms his legendary ability to create the work to the site: any site. In spite of the intimate performing space at St. Mark's, the actors wore close-contact mikes. It certainly wasn't because their voices couldn't be heard without amplification; it constituted yet another layer of aesthetic distancing.

In an interview conducted by David Savran in 1987, Foreman was asked what his plans for the future were. 'I have absolutely no goals anymore,' he responded, 'except maybe to get out of the theatre. I think one should change, and the remaining opportunities for change in the theatre are not that great.'[34] In 2005, Foreman said – not for the first time – that he was quitting theatre; it eventually became clear that meant that his emphasis would be on film in the future. More precisely, Foreman intended to create works that coupled film with performance, an aesthetic he had introduced in *Film is Evil* (1987) with the 16mm film *Radio Rick in Heaven and Radio Richard in Hell*. Following the 'retirement' announcement, Foreman created three pieces involving film at St.

Mark's in three years, beginning with *Zomboid!* in 2006, with the hybrid subtitle 'Film/Performance Project No. 1'. There are, by Foreman standards, dramatic shifts in the lighting that effectively block either the film actors or the live actors out of view at any given moment and, while both sets of actors speak familiar tropes of Foreman dialogue, the effect is one of experiencing parallel planes of existence. It becomes difficult at times to pinpoint who is speaking and from what direction, which further enhances Foreman's desire for distancing. Always keeping his following guessing, Foreman came out of retirement and returned to theatre – just theatre – in 2009 with *Astronome: A Night at the Opera* (2009), with music by the composer John Zorn.

Foreman has complained about the limitations of theatre and repeated his intention to retire ever since, although he has continued to produce video, film and theatre work: in 2012 he directed and produced a feature-length film, *Once Every Day*, and the play *Old-Fashioned Prostitutes* was produced at the Public Theatre in New York City in 2013. He has produced some 20-odd productions since making that retirement threat in 1987 – and he hadn't even begun his late period residency at St. Mark's in the East Village. After some fifty productions over forty-eight years, Foreman may have slowed down – he is, at this writing, seventy-eight years old – but he is unlikely to quit outright as long as he has breath and continues to believe, after Wittgenstein, that 'ordinary language is all right'.

Afterword

Mike Vanden Heuvel

All historical narratives are retrospective and therefore partial. The significant developments in American theatre addressed in the preceding chapters define many, but certainly not all, of the possible lines of flight one could follow in proposing an overview of the period. The devolution of Broadway as the sole crucible of 'American drama' and the ensuing rise of Off- and Off-Off-Broadway as the source of new playwriting – to be followed in turn by the rapid growth and development of the resident non-profit theatres beyond New York – was perhaps the decade's defining trend. The emergence of a new, youthful and more diverse cohort of American playwrights, including those covered in these pages but including many others, marked a generational turn that affected everything from dramatic content and form to the means by which these artists sought and accumulated cultural capital (as well as how and where that capital might be exchanged).

At the same time, one might easily imagine different points of focus taking centre stage to produce an alternative (yet admittedly still partial) synopsis of the decade. Were one to buy into the tired stereotype of the 1970s as an afterthought to the previous decade, then plays casting a backward glance and assessing the effects of the radical 1960s on the quiescent 1970s – liberating or malaise-producing – would assume a central role: for instance, Robert Patrick's *Kennedy's Children*, the Open Theater's *The Serpent*, Michael Weller's *Moonchildren*, Ed Bullins' *The Taking of Miss Janie* and Lanford Wilson's *Fifth of July*. Turning in the opposite direction, a selection of plays and contexts that looked forward to what lay over the horizon in the 1980s might be the organizing principle. In this case, a deeper analysis of gay and lesbian themes and playwrights, and the degree of institutional support for gay artists within American theatre during the 1970s, would illuminate the growing lesbian and gay rights movement (and reactions against it) as well as the response to AIDS that would dominate the next decade. Or, in anticipation of the economic recovery of the early 1980s and the new corporate decadence it spawned, plays from the 1970s exploring the ruthlessness of competition and the enlarged appetite for consumption might come to the fore: Mamet's *American Buffalo*, for instance, leading the way toward his later work in this vein (*Glengarry Glen Ross*, 1984, and *Speed-the-Plough*, 1988), or possibly John Guare's exposure of celebrity culture culminating in *Six Degrees of Separation* (1993).

Perhaps most compellingly, one might look for dramatic writing and developments in theatre funding and support from the 1970s that better map the rise of the evangelicalism and rise of the Christian Right that would pave the way for Reagan and later the Newt Gingrich-led 'Contract with America' Republican Congress of the 1990s. Here, the shift in focus would have to be substantial: the paucity of overtly conservative plays addressing the typical concerns of the Right – abortion rights, anti-communism, free markets and the morality of business, the unchecked spread of entitlement programmes and rights movements – that characterizes the American theatre after the 1930s certainly limits the number of representative plays of the 1970s as well. Yet, if one limited the definition of 'conservative' to the fundamental notion of sustaining respect for traditional values and expressing nostalgia for a time before modern liberalism appeared to encroach on these beliefs and render the world unstable, a very interesting history of American theatre of the 1970s might be conceived. The traditional American musical (that is, with no rock music, no nudity, and beaming casts of healthy dancers and singers) that saw many popular revivals during the decade might be positioned as the 'real' expression of American values, and Broadway not so much the declining engine of new work as the steady bastion of traditional forms of popular art. *Grease*, with its evocation of an anodyne 1950s, and even Off-Broadway shows like *Godspell* might also provide evidence from new musicals. Plays by A. R. Gurney and Horton Foote could be deployed, as much for their nostalgic evocation of orderly worlds – the first metropolitan and east coast, the second Southern-rural and folksy – as for the voice they adopt to delineate those lost worlds: urbane and detached in the case of Gurney, ruminating and bemused in Foote. As for setting the stage for the more radical expressions of conservatism in the 1980s, such as the Christian Right, one would either need to turn away entirely from the traditional centres of theatre production to focus on rural regional theatres and even church-based dramas (or the spectacle of evangelical worship itself), or else assess the decade's dramatic output critically from a conservative position that would treat American drama of the 1970s as evidence of the general breakdown of aesthetic, political and cultural standards engendered by liberalism.[1]

Here too, Mamet's work of the decade could become a central case study, given his turn away from castigating the conservative agenda of the business world in *American Buffalo* to his playwriting in the 1980s attacking political correctness (such as *Oleanna*, 1992). That would lead, ultimately, to the announcement in his 2011 book *The Secret Knowledge* that, post 9/11, 'I am a new-minted Conservative.' Mamet's influence on the arrival of openly conservative playwrights like Jonathan Reynolds (author of the 1984 *Stonewall Jackson's House*, which could not find a producer until 1997 and yet was a Pulitzer Prize finalist, and *Girls in Trouble* [a counterargument to pro-choice feminists], 2010) and even a British-born American author like Lionel Chetwynd (*Reagan*, 2008) might make for a fascinating look back on the 1970s.

Thus, while every choice of foci will produce a slightly different narrative of the decade, the broad themes and representative playwrights selected here tell a compelling story of the nation's preoccupations, its anxieties and its hopes. Yet it is telling that, for all their prominence during the 1970s, among this book's case studies only Richard Foreman could be said to have sustained a regular career devoted to producing drama through the ensuing decades and into the present. In what follows, I will attempt to parse some of the reasons for, and the consequences of, the divergent trajectories followed by dramatic writers who dominated part or all of the 1970s, but whose work for theatre would find uneven presence and weight in the decades that followed, even while they remained prolific.

Nobody hit the ground faster after the end of the 1970s than Sam Shepard. With his Pulitzer for *Buried Child* in 1979, *True West* heading for its first (albeit unsuccessful) production at the Public Theatre in 1980 and his film acting career escalating – after his success in Terence Malik's *Days of Heaven* (1978) and with future roles in *Resurrection* (1980), *Raggedy Man* (1981) and *Frances* (1982) – Shepard entered the 1980s on the cusp of celebrity stardom. His multifaceted career peaked in 1986, 'when *A Lie of the Mind* was playing off-Broadway, *Fool for Love* was being filmed in Hollywood and he was acting in *Crimes of the Heart*'.[2] By then he had also received an Academy Award nomination for his iconic role in Philip Kaufman's blockbuster film *The Right Stuff* (1983); obtained plaudits for his performance alongside Jessica Lange in the movie *Country* (1984); seen the film based on his writings (*Paris, Texas*, in which he also played an uncredited role) win the top prize at the Cannes film festival; and published a book of non-fiction (*Motel Chronicles*, 1982).

After leaving his wife O-Lan and son Jesse in 1983, he moved with Lange into a world of Hollywood paparazzi relieved by bouts of seclusion. As a result, as Shannon Skelton notes, '[as] Shepard achieved wider recognition as a playwright and actor in the 1980s, essentially becoming a celebrity-artist, attributes associated with Shepard's persona became magnified and gained further currency through mechanical reproduction'.[3] With his film personas now blending with his status as the renegade playwright who stormed both Off-Off-Broadway and eventually achieved delayed mainstream success on Broadway – and particularly one who often wrote about rebels and their desire for authenticity and individualism – Shepard had truly achieved iconic status. Yet he chose this moment to leave playwriting behind as he explored more film options, writing and directing *Far North* in 1988 and taking leave of playwriting until the 1991 *States of Shock*. He made only a ghostly appearance when the revised version of *Buried Child* transferred to Broadway from Chicago's Steppenwolf Theatre in 1996, Shepard's first foray into the Great White Way.[4]

Since then, his output has been irregular and uneven. Les Wade, who has closely tracked Shepard's late work, took stock of it in the late 1990s in the context of a changing America of ever-diversifying points of view and audiences. Yet Wade could still hopefully conclude, 'It remains to be seen if "the American theatre's great white hope," who burst upon the scene in the counterculture days of the sixties, will thrive and prosper in the multicultural America of the next millennium.'[5] But a scant five years later, in his essay '*States of Shock*, *Simpatico*, and *Eyes for Consuelo*: Sam Shepard's Plays of the 1990s', Wade's tone is more sombre:

To all but the most loyal of Shepard devotees, it seems that the playwright has entered a state of decline, at best a state of transition ... In virtue of his sporadic productivity, one might conclude that Shepard has willfully spurned the role of Great American Playwright, that he has eased into an emeritus mode. However one might assess the recent artistic activity of Sam Shepard, I suggest that he is no longer perceived as the most important dramatist working in America today.[6]

The long-standing aporias in Shepard's work, the almost exclusive focus on the plight of the white American male struggling to free himself from the shackles of family, commitment and circumscribed national identity, were often critiqued even during his rise to literary eminence, and might explain how by the late 1990s Shepard could seem out of step. These coincided with developments in his own life as age, relocation and retrospection fuelled a reappraisal of his earlier work and its concentration on the male *isolato*. After *True West* he penned two more family plays that many see as codas to the family trilogy, but that certainly offered new directions. In some respects, the plays continue his ironic use of a quasi-realist structure unravelled by the presence of the fantastic, the grotesque and the gothic, but they do not explicitly evoke conventional myths to be deconstructed. Both *Fool for Love* (1983) and *A Lie of the Mind* (1985) are largely realistic, the first taut and spare (and thus in line with Shepard's concurrent 1984 screenplay for *Paris, Texas*) and the second sprawling and unhurried. Both utilize characters whose voices register on a different plane than the protagonists' and lend an air of surreality to the realist underpainting. The Old Man is a haunting presence in *Fool for Love*, and advocates a realism that is, ironically, completely subjective and in a sense opposed to the typically male emphasis on ego and power. In the latter play, Beth's aphasic speech patterns mine a deep level of signification and affect that comes from elsewhere (literally, she feels, from her belly). But Shepard, if not deeply examining female character itself but to some degree the female side of his male characters, nevertheless explores the self-damaging 'lies of the mind' that males concoct to bind themselves in abusive relationships and offers images of release and atonement not found in the family trilogy. But while pacts that imprison family members in hopeless relations are broken in these plays, real freedom remains elusive. Characters learn, as Rosen says, 'to let go' – of memories, kinship ties, cycles of desire and violence – but remain bereft of direction.[7]

However, Wade's analysis of the plays from the next decade reveals a strange twist: against Shepard's earlier output and the public persona it helped create, these plays even more forcefully 'express a concern for interconnectedness that is new to his writing, one that militates against individualism and ego assertion. These plays expose the deleterious effects of self-absorption, of masculinist power-grabs, and reveal a yearning for mutuality.'[8] *States of Shock* (1991), which fared badly with critics and audiences, rather too overtly exposes how Stubbs, the wounded veteran, can only feel whole again when his 'thing' (sexual potency) comes back and he is able to reacquire his connection to the putative father who, in this case, is the fascist Colonel. Similarly, *Simpatico* (1994) explores the damaging effects of male interaction, investigating, as James Crank says, 'ways in which men can express their power over other men and how that power often wounds both parties'.[9] At a time when subcultures like skateboard aficionados were popularizing the term 'bromance' to describe homosocial bonding in fairly stereotypical – and mostly positive – ways, Shepard's analysis may appear almost counterintuitive.

According to Shannon Skelton, these qualities abide in Shepard's 'late phase' as well, as the playwright-turned-actor-turned-director-turned-'It' celebrity figure continued to push against his own established dramatic forms by exploring, across a range of media, the 'corpus' of his own mythicized identity constructed from his collective artistic output. Thus we find Shepard, for instance, questioning his long-held faith in authenticity in plays like *Kicking a Dead Horse* (2007) and his understanding of male homosociality in the 2009 *Ages of the Moon*.[10] This tantalizing shift in Shepard's writing and public persona after his last true success, *A Lie of the Mind*, leads Wade to wonder, 'Is his decline in critical regard a result of his meager output, or the result of audience fatigue with his high-octane machismo? Or is there an implicit desire for the old Shepard, which prejudices reception of his more recent work?' (259–60).

I submit that this question, in different ways, stalks the playwrights featured in this book as well as others who grappled with the ongoing crises of 1970s America, exploring its bitter malaise, its loss of place in the geography of global power following Vietnam and its failure to live up to the utopias offered by both Right and Left during the 1960s. The different strategies taken by Shepard, Rabe, Shange and Foreman to engage with this reality – whether by exposing empty national myths, excoriating the latent violence of the American character on the battlefield and at home, mobilizing the new form of the choreopoem to resist the disappearance of one's language and existential being, or turning inward to confront consciousness itself as the hapless instigator of these confusions – established them as leading dramatic voices of the 1970s. But how would these approaches fare in the bright light of the new 'Morning in America', when Rambo replaced Pavlo and the film *Die Hard* would become a Christmas classic? When the feverish outbreak of entrepreneurial capitalism and the mantra 'Greed is good' rendered the empty refrigerator of the Starving Class more or less invisible?

In Shepard's case, it may be that a hard-earned rapprochement with 'mutuality' simply arrived at the wrong cultural moment, and one wonders whether the spectacle of America's leading cowboy playwright exploring his feminine side or aging into a more retrospective mode simply went against the grain of the time. And in the initial response to 9/11, with public cries to 'cowboy up' to terrorism, the subtle shifts in Shepard's work toward more nuanced understandings of homosociality, of the 'other', and father and son relations encountered trouble finding an audience. Ironically, Shepard may be remembered best in the twenty-first century for his non-fiction work, including the remarkable collection of letters published in 2013 as *Two Prospectors: The Letters of Sam Shepard and Johnny Dark*.[11] Along with the accompanying film, *Shepard and Dark* (dir. Treva Wurmfeld, 2012), the collection reveals Shepard seemingly out of step with himself and the contemporary world, and a far cry from the self-confident persona one might associate with a film character like Chuck Yaeger. The Shepard 'corpus' of the twenty-first century of which Skelton writes seems one riddled by doubt and engaged in attempting, through his writing, to come to grips with the past 'body' of work on which his reputation rests.

David Rabe, too, entered the 1980s riding his success from the previous decade and scored a hit with the 1984 *Hurlyburly*, considered by many to be his most sophisticated work. His vision, bordering on the tragic and consistently anti-heroic in its depiction of an America bedeviled by violence, racism and an inability to come to terms with its collective history, seemed poised to establish a much-needed counterpoint to the Reagan mantra that 'ours is not a sick society'.[12] After assessing Rabe's work to the mid-1980s, Philip Kolin ranked Rabe as 'one of the most powerful voices in American theatre' with an established reputation in both America and abroad. Concluding his excellent resource *David Rabe: A Stage History and a Primary and Secondary Bibliography*, Kolin remarked:

> In one interview Rabe told his listener that he had several boxes of unfinished plays and fiction at his home. Surely among these foul papers are several shining plays and at least that one novel he has promised the world for so many years. David Rabe is one of America's greatest living writers whose future is as bright as it is necessary to the American theatre.[13]

But like Shepard, Rabe soon found himself producing varieties of non-dramatic writing, married to a prominent Hollywood actress (and eventually father to the actress Lilly Rabe) and thereby increasingly drawn to film writing and other creative outlets that seemingly offered him greater satisfaction but led to a decline in his dramatic output. After his marriage to the actress Jill Clayburgh in 1978, Rabe turned to writing screenplays, the first of which to see production was the 1981 *I'm Dancing as Fast as I Can*, in which Clayburgh starred. Other opportunities presented themselves: after the mainstream success during the 1970s of anti-Vietnam War films (*Coming Home*, 1978; *Apocalypse Now*, 1979; and even the film version of the decade-old musical *Hair* in 1979), a slew of movies revising those histories and proposing more heroic narratives for remembering the war appeared, most notably the *Missing in Action* series starring Chuck Norris and the Sylvester Stallone *Rambo: First Blood* franchise. Rabe might have seemed the best hope for countering these revisionist film histories, and indeed *Streamers* was adapted by the playwright for film and directed by Robert Altman in 1983. Rabe then followed this with the anti-heroic *Casualties of War* (dir. Brian DePalma) in 1989. He also saw success with his script for *The Firm* (1993), a legal thriller directed by Sydney Pollack and starring Tom Cruise and Gene Hackman, based on the John Grisham bestseller of the same title. *Hurlyburly* was released as a film in 1998, and

Rabe's film adaptation of *The Boom Boom Room* appeared the following year.

But with his success writing screenplays, Rabe seemed less interested in and engaged with the theatre, and he consequently turned more to fiction, publishing four novels and a children's book between 1993 and 2010. When he returned occasionally to playwriting in the 1990s, it was first in the form of a prequel to the burned-out souls of *Hurlyburly* in the play *Those the River Keeps* (1991). It received savage reviews and closed almost immediately. Later attempts to reclaim his central place among American dramatists – *The Dog Problem* (2001), *The Black Monk* (2004), *An Early History of Fire* (2012) – were similarly dismissed. As a result, Rabe is seldom evoked as a representative, much less a central, contemporary American dramatist, and he has unfortunately all but disappeared from the twenty-first-century critical canon.[14]

So while it may be the case that Rabe has found more diverse outlets for his work – some less risky and more remunerative than playwriting – it may also be that his excoriating brand of drama could not find resonance in an America emerging from a period of malaise into a more economically stable and politically conservative time. While contrarian voices are always necessary, and American theatre has provided these in abundance throughout its history, the particular crises facing the nation during post-1970s – particularly AIDs, the continued push for equal rights and the confrontation with global terrorism – may invite a less corrosive form of critique than the sort Rabe has traditionally offered. Thus, while Tony Kushner's *Angels in America* could engage with America in the age of AIDs by suggesting a shared (if divisive) language and history and thereby, in David Savran's phrase, 'reconstruct the nation',[15] Rabe's work has seldom shown interest in such renovation. Coming to prominence in a decade when playwrights were driven to uncover the deepest sources of America's defects and to expose them ruthlessly, Rabe seems not to have deviated from that course and thus can find himself out of step with a cultural politics of rapprochement.

Such tendencies are always in flux, however, and it may be that with renewed anger stemming from the 2008 financial collapse and the newly contentious politics of race emerging at the same time as a renewed populism, Rabe will find new audiences for his scathingly critical plays. Or, he may soften his tone in the manner of Shepard: his latest play, *Good for Otto* (2015), dealing with depression and other forms of mental illness, recently received strong reviews (albeit at Chicago's smallest Equity theatre, the Gift), with Charles Isherwood complimenting Rabe on a 'return to powerful form'.[16] There are both similarities with Rabe's past work – the play investigates the deepest recesses of human suffering and the ultimate message is one of exerting tough love, first and foremost, on oneself – but also stark departures: in an interview, Rabe is 'at pains to point out that the work is no piece of realism but an experimental composition that looks at the topic of mental health "in a free-flowing way"; and is, at times, "funny"'.[17] The formal experiment may owe something to his work on film screenplays, but equally interesting is the shift in tone toward something suggesting compassion for his subjects, similar in some ways to the shift toward 'mutuality' in Shepard's late work.

Ntozake Shange, similarly, positioned herself during the 1970s as a uniquely oppositional voice within American playwriting, critiquing the language and structure of conventional drama as complicit in the denial of black and female experience. Her rejection of conventional theatre – even in many of its non-commercial manifestations – left her little room for dialogue with mainstream audiences, although this was always based on a strong ethical choice. Sandra Richards notes how Shange deployed the notion of 'combat breath' in positioning her theatre work during the 1970s:

> Shange borrows the term 'combat breath' from Frantz Fanon. In analyzing Francophone African colonies, the social psychiatrist had argued:
>> There is no occupation of territory, on the one hand, and independence of persons on the other. It is the country as a whole, its history, its daily pulsation that are contested, disfigured, in the hope of final destruction. Under this condition, the individual's breathing is an observed, an occupied breathing. It is combat breathing.[18]

Given Shange's overt dismissal of the 'minstrelsy' that American theatre propagated in its staging of black theatre, and her development of the choreopoem form to challenge that practice and the politics behind it, it was never likely that she would return to Broadway (indeed, she has spoken often of her discomfort at having *for colored girls...* produced there at all). After her whirlwind arrival in the New York theatre scene in the late 1970s, her work appeared more often in regional theatres and university drama departments and by performance collectives that share her feminist and Third World commitments, where combat breath might find room to exhale. As well, as Neal Lester's chapter in this book shows, her work from the 1970s has a vibrant cultural life in the form of the many adaptations it has spawned (see Chapter 5).

Yet here again, her absence from the putative 'centre' of American theatre can be read as the resounding success of the 1970s devolution away from the notion that such a centre exists, or should exist. Shange, like Shepard and Rabe, remained prolific until her stroke in 2004, and even today continues to write in a variety of forms. And, because her work transcends conventional genres, even her non-dramatic writing is always in its way a mode of performance writing, and always engaged in a transmedial relocation to new platforms: *From Okra to Greens* began as a 1978 performance piece at Barnard College before being published as a selection of poems in 1984 and then appearing in 1985 as a performance text with the subtitle *A Play with Music and Dance*. Indeed, in her poetry she prefers 'letters that dance ... I need some visual stimulation, so that reading becomes not just a passive act and more than an intellectual activity, but demands rigorous participation' – a sentiment that would characterize a choreopoem as well.[19] She has worked in multimedia, publishing poems with accompanying photographs (*The Sweet Breath of Life*, 2004). Despite not ever working directly in either film or video, she is included in the anthology *Black Women Film and Video Artists*, where P. Jane Splawn makes the case for her work being thoroughly immersed in visual culture.[20] Her novels, especially *Lilliane: Resurrection of the Daughter* (1994), are expressed in deeply sensual language, and *Lilliane* – a novel in the form of 12 monologues – found a second life as the basis for a collaborative text with the poetry of Jimmy Santiago Baca to form an experiment in 'performative storytelling' (*A Place to Stand*) presented in San Francisco in 2007 (with Shange's daughter, the actress Savannah Shange, in the lead). In the meantime, she continued to produce choreopoems late into her career, such as *The Love Space Demands* (1991). Her four children's books of the 1990s – *Whitewash*

(1997), *Float Like a Butterfly* (2002), *Ellington Was Not a Street* (2003) and *Daddy Says* (2003) – have a devoted following. In 2010 she collaborated with her sister, the playwright Ifa Bayeza, to write *Some Sing, Some Cry: A Novel*. Finally, of course, there is the interest in Shange's earlier work spawned by the 2010 Tyler Perry film adaption of *for colored girls*.

Distinct from Shepard's anxious desire to be made new and to escape the trauma of the past (whether embodied as memory, family or myth), Shange's legacy thus seems more future-oriented. Her corpus, the body of her work, finds new rhythms by which to move, whether in her own multidimensional work or in the art she inspires in others. When Will Power interviewed Shange in 2007 (during a retrospective of her work at New York's New Federal Theatre), he wrote:

> What we in the hip-hop theatre and spoken word movements owe her is both enormous and obvious: Shange is one of the supreme pioneers of her generation in terms of presenting verse on stage; in terms of actors melding speech, song and movement to create character and story; in terms of performers using various extensions of their spirit to share an experience on stage. From our vantage point, she's the matriarch of the whole thing.[21]

Power speaks of being mentored by Shange's collaborators (Laurie Carlos, the DJ Avotcja) and eager to carry on their work using the digital tools of his own generation. It would not be a stretch to suggest that Shange's work was always concerned with remediating dramatic language and conventional narrative by breaking it down to its beats, before relaunching it as a series of pulses to be felt rather than developed as 'dramatic' material with a teleology. This is the basis of hip-hop as well as of art in the digital age. As she told Power:

> I don't understand storylines, I understand language, or at least I used to. I can write, I can move. But I'm not interested in what happens – I'm interested in how it sounds. In order for a play to work, there has to be drama: you can't say what happens, you have to see it happen. But in narrative there isn't always drama. I can write really good scenes, but that doesn't mean anything happens.[22]

Shange, then, despite being relatively absent from the putative centres of American 'drama' and 'theatre', might be finding continued success as a 'performance writer' beyond the 1970s simply because her work was never tied to the (Western) literary, *belles lettres* tradition in the first place and thus finds connections to new forms of multicultural and transmedial multiplatform writing.

And so we come finally to Richard Foreman. The chapter by Geoffrey King and Craig Werner in this book concludes with a discussion of Foreman's work since 1981. Here, I will comment only on the irony that Foreman, among the four case studies in the volume – the idiosyncratic auteur working outside most of the conventional structures and institutions on which the usual definition of theatre depends – has remained most single-mindedly devoted to making theatre beyond the 1970s. Despite temporary forays into film, and the more constant expressions of a desire to leave theatre aside as far back as 1987, Foreman remains a man almost utterly devoted to making theatre. As he wrote in *Unbalancing Acts* (1992), 'essentially an artist does one thing throughout his career, but over the years he discovers its various implications and expands upon and deepens aspects of what has always been present in his work'.[23]

What is one to make of this persistence? Perhaps Foreman simply began his career making theatre at the end of the spectrum opposite from Shepard and Rabe, and some distance even from Shange: the early influence of film is interesting, given that it is toward film that Rabe and Shepard have been drawn, though a cinema of a vastly different nature from the Jonas Mekas/Godard school that attracted Foreman. But to a degree Foreman's work – in some ways closer to Shange but more self-consciously – represents the infiltration of theatre by the aesthetics and techniques of film, and so in a sense he has always been a servant of two masters. The difference is that Foreman, coming to theatre via the 1960s cross-disciplinary arts movement, combined the two art forms, recognizing from the moment he founded the Ontological-Hysteric Theatre that theatre was never a coherent formula of aesthetic and artistic practices but a mixture of discourses that may be inflected in innumerable ways. The ironic title of his theatre, evoking the purity and completeness of ontology only to undercut it with the hysteric's fitful movement, noise and instability, expresses clearly that his goal is not to remedy the split personality but to constantly rejuvenate it. Thus, instead of forsaking theatre for the different satisfactions of film writing, Foreman can consummate both desires in his mixed art form (the recent turn toward coupling film and performance after 2005 might substantiate this).

Like Shange's, then, Foreman's post-1970s work seems vital because it accepted from the beginning that writing 'for' the theatre need not be restricted to constructing traditional, dialogue-based texts built around 'drama' in the usual sense of that word. Like the choreopoem, Foreman's kinetic texts partake of developments in performance writing that stretch the boundaries of the traditional dramatic codex, and these forms are strongly connected to the 'radiant texts' of the digital age.[24] While Shepard and Rabe forcefully extended the realist form – one of the signal achievements of playwriting in the decade – they remained within the remit of dramatic writing conventionally understood. It is therefore interesting to contemplate whether their struggle to find a place in the shifting landscape of post-1970s theatre is related to the forms in which they choose to express themselves, or the content (focused primarily on the dilemmas of the contemporary white American male) they are drawn to.

Documents

This chapter provides excerpts of primary and secondary readings intended to help the reader discover resonances with material from the preceding chapters. David Rabe's work in the 1970s is closely linked to the Vietnam War, so sources contextualizing the conflict as well as reactions to Rabe's use of violence in the plays are provided. Given the abundance of existing primary and secondary material on Sam Shepard, the focus here is on influences that helped to shape his writing in the 1970s. Richard Foreman's work is likely the most unfamiliar to a general readership, so commentary on the manner of making his performances is highlighted. Shange's signal contribution during the decade was the genesis of the choreopoem, so issues of form and language take precedence.

David Rabe

Rabe's work of the 1970s is indelibly linked to the Vietnam War and his experiences in the armed services. The decade saw first a slow trickle and then an outpouring of literary and dramatic writing on the war.[1] *Notable among these was Michael Herr's* Dispatches, *which began as a series of articles for* Esquire *magazine in the style of the 'New Journalism', featuring a strongly subjective point of view. Herr converted these into his non-fiction book in 1977. (It would later find life as a rock musical of the same title directed by Elizabeth Swados and produced at the Public Theatre in 1979.) In the first passage, Herr comments on the collapse of myth and the brute (sur)reality of Vietnam, a trope deployed by Rabe as well.*

There wasn't a day when someone didn't ask me what I was doing there. Sometimes an especially smart grunt or another correspondent would even ask me what I was *really* doing there, as though I could say anything honest about it except 'Blah blah blah write a book.' Maybe we accepted each other's stories about why we were there at face value: the grunts who 'had' to be there, the spooks [non-military advisors] and civilians whose corporate faith had led them there, the correspondents whose curiosity and ambition drew them over. But somewhere all the mythic tracks intersected, from the lowest John Wayne wetdream to the most aggravated soldier-poet fantasy, and where they did I believe that everyone knew everything about everyone else, every one of us there a true volunteer. Not that you didn't hear some overripe bullshit about it: Hearts and minds, Peoples of the Republic, tumbling dominoes, maintaining the equilibrium of the Dingdong by containing the ever encroaching Doodah; you could also hear the other, some young soldier speaking in all bloody innocence, saying, 'All that's just a *load* man. We're here to kill gooks. Period.'[2]

Later, Herr reflects on the causes of the war – a national obsession during the 1970s – and once again is compelled to return, like Rabe, to myth as an agent.

Anyway, you couldn't use standard methods to date the doom; might as well say that Vietnam was where the Trail of Tears was headed all along, the turnaround point where it would touch and come back to form a containing perimeter; might just as well lay it on the proto-Gringos who found the New England woods too raw and empty for their peace and filled them up with their own imported devils.

[...]

Straight history, auto-revised history, history without handles, for all the books and articles and white papers, all the talk and the miles of film, something wasn't answered, it wasn't even asked. We were backgrounded, deep, but when the background started sliding forward not a single life was saved by the information. The thing had transmitted too much energy, it heated up too hot, hiding low under the fact-figure crossfire there was a secret history, and not a lot of people felt like running in there to bring it out (51).

Rabe is often presented as having been 'discovered' and 'launched' by Joseph Papp and the Public Theatre; but it bears recollecting that Rabe energized the Public as well at a key moment in its evolution into a producing powerhouse. In John Zeigler's fine Regional Theatre: The Revolutionary Stage,[3] *the confluence of Rabe's arrival, the fruition of Papp's Shakespeare in the Park initiative and the complex relations between Off-Broadway and Broadway come to a head to convey some of the wheeling and dealing dynamism of the New York theatre of the 1970s. One consequence was the decision to bring Rabe's shocking portrayals of the effects of the war into American homes via a series of taped television broadcasts.*

Joseph Papp was beginning to cut a very wide swath. When financial straits threatened the [Shakespeare] festival with extinction in 1971, Papp pointed out that the problem was caused by the renovation and operating expenses of the Public Theatre as a public trust; he got the city to buy the building [the former Astor House Library] from the festival for $2,600,000 and to rent it back for $1 a year. When other institutional theatres in the city were threatened financially (including the Repertory Theatre of Lincoln Center), it was usually Joseph Papp who rose up to spearhead attempts to save them, thereby placing himself in a position almost above competition. His emergence was climaxed in 1972, when virtually all attention was focused on him and his festival. On Broadway, his production of David Rabe's *Sticks and Bones* (transferred from the Public Theatre) and his rock musical version of the *Two Gentleman of Verona* [book by John Guare] (transferred from Central Park) won Tony Awards as the best play and the best musical, and the profits of the latter were subsidizing the losses of the former. (Papp was also grandly turning back 5 percent of *Verona's* Broadway profits to the city as a gesture of gratitude for the more than $5,000,000 in municipal support over the years.) Two more productions – Jason Miller's *That Championship Season* (from the Public Theatre) and *Much Ado about Nothing* (from Central Park) – were installed on Broadway in the fall of 1972. Miller's play, realistic and even old-fashioned, was Broadway's only sell-out ... Meanwhile, CBS television engaged Papp and his festival to produce thirteen 'specials' in prime time over a four-year period and provided more than $7,000,000 for the project, starting with a taping of *Much Ado*. This development more than any other put a national constituency at Papp's disposal; it was a startling and brilliant coup ... One after another, the traditional and even the special awards were bestowed on Papp. *Newsweek* featured him in a major article and put his picture on the cover with the banner headline: 'New Life in the American Theatre.'

Papp's television initiative did not proceed without controversy when it came time to broadcast Rabe's Sticks and Bones. *By situating his plays within the culture of the military (or, as in* Sticks and Bones, *having that world infiltrate the domestic sphere), Rabe invited themes of violence into his dramatic world. Much as the Living Theatre's* The Brig *(1963) cast light on the dehumanizing training of the Marine Corps, Rabe's plays investigated not just the real violence of the Vietnam War, but also the cruelty enacted upon men (and their language) in order to prepare them to perpetrate violence in Vietnam. Rabe's directness in bringing this violence back home created tensions in American culture as it struggled to address the latent and manifest guilt caused by the incursion into Vietnam and the effects on US military men and women. Audience reactions to his plays were notorious, as indicated from an interview with David Savran:*[4]

> **DS** Walter Kerr described an infuriated audience in New Haven when *Streamers* was first done. What do you remember of that?
> **DR** Mike Nichols directed it so I don't know what they were expecting. *Streamers* – they could have expected a party. You get a very raw reaction because they don't have any preconceptions. The first reactions were sometimes quite extreme ... One time a whole busload of people walked out. They probably just thought the bus was going to leave, I laugh about it now but it was very hard to take. *Sticks and Bones* was not dissimilar. The actors in *Sticks and Bones* used to say they needed combat pay to go on stage, because the audience's emotions were so confused and hostile to some of what went on, particularly at the end of the play. When we got *Streamers* to New York, we got it more under control. But there were always people walking out, fainting.

When it came time to broadcast Sticks and Bones, *Rabe's reputation for driving spectators to faint and walk out of theatres was well established. Initially, CBS executives saw the potential of large audiences when the proposed airdate coincided with the return of American former POWs from Vietnam, but the atmosphere quickly changed. Helen Epstein describes the tumult.*[5]

On January 24, the day *Sticks and Bones* was to have its first screening at the offices of CBS, the *New York Times* carried the banner headline: 'VIETNAM ACCORD IS REACHED; CEASE-FIRE BEGINS SATURDAY; P.O.W.'S TO BE FREE IN 60 DAYS.' ... Rabe's play was about the return of a damaged Vietnam veteran to his unscathed family. That evening and for most of the next few weeks, television news would feature the real families of real American POWs and their return home ...

[Days later] Papp stopped the car by a newsstand. *Time* and *Newsweek* were both carrying advance reviews of the televised *Sticks and Bones*. The show 'will drive a nail into your forehead and leave your face hanging like a sack from it all weekend long,' reported *Newsweek*. 'I cannot recall anything on commercial television of an intensity comparable to this production.' The *Time* reviewer wrote, 'The greatest national trauma since the Civil War, the U. S. involvement Viet Nam has yet to be exorcized in drama or fiction. *Sticks and Bones* ... is strong stuff for commercial TV, stronger even than it seemed on the New York stage.' The night before, Papp had received phone calls from two reporters checking out a rumor that CBS had canceled the show, but since then he had not thought about it.

... As the group was boisterously reading through the reviews, a waiter told Papp he had a telephone call. The producer took it at the front of the room.

On the line was Robert Wood, president of CBS Television.

'Great reviews, huh?' Papp later remembered greeting him.

'I have bad news,' was Wood's reply. 'We can't put that show on.'

He had just sent a telegram to the general managers of all the CBS affiliates explaining that *Sticks and Bones* had been previewed twice for the managements of CBS-affiliated stations, with most of them responding favorably to the powerful show. But a cease-fire had since been declared in Vietnam. The telegram made clear his position that presentation at this time might be unnecessarily abrasive to

> The feelings of millions of Americans whose lives or attention are at the moment emotionally dominated by the returning POWs and other veterans who have suffered the ravages of war.
> Never has there been a greater or more serious and responsible sense of concern expressed by our affiliates about a projected program and the timing of the broadcast. It is the conclusion of the CBS Television Network, therefore, that the broadcast of *Sticks and Bones* should be postponed and broadcast at a later date, to be announced, when the context of its showing will be less distressing and its possible application to actual events less immediate ...

Papp did not let Wood read his telegram. Instead he began to shout into the telephone receiver about censorship, government pressure, the First Amendment, the obligation of a network to its viewers.

The episode revealed the changing relationship between theatre and television, the latter of which had to this point benignly remediated live performance by making it available for a larger audience. But in the fraught context of the 1970s and Vietnam, the different demographics and institutional structures of television were revealed. Before the situation with Sticks and Bones *escalated, Wood had cautioned Papp*:

'Joe, you don't realize, television just isn't like theatre,' Wood had said, trying to explain to Papp what seemed obvious to him. 'Television is like a large battleship. You have to make a slow turn. There are two hundred affiliates we have to watch out for. And we've promised them *Romeo and Juliet*' (274).

Finally, an indicator of how far up the CBS chain of command the issue rose was an article by Albin Krebs in the New York Times:[6]

Responsibility for the indefinite postponement, made on the announced ground that showing the play at a time when Americans were rejoicing in the return of prisoners of war might be 'abrasive,' was firmly taken at the time by Robert D. Wood, president of the

TV network ... It was learned from two well-informed, independent sources, however, that Mr. Paley [CBS Chairman], after viewing the program for the first time on March 5, objected strenuously and told other CBS officials it would have to be postponed to a later date.

Philip Kolin, interviewing Rabe for the Journal of Dramatic Criticism and Theory *in 1989, looked back over two decades of Rabe's career and brought up an issue that remained significant: 'the question of genre' as Jon Dietrick states in his chapter in this book. Here, Kolin pressed Rabe on his preference for 'mixed' forms:*

> **PCK** I know you're no Aristotelian, but there's a remarkable mixture in your plays of pity and fear that some of your most famous characters evoke, Pavlo, for example, Carlyle ... Would you comment on these different responses, this sense of empathy and the sense of horror that audiences feel? Why, for example, should an audience both loathe and feel sorry for Carlyle?
>
> **DR** I think that strict Aristotelianism really interferes with the arousal of emotions, of the very emotions he seems to want. I'm very opposed to the ideas of Aristotle. He's managed to interpose a definition between the experience of the play and the play itself. You actually end up with people wondering whether people wrote tragedies, which is truly absurd. It's sort of sanitizing tragedy as if isn't supposed to be about inevitable horror. If tragedy is about destiny, and inevitability, if it's about fated dooms, how can it be about appropriate behavior, I mean, behavior that is capable of avoiding tragedy – moral lessons so to speak – how can it be about moral instruction and proportional events and emotions? It is not about reasonable failure but inevitable irrationality.

The mixing of forms sometimes created critical confusion when Rabe's plays were read as simple tragedy. In the same interview, Rabe speaks to a common misapprehension that dogged productions of Sticks and Bones*:*

PCK What about a play like *Sticks and Bones*? What should the audience be doing or meditating on at the end of that play?

DR The end of the play is very confrontational. It's very much an assault and again, if the play's done correctly, the audience will be compelled from the beginning of the play through the end to identify with Ozzie. That has rarely been grasped. Most people who came to the theatre at the time of the first production were people with a liberal point of view so they wanted to identify with David and be sympathetic to him. They shunned the parents, but I think the real core of the play is Ozzie. He's the one on the journey. David comes into the play wild and angry; he's trying to compel Ozzie into action. So I think if you were identifying with Ozzie and you reached a point where you too were saying 'Shut up' to David and then they did that to him, had him cut his wrist, you would be an accomplice in a ritual and you would have to see something about yourself. In other words, Ozzie fails; it's too much. He doesn't change. He opts for the way he has been. In many ways it's Ozzie's tragedy as well as David's. For them both there could be a point where we say, 'Oh no, don't do that,' particularly for Ozzie when he agrees to help them cut David's wrists. But David's demands are unlivable. The truth of the matter is that what David's asking for is impossible. He's gone too far. He's asking for a form of insanity. In the horror of the ending, there is a conflict between David's extreme point of view and Ozzie's extreme withdrawal from that point of view. It's a very confrontational play that basically says that society, or the status quo, is sick and when it's reestablished, it's sicker. This character David comes in and tries to shatter it, almost does, but in the end, he made a fatal mistake and underestimates something and is then himself drawn into the society. Are they all dead? I wouldn't suspect or suggest that *Sticks and Bones* could offer the kind of tranquility that I think is possible in *Goose and Tomtom* or *Hurlyburly*.

Sam Shepard

Shepard's early work is often analysed in relation to Antonin Artuad's 'Theatre of Cruelty'. Shepard had written that 'The power of words for me ... is in their capacity to evoke visions ... Words as living incantations, living, breathing words with the power to change our chemistry ... Language can explode from the tiniest impulse ... In these lighting-like eruptions words are not thought, they're felt.'[7] In an essay linking Shepard to Artaud, John Glore's close reading of a key speech from Curse of the Starving Class *explicates how the playwright reached for such incantation:*[8]

The play begins with an expository scene in a realistic mode. Wesley and his mother, Ella, argue about her harsh treatment of his father, Weston, the night before. In a matter of moments we already have a sense of their characters, their relationship, of plot elements coalescing to begin a story. This could be a scene from any typical play of the overwrought, American realist school. But then Wesley abruptly launches into a three-minute monologue, almost a soliloquy, in which he describes the events of the preceding night as experienced from his vantage point, lying awake 'in my bed in my room in this house in this town in this state in this country.' Here we can sense what Shepard means when he repeatedly insists that he writes from 'inside' his characters. Wesley speaks only of sensations: the smell of blossoms, the sound of animals, the feel of the bed, the sight of his model airplanes hanging above him.

This monologue, entirely descriptive, vivifies a single, complete, developing image of actions and emotions; it is an isolatable unit, a structure with a beginning, middle and end. Its rhythm builds, accelerates, cascades over shorter and shorter pieces of information, sentence fragments that become distilled until they contain only the most essential details: 'Bottle crashing. Glass breaking. Fist through door. Man cursing. Man going insane. Feet and hands tearing. Head smashing. Man yelling. Shoulder smashing. Whole body crashing. Woman screaming.' The accelerating rhythm of the speech echoes the acceleration of Wesley's heartbeat, which doesn't calm until the end of the event, when Wesley speaks his first full sentence since the middle of the monologue: 'Then, far off the freeway could be heard.'

Shepard finds another species of that Artaudian magic in music, especially rock and jazz. When he was invited, in 1975, to concoct a script for a planned film of the Bob Dylan Rolling Thunder Review (a tour featuring a number of performers in support of Dylan), Shepard recorded his impressions of the live shows and the carnivalesque atmosphere between them, published as The Rolling Thunder Logbook.[9] *As the following excerpt clearly reveals, Shepard brought his own preoccupations regarding authenticity and the shocks that live performance might elicit:*

Then comes the blockbuster. Dylan moves up on the platform to the rickety old upright piano used for years for the sole purpose of producing middle-class pablum [sic] Big Band sounds of the 30 and 40s. He sits, stabs his bony fingers into the ivory, and begins a pounding version of 'Simple Twist of Faith.' Here's where it's at. The Master Arsonist. The place is smoking within five minutes. The ladies are jumping and twitching deep within their corsets. The whole piano is shaking and seems on the verge of jumping right off the wooden platforms. Dylan's cowboy heel is driving a hole through the floor. Roger McGuinn appears with guitar, [Bob] Neuwirth, the whole band joins into it until every molecule of air in the place is bursting. This is Dylan's true magic. Leave aside his lyrical genius for a second and just watch the transformation of energy which he carries. Only a few minutes ago the place was deadly thick with tension and embarrassment, and now he's blown the top right off it (31).

In a later entry, Shepard locates the confluence of music, myth and performance:

A strong recurring feeling I get from watching Dylan perform is the sense of him playing for Big Stakes. He says he's 'just a musician,' and in his boots he needs that kind of protection from intellectual processes, which are a constant threat to any artist. Even so, the repercussions of his art don't have to be answered by him at all. They fall on us as questions and that's where they belong. Myth is a powerful medium because it talks to the emotions and not the head. It moves us into an area of mystery. Some myths are poisonous to believe in, but others have the capacity for changing something inside us, even if it's only for a minute or two. Dylan creates a mythic atmosphere out of the land around us. The land we walk on every day and never see until someone shows it to us (62).

As with Rabe, issues of genre become important to Shepard's work of the 1970s as he modifies and reanimates realism into something malleable enough to capture the chaotic dynamics of modern American life. Surveying the scene in 1979, Robert Brustein perceptively noted that, while some European drama (particularly the Absurdists) had followed the lead of Ibsen's late plays – his example is The Master Builder – *in undermining causal logic, American playwrights like Miller were still invested in a politics of 'liberal reform democracy' that required causality as away of uncovering the exact source and cause of corruption and guilt:*

In short, the premises underlying Miller's themes and actions are not Ibsenite in the least. They belong to the 18th Century, which is to say the age of Newton, rather than the 20th, which is the age of Einstein ...

So prevalent is this pattern in mainstream American drama that even now, towards the end of the 1970s, our most highly acclaimed playwrights are still shaping their works to sequential diagrams ... More often than not, American mainstream dramatists continue to explore the causes behind their effects; the event to be excavated is still the guilt of the (generally older generation) protagonists; and the drama retains the air of a courtroom, complete with arraignments, investigations, condemnations, indictments, and punishments.[10]

Brustein took Rabe to task for not entirely escaping the Newtonianism of Miller in his Vietnam plays and instead concluded that '[w]ith Sam Shepard, the American theatre takes a step beyond the Newtonian universe into a world of dreams, myth, and inner space. With [auteur director] Robert Wilson, it leaps into the universe of Einstein, developing new dimensions of outer space and fractured time' (27). William Demastes and Mike Vanden Heuvel suggest that Shepard's work is not only post-Newtonian but also post-Einsteinian: a realism that operates not relativistically and in line with Absurdism – at the opposite end from Newtonian causality – but in the liminal space between order and relativity, and in accord with the dynamics of nonlinear ('chaotic') systems:

Controlled anarchy [a phrase Shepard used to describe his preferred acting style], in fact, is a term applicable to most of Shepard's work, a characteristic that distinguishes his work from earlier American dramatists whose instincts tend toward visioning a world of culture that *controls* anarchy. That earlier American dramatic sense of a need for order reflects an American cultural desire for control in general, the need to maintain an order in pursuit of its 'manifest destiny,' a cultural imposition of a sort of determinism over the events with which it engages ... Shepard's implicit argument is profound and reverberates to the very foundations of our cultural edifice. Reversing American mythic history, Shepard intimates that we must release ourselves from an order that excludes the noise of real experience. The new 'order' that Shepard posits is one that sees the necessity of welcoming a dynamic tension between order and disorder, a decentered vision of the notion of order as control. Such unpredictable interferences are inevitable and are therefore actually determinist. Hence, the appropriateness for Shepard's turn to realism and an 'apparent' naturalism. But, like Rabe's realism, Shepard's realism is not Zola's; it is a chaos-informed realism.

True West is an excellent case in point, the play's very title suggesting its cultural engagement with American myth. Austin and Lee are, respectively, paragons of culturally prescribed order and a 'natural' disorder. Separately, the two brothers have stagnated into sterile, unproductive existences. Austin is a product of a culturally triumphant 'real' West and Lee of a natural 'untamed' West. It should be noted that while several critics have seen the play as a psychological study of two halves of one self, Shepard has rejected such an interpretation because in many ways Austin and Lee are not 'selves' at all ... What Shepard argues, more precisely, is that the real West – developed, paved, orderly – must reengage with the untamed West – vital, wild, nonlinear.[11]

Despite the unlikelihood of Shepard having become conversant with nonlinear dynamics and chaos theory, some form of 'orderly disorder' exists at the root of his conception of character, given the transformations we witness in them. Shepard prefaces his play Angel City *(1976) with this 'Note to the Actors':*

Instead of the ide of the 'whole character' with logical motives behind his behavior which the actor submerges himself into, he should consider himself a fractured whole with bits and pieces of character flying off the central theme. In other words, more in terms of collage construction or jazz improvisation.

Bonnie Marranca uses the 'Note' to develop further correspondences between Shepard's notion of character and jazz:

The appeal of jazz is more than structural. As an approach to composition it embodies an attitude that is at the heart of Shepard's work: spontaneity of expression. Not chance, but improvisation ... ... The jazz artist teases the audience into following his rhythm for as long as he can keep it going, lifting them to a tantalizing high, taking them down, bringing them up again, one tempo to another, a little bit at a time as if they were caught up in a sexual embrace with music that continuously forestalls the orgasmic response of applause and shouts. The most powerful solo parts in Shepard's plays have that same erotic effect which is what makes his writing sexy though there's no actual sex in them: it's the rhythm of sex not the representation of it.[12]

As noted in the chapter on Shepard in this book, the playwright continued to work in non-conventional performance modes even as he turned to the more realist plays of the family cycle. One such collaboration in the 1970s involved the former artistic director of the Open Theater, Joe Chaikin. Shepard would go on to create several additional works with him, including Savage/Love, *and continued to collaborate after Chaikin suffered a stroke in 1984 and became partially aphasic. Joe Chaikin died in 2003. Eileen Blumenthal observed both artists in 1979, when their collaboration brought Shepard's musical approach to language to the fore.*[13]

After the Open Theater disbanded, Shepard suggested to Chaikin that they create a piece together ... They had decided to proceed without an ensemble – to make something between the two of them which Chaikin would then perform.

Asked if he [Shepard] felt pressed into someone else's way of seeing – particularly since these joint creations are closer in form and mood to Chaikin's work than his – Shepard said that his enormous respect for Chaikin prevented that being an issue:

When you're collaborating from someone who you can learn from, it's very different from collaborating with someone who you're struggling with in some kind of competitive way. Like you're showing each other your chops. Musicians call it chops. If you can play a scale 16 ways, you've got chops – and there are ways of playing together where you show that off. But when you're working with someone who actually has an experience that penetrates deeply, and you know you can learn from it, the relationship isn't that way. I feel like I'm an apprentice to Joe ... I feel like he's my elder.

[...]

Shaping the dozen-plus sections of *Tongues* into a performance piece, Chaikin and Shepard used principles drawn more from musical composition than traditional dramaturgy. Rather than looking for a story line, consistent characters, or an Aristotelian beginning, middle, and end, they worked with statement, development, and counterpoint ... Shepard brought a selection of musical instruments to the theatre (by now they were working in the Magic Theatre, where *Tongues* was first performed), and they started to jam and experiment. They devised a percussion accompaniment on traditional and invented instruments – bongos, cymbals, maracas, an African drum, a tambourine, bells, chains, pipes, brass bowls, kitchenware. The voice addressing the blind one was accompanied by the high, eerie whine of a brass bowl being vibrated by a soft mallet – a sound which suggested the noise of a mosquito ... Both men wanted to keep focus on Chaikin while making the music an integral part of the performance. They had already decided that Chaikin would face front in a chair, motionless except for his head, his lap covered with a blanket. Now Shepard sat behind him, back to back, on a low platform, the instruments arranged around him. As he played he periodically held his arms and instruments out, so that they could be seen over the top or around the sides of Chaikin's chair.[14]

Given Shepard's dedication to principles of rhythmic language, transformational acting and shifting identity, his equal commitment to authenticity provides a number of interesting conflicts within his plays. Jeanette R. Malkin's Memory-Theatre in Postmodern Drama *agues that, under the conditions of contemporary life, the very machinery and function of memory (private and cultural) have been altered. In her reading of Shepard, she describes how the playwright dramatizes the conflicts that arise when dual operations of memory seem to be pitted against one another.*

Shepard's situation is a paradoxical one. A product of postmodern America and postindustrial capitalism, his dramatic language reflects this world on conflated, ungrounded, open, and constantly shifting images that grant stylistic freedom and allow imaginative release. At the same time, Shepard cannot escape a concomitant angst and longing in the face of this foundationless world, anxieties expressed through images of claustrophobia and the desire for escape. An aspect closely connected to this paradox is his presentation of identity, private and public. Shepard's characters are caught in the bind of seeking postmodern release from culturally induced determinations of personality – and thus are constantly transforming. At the same time, they have the modernist need to find sustenance in a memoried past, often expressed in long, monologic fables, or through nostalgic imaginings of the past … The need to reinvent the self is thus an urgent reaction to the formulating forces of societal pressure and tradition, viewed by Shepard as prisons to be struggled against. Among those forces is also memory … 'That's isn't me! That never was me!' says Dodge when reminded of the pictures of his youth: 'This is me. Right here. This is it. The whole shootin' match' (*Buried Child*).[15]

Memory continues both to haunt Shepard and generate much of his late writing. In Two Prospectors: The Letters of Sam Shepard and Johnny Dark, *Shepard – who once stated he will never pen a memoir – allows an unprecedented glimpse into his inner life through a series of letters exchanged with a long-time confidante. (A 2012 film by Treva Wurmfeld,* Shepard and Dark, *documents the tension-filled process of assembling the book.) The process of collating the correspondence and revisiting his past cast a Beckettian shadow:*

Dear John,
    Sat down yesterday to go through a stack of letters I saved back of yours & at last put them in some kind of chronological order

but I wasn't ready for the deep sorrow in re-visiting our past lives. I guess it's that feeling of life just slipping through your fingers like so much sand – no regrets really – how else are we going to live? I've never really felt very courageous about it all – in fact terror is closer to my real response toward the world & people in general. In the words of Master Beckett:

> 'world world world
> & the face grave
> clouds against the evening'[16]

To find oneself at this stage of life is very interesting and a little disturbing ...

Yr amigo
Sam

As the correspondence winds down after Shepard's relationship with Jessica Lange ended, Shepard evokes the desires of his own earlier dramatic creations:

John –
  ... Some scary part of me actually believes it's possible to burn bridges & start completely new. My favorite line of Bertolt Brecht: 'A man can make a fresh start with his last breath.'[17] Maybe it's some hang-over impulse from my Puritan Father's heritage – this American notion that you just leave a place when you're not welcome & start from scratch. Create a whole new country & damn the torpedos! – damn the Indians! – Damn the buffalo! – damn the environment! Fuck 'em all – God says we're entitled to this place.

In early 2011, Shepard dropped out of the project to publish the correspondence, writing to Dark:

I've just realized that I have come to the end of this obsession & long to be free of it. I'm no longer interested in poring over the past – re-making the past – goofing on the past – reminiscing about the past or re-writing the past. I need to move on to my own stuff & leave this behind. It may be some emotional territory I'm going thru that has prompted this – in the same way leaving Jessica but in any case this whole phase of things is over & done with, for me. Finished.

Ntozake Shange

In a 1979 essay in The Black Scholar, *Robert Staples criticized both Shange and Michelle Wallace (author of the study* Black Macho and the Myth of Superwoman*) for their negative representations of black males. It was an odd pairing – Wallace criticized the 'sentimentality' of Shange's play in a* Village Voice *review after the Broadway opening – but the essay resonated with other critiques by male black critics and occasioned spirited responses from feminists:*

In Ms. Shange's play, we witness the abuse of black women by black men; to waiting for men who do not show; to the horror of watching him drop her baby out of a window. At the end of her play, black women are exhorted to love themselves because, presumably, nobody else will ...

What is curious is the reaction of black women to this play. Watching a performance one sees a collective appetite for black male blood. The reaction, however, is not unanimous, as many women are greatly disturbed by the play and its vicious assault on black men. Particularly upset are the happily married women who have no pent-up frustrations which need a release. At the end of the play, what I find unsettling is Shange's invitation to black women to love themselves. This seems, to me, no less than an extension of the culture of Narcissism. She does not mention compassion for misguided black men or a love of a child, family and community ... A black woman who loves only herself is incapable of loving others. What greater way to insure being alone the rest of your life than the self-centered posture so eloquently expressed in Ntozake Shange's play?[18]

The issue of the representation of males in 1970s feminist works of art and literature, and in particular the representation of black men by black and Third World feminist authors, created much debate. An early intervention on Shange's behalf in defence of her work from Staples' charges came from Sandra Hollin Flowers, who referenced specific poems from for colored girls ...:

Even 'Latent Rapists' (pp. 17–21) and 'Abortion Cycle #1' (pp. 22–3), which seem to deal exclusively with women's issues, are of political significance to black men. It is difficult to politicize rape among black women, for instance, because the feminist approach began with a strongly anti-male sentiment, whereas the black community is highly male-identified. Furthermore, blacks have their own historical perspective on rape – thousands of black men who were lynched for 'rape' of white women. The history of these persecutions, however, does not remove the black woman's need for a political consciousness about rape, such as the traditionally feminist one Shange articulates. By the same token, Shange has sensitively portrayed the trauma of abortion, a trauma which, to some extent, probably exists in every case, no matter how strongly a woman might advocate the right to choose an abortion. Still, the black movement's rhetoric linking birth control to genocide cannot be lightly dismissed. These considerations ought to make clear the delicate balance between blackness and womanhood which Shange manages to strike in *Colored Girls*. Maintaining this balance is no easy task, and the black woman writer of some political consciousness is under tremendous pressure not to sacrifice issues of blackness to those of womanhood and vice-versa.[19]

for colored girls... *was also ostensibly a play concerned with suicide rates among young black women, and constructed so as to repair the self-esteem of this at-risk population. Andrea Benton Rushing addressed the issue directly in a 1981 article, citing a study reported in a 1973 article in* Ebony. *Responding to the study's forecast that 'suicide rates among black women will continue to rise', Rushing – while admiring the choreopoem's moving depiction of black female culture – questioned the absence of traditional black support networks in the lives of the choreopoem's characters, and by taking a sociological perspective on it suggested generational, class and cultural differences among black feminists:*

... although the Macmillan version of the play is dedicated to Shange's grandmother and great-aunt, the ladies of the rainbow have no mothers, aunties, grandmothers, sisters, cousins, godmothers, play aunts, or play sisters. They have no christenings, funerals, or weddings to go to and be buoyed and challenged by, no neighborhood's pride to push them on to college, no families (nuclear or extended) to harass and nourish and soothe them. They are as isolated and alienated as the typical middle-class, single white woman in contemporary America, and that is probably part of the reason the play succeeds with white audiences.

... 'For Colored Girls' [sic] has no knowledge of that 'old-time religion' that was good enough for mother, of the voices of Mahalia Jackson, Clara Ward, Albertina Walker, and Dorothy Love Coates. It is ignorant of black women on the mourner's bench praying struggling souls 'through,' serving on stewardess boards, superintending Sunday schools, frying chicken by the crate to pay off church mortgages. Its ladies of the rainbow in their bright chitons with their exquisitely articulated anguish don't know the 'Old Ship of Zion,' the 'Beautiful Garden of Prayer,' or 'Amazing Grace.' They are cut off from the rich tradition of faith which sustained a slave people through fire and brimstone and a half-free people through Reconstruction, lynching, legal segregation, second-class citizenship, and all the other travails of our stay in this Babylon.[20]

Shange has been a popular interview subject over the years. Serena Anderlini discussed Shange's preoccupation with form and the sources for her radical reworkings of theatrical structure:[21]

Anderlini – What about black American history?
Shange – My parents used to be called 'race people.' Life was dedicated to the betterment of the race; heroes or achievers of any kind were seen in terms of how they portrayed the race in the eyes of the Anglo, who saw us as 'Sambo.' Black people a generation or two before me found 'Sambo's' images embarrassing – not realizing that maybe that art form was the foundation of what came after. Before the baby-boom – before those of us who were born during world war two and after – 'Sambo' types were all there was. There was no respect for black opera singers, for black poets.

Paul Lawrence Dunbar is a genius because of his dialect poems; but he was most proud of sonnets he wrote because that to him meant he was a poet: he could not accept that his dialect poems were classics, that they would remain so forever. There was so much prejudice and make-believe about black people at that time that the only way he could respect himself was by writing sonnets; that to me is very painful. I was raised to listen to his dialect poems, and Langston Hughes's and Chuck Berry's.

[...]

Anderlini – Speaking about *colored girls*, years ago you said that was a 'distillation of years of work in common.' What do you think today?
Shange – The collective effort was that of 20 to 30 feminist writers in the San Francisco Bay area, to remedy and explain, explicate and extrapolate our situation as women. That was the collective effort. The work itself is individual. The stamina and courage – if there is courage involved in it to tackle issues that might be painful or unattractive – comes from that collective effort, but the work itself is individual. Judy Grahn, Susan Griffin, Sonia Sanchez, Janice Marcantoni, Jessica Hegedorn, we were a collective of black Asian and native American [sic] women working at the same time. We read our works at the same readings. For the most part they were about our own experiences. We gave each other the strength and the environment to do that.
Anderlini – Do you think that a similar situation would be possible today?
Shange – It would be impossible today. Those of us who grew up in my age group – in their late thirties – are much more sophisticated than we used to be. We are also involved with families and relationships of some sort, and we are not as available to one another as we used to be. We all used to be single and free. Free to do whatever, and that's no longer true. It is also no longer true that there haven't been great frictions in the feminist movement, between gay women and straight women, for instance. But when I was working there was no such thing. That didn't exist.
Anderlini – Can you describe the difference between theatre and performance art?
Shange – I can change performance art when I want to. Before performance theatre we had the same thing every night. The same lines. I don't like that. [C]*olored Girls* was never the same at any reading I did in California. My character moved every night, and she had more and more things around her. By the last two weeks

I was really feeling very accomplished: I knew I hit some new things.

Doing the same thing every night, that's not an adventure for me. I'd find out how I use my fingers, I'd find out how I held my cigarette. I discovered things.

Shange's critiques of American theatre were the sharpest since Albee's, and she was among the first to decry the appearance of black culture on Broadway almost exclusively in the form of revues, saying 'with the advent of at least 6 musicals about the lives of black musicians & singers/ EUBIE, BUBBLING BROWN SUGAR, AIN'T MISBEHAVIN', MAHALIA, etc.)/ the lives of millions of black people who don't sing & dance for a living/ are left unattended to in our theatrical literature'.[22] *In the same essay she pressed her point by arguing that it was not only a matter of content but form as well:*

In other words/ we are selling ourselves & our legacy quite cheaply/ since we are trying to make our primary statements with somebody else's life/ and somebody else's idea of what theatre is. I wd suggest that: we demolish the notion of straight theatre for a decade or so, refuse to allow playwrights to work without dancers & musicians. 'coon shows' were somebody else's idea. We have integrated the notion that drama must be words/ with no music & no dance/ cuz that would take away the seriousness of the event/ cuz we all remember too well/ the chuckles & scoffs at the notion that all niggers cd sing & dance/ most of us can sing and dance/ & the reason that so many plays written to silence & stasis fail/ is cuz most black people have some music & movement in our lives. We do sing & dance. This is a cultural reality. That is why I find the most inspiring theatre among us to be in the realms of music & dance (19).

In a long interview with Claudia Tate, Shange went on to describe the differences between her work and the mainstream of American theatre:

Taking risks in performance is virtually prohibited in this country. I think I should take a lot of risks. It was risky for us to do the minstrel dance in *Spell #7*, but I insisted on it because I thought

the actors in my play were coming from pieces they didn't want
to be in but pieces that helped pay their bills. Black characters are
always being closed up in a 'point.' They decided, for instance,
that *Spell #7* by Zaki Shange is a feminist piece and therefore not
poetry. Well, that's a lie. That's giving me a minstrel mask. That's
forcing me to fulfill somebody else's idea. So I put that dance in
there because that's how I felt. I felt trapped, and I felt parodied
and ridiculed and exploited. I had the minstrel dance because that's
what happens to black people in the arts no matter how famous
we become. They still refer to Alvin Ailey as if he were a freak; he
had a company for twenty years. They still act as if Carmen De
Lavallade was the last African ballerina, and she has trained at
least fifty people herself. It's this box, these stereotypes, that people
expect, so I put them in a minstrel dance.

Black Theatre is not moving forward the way people like to
think it is. We're not free of our paint yet! The biggest moneymakers – *The Wiz, Bubbling Brown Sugar, Ain't Misbehavin'* – are
all minstrel shows. So that's why I did the minstrel piece.

*In a famous mock-serious article, 'Ntozake Shange Interviews
Herself', for* Ms. *magazine in 1977 after she had taken the New
York theatre world by storm, Shange asked herself how she had
absorbed the ethos of black popular music as a young girl (an
'ikette' would be a devoted follower of Ike and Tina Turner):*[23]

There waz a time in my life when rhythm & blues was my only
reality. From the time I was eight until I was about thirteen years
old I wd sit by the radio in st. Louis & listen to george logan's
show, till my mother insisted I had enuf of that niggah music.
Saturdays were spent at vashon high school or at summer high
school (all colored) watching Jackie Wilson tear his clothes off,
dancing in the aisles to ben. e. king, the olympics, the shirelles.
The only black folks with the public aura were on the stage. no I
cd never really sing, but I've always been able to 'shake that thing.'
ike & tina turner were big big in st. louis. the ikettes got ta wear
lil slinky skirts & be on the stage where smokey robinson wd bend
over and whisper abt 'bad girls.' 'she's not a bad girl because she
wants to be free / uhmmm she wants to be free.' that waz what I
wanted/ to be free to dance and smile at the people having such
a good time listening to tina turner talk abt 'i'm justa fool / you

know I'm in love.' i imagine her songs were for me what edna st. vincent millay's sonnets were for a terribly romantic lil white girl thirty years ago.

Richard Foreman

Given the excellent selection of primary and secondary sources available in Gerald Rabkin's Richard Foreman *in the PAJ 'Art + Performance' series,*[24] *the focus here is on thematic bundles that provide information on Foreman's idiosyncratic methods of theatre-making. As well as information on his scenography and use of performers, a representative excerpt has been selected from his voluminous notebooks, many of which are available via open access (with a few stated provisions) on the Ontological-Hysteric website (www.ontological.com). There, readers are told, 'This website contains hundreds of pages of unedited text which Richard Foreman is making available freely for use by theatrical authors/ directors from which to create plays of their own.'*[25] *Selections provide further information on Foreman's primary themes and obsessions, and resonate with other entries: but all are presented in the spirit of Foreman's own stated purpose of generating possible 'cells' for other writers.*

Foreman explains on the website that 'in the texts that follow, there are some repetitions for which I apologize. The spelling is TERRIBLE – please excuse that, and the obvious typos also, which you should feel free to adjust. Sometimes you won't be sure if it's a typo or an artistic choice. That's for you to decide, but be open to the fact that a word or reference seems askew may indeed be what I intended.' For those reasons, the text below has not been edited.

From the Notebook entitled 'Theory':

The now.
Any attempt to grasp the incomprehensible hinders
(don't screw up the brow with effort, to AIM, just be in the dispursion, relaxed)
Every point has density of expanded to all
as if center goes to outside again and again

amdf outside is so re-packed to center, like heart beat?
So play pulsates> Item: fills out: new item: fills out; new item; fills out ...
God is vast point, God expands by making points re-vast

like mandela, like heart, like torus

God is potentia, WE pull things out for him to re-vastify

To STRAIN is to cut down to tunnel vision. But to 'wide', effortless ...

Just relax effort, so you inflate to globe head (from inside, all your thought-strainings)
pushes world away,
your acts FLOATED by inner expansion
Open the chest book.

Allow inflatedself-absence
to float acts into the world

REAL world (not one we live in, by conceptualizing and perceiving) is symbol for non-fear, non dream-construct.
Real it by light superimposition. That 'being here which is out of 'here'.
Let's be an erruption of source.
Whereas dream world clogs the expansive flow.

When a meaning triumphs over others
Meaning dies. Only is meaning alive if meaning hovers, weaves in and out with many others.
Meaning is 'man' made, if it's expressable.
Ok. But see how it immediately splits, self-contradicts, meanders.

So: meaningless is all meanings in play.

What's it about? Everything.

The peculiar understanding of text that allows Foreman to construct his writings in unconventional forms (fonts, layouts, spacing, placement of text on the page, the inclusion of charts, drawings and doodlings) seems very Postmodern. But critics have uncovered a number of possible forebears, many pointing to the influence of Gertrude Stein.[26] *More recently, Hans-Thies Lehmann has suggested that Foreman's work is an important precursor to 'postdramatic' theatre, which shares Foreman's desire to undermine conventional dramatic content and theatre's typically representational mode of presentation. Lehmann cites Foreman's debt to Stein but also his remediation or overwriting of her style:*

When Gertrude Stein speaks of her idea of the 'Landscape Play,' it appears as a reaction to her basic experience that theatre always made her terribly 'nervous' because it referred to a *different* time (future or past) and demanded a constant effort on the side of the viewer contemplating it. Instead of following it with 'nervous' – we may as well translate this with 'dramatic' – tension, one ought to contemplate what was happening on stage as one would otherwise contemplate a park or a landscape. Thornton Wilder remarked: 'A myth is not a story read from left to right, from beginning to end, but a thing held full in-view the whole time. Perhaps this is what Gertrude Stein meant by saying that the play henceforth is a landscape.'[27]

In Stein's texts the – relatively sparing – explanations of her theatre concept are repeatedly linked to actual landscapes. If it is often tempting to describe the stagings of the new theatre as landscapes, this is rather due to traits anticipated by Stein: a *defocalization* and equal status for all the parts, a renunciation of teleological time, and the dominance of 'atmosphere' above dramatic and narrative forms of progression. It is less the pastoral than conception of theatre as a *scenic poem as a whole* that becomes characteristic. Elinor Fuchs rightly remarks that it is above all 'the lyrical mode, essentially static and reflective, that is the key to linking Foreman back to Stein and Maeterlinck, and horizontally to [American theatre auteur Robert] Wilson and many of his contemporaries creating landscape stagings.'[28] Gertrude Stein simply transferred the artistic logic of her texts to her theatre: the principle of a 'continuous present,' of syntactic and verbal concatenations that mark time seemingly statically (similar to later 'minimal music') but in reality continuously create new accents in subtle variations and loops ... Just as in her texts the representation of reality recedes in favor of the play of words, in a 'Stein theatre' there will be no drama, not even a story; it will be not possible to differentiate protagonists and even roles and identifiable characters will be missing. For postdramatic theatre Stein's aesthetics is of great importance, although more subconsciously so outside America. Bonnie Marranca emphasizes her effect on the avant-garde and performance.[29] After the performance of *Ladies Voices* by the Living Theatre in 1951 (!) [sic] and the occasional performance of other pieces by Gertrude Stein by theatres and companies like the Judson Poets Theatre, La MaMa, the Performance Group and others since the 1960s, it was Richard Foreman (in Germany renowned for his *Doctor Faustus Lights the Lights*, performed in 1982 at the Freie Volksbühne, Berlin) and Robert Wilson who from the 1970s carried a use of language inspired by Stein into the theatre.

Foreman's scenography comprises more than simply set, costume and lighting design. Guy Scarpetta introduces the notion of 'scenic writing' in regard to Foreman's use of space and objects:[30]

It is impossible to isolate one purely scenographic element in Foreman's work. His scenography, in a strict sense – his scenic 'writing' or design, concerning the space, décor and costumes – never ceases to overwhelm traditional functions. There is, without a doubt, one major singularity to Foreman's style: scenic 'writing' is everywhere. Spatial tracing is not simply a phase in the spectacle's preparation – it persistently shows itself off and sets the resulting production in motion.

Foreman's scenography is not a code that one can contrast with others in polymorphic theatre – it cuts across all theatrical codes. Foreman's art, at base, is an art of 'contamination.' The décor intervenes in the action; it is a 'performer.' Characters assume a purely spatial, rhythmic, decorative function. Costumes and props play a dramatic role. In this manner, Foreman explodes the classical oppositions on which theatre has been based, oppositions between décor and action, between animate and inanimate, between the accessory props and the essential ones, between scenographic space and spectacular time. His theatre requires new instruments of analysis; it becomes necessary to think in terms of energy, tension, lines of force and variations of intensity.

Notions like 'variations of intensity' naturally evoke Foreman's best-known performer, Kate Manheim. As the chapter by Geoffrey King and Craig Werner in this book points out, Foreman's work during the 1970s will forever be associated with her acting. Don Shewey describes Manheim as having an 'eerie, spaced out style of delivery and a romantic, Garboesque presence that combine to make even Mr. Foreman's loftiest philosophical concerns urgently personal'.[31] *That persona, it turns out, contains multitudes: first, Richard Foreman on Kate Manheim:*

'What's interesting is that she brought something to my work that I would have rejected,' he said. 'She came to America 10 years ago and got hooked on all these television serials that I would never deign to watch. She loved "I Love Lucy" and "The Honeymooners" and so forth. And the injection of that kind of energy into my pretensions of rarefied intellectual art ... has been tremendously healthy. I'm terribly interested in using the lowest kind of theatrical shtick, but using it in a way that, I hope, has rather subtle, elegant theatrical points to make.'[32]

In a 1977 interview with Florence Falk for the Soho Weekly News, *Manheim discussed her performances, but equally interesting is the way her work is positioned by the interviewer, which gives a sense of how Manheim's persona was read and responded to during her formative years with the Ontological-Hysteric Theatre:*

In Foreman's plays the complementary rituals of exhibitionism and voyeurism liberate Manheim/Rhoda's imagination. Foreman's erotic landscape is a sanctified area in which the proximity to mystic insight might be apprehended. Manheim/Rhoda's performance is a kind of sexual act.

During the course of our conversation there is no hint of the aloof Rhoda who moves through Foreman's plays like a cat in heat, leaving behind and odor of innocence and experience. As Rhoda, she is like Blake's 'little girl lost' who has come into the 'desert wild' and is utterly seduced by it; indeed, she cannot, will not, seek escape from its 'pathless ways.' Hounded and beleaguered by male and female predators, Manheim/Rhoda waits in every place to be raped into the exultant experience of the unknowable.

[...]

In every play Manheim/Rhoda endures physical as well as psychic assaults. In *Pain(t)* (1974), Rhoda and Eleanor enter the 'ring' at the sound of a bell, fight, and release their hold only when the 'round' is over; in *Book of Splendors* Rhoda is rammed into tubes and shoved against walls. Just to show how close the link is between Manheim and Rhoda, it is amusing to learn that this fall Manheim started seeing a masseur to handle her 'body problems.'

I asked Manheim whether she thinks one has to be a masochist to play Rhoda. 'Probably, but I am a conscious masochist, not an organized one. There's something about my acting that I see as an exercise in death, or perhaps I'm learning to die through the physical suffering that takes place on stage …'

[...]

It occurs to me that Manheim sitting opposite me in her mauve smock and Rhoda, lost in her sack dresses, are indistinguishable. Even nudity is part of the costume. Dress and undress together constitute her individual style, her special 'chic' – [Parker] Tyler's word for 'the soul of matter insofar as matter achieves final form.' What costume could be more appropriate to the part-child, part-goddess figure of Rhoda?

In her groundbreaking 1988 study, The Feminist Spectator as Critic, *Jill Dolan analysed Foreman's positioning of Manheim, especially when she performed nude, as an object of the 'male gaze'. Critiquing the deployment of female nudity in his early work – particularly* Sophia = (Wisdom) Part 3: The Cliffs, Pain(t) *and* Book of Splendors *– Dolan emphasizes that 'the intent here is not to condemn the work for trading in the currency of female sexuality, but to show that the preponderance of female nudity implies ideological assumptions that Foreman elsewhere denies'.*[33]

Foreman, then, does control the spectator's gaze to some extent. The female nude is constructed for the male spectator's gaze as a seductive image that Foreman can withhold, obscure, or offer at will …

For Foreman, the spectator's theatrical experience can only

concern the process that is constructed in front of them at the eternally present moment: the reality of the stage picture assembled in time and space, tableau by tableau. His work appeals to immediate perceptions, which he assumes can be purely aesthetic, and can occur in forms and structures that are themselves pure, unencumbered by ideology ... But what would perceptions be without ideology?

... The problem with Foreman's theory of aesthetic rigor and his goal of altering consciousness by changing perceptual patterns is that it presupposes a spectator who is willing to be changed by the works in such a way. A spectator with different, but equally strong, ideological commitments might resist the formal manipulations of the work; she might read into Foreman's pictures in a way that belies his intent.

Foreman attempts to deconstruct the signs he chooses to their phenomenological essence, but for a feminist spectator observing his use of women he cannot go far enough. A woman is never 'a woman is a woman is a woman,' particularly when she is part of a representational frame. An image of a woman cannot merely denote, as might the essential signs Foreman attempts to construct. Placing a woman in a representation always connotes an underlying ideology and presents a narrative driven by male desire that effectively denies women's subjectivity.

Even as he tries to empty his work of anything but pure phenomena, Foreman reveals his operative ideological assumptions ... Foreman's construction of women is not natural or meaningless; it reflects the discourse of women's objectification in the history of representation.

The matter of 'objectification' takes on a more complex light in terms of Manheim's own contributions to the Ontological-Hysteric Theatre, which Foreman discussed in an interview with Ken Jordan in 1990.[34]

    KJ 'Hotel China' was also the first play Kate was in, though she didn't play Rhoda.
    RF Yes ... I've just given an intellectual program for the increasing complexity, the increasing speed, the increasing eroticism of the work. Yet all of these things at the same time can be traced to her influence. Because I was living

with Kate, and a lot of our own psychological sexual interaction and fantasies were plugged into the work because of her presence in the work. She wanted to take her clothes off, she wanted to dare that, and it was important to her as a performer to do that a lot, to be in sexual situations on stage. She wanted to be performing in a livelier rhythm. She wanted to do more dances, eccentric things. So ... at the same time, serving her needs and her desires to do the work in the direction that could also be justified in terms of changing intellectual interests on my part.
[...]

KJ In your use of nudity and erotic behavior, there was a tension between that open sexuality and a coldness in the presentational aspect of the performance, which is opposed to a personality oriented theatre where eroticism is framed differently.

RF It was cold to make the fact of eroticism more present, more palpable, more shocking in a sense ... If the eroticism is presented in a more presentational, naked way, then the audience hopefully has to say, Do I feel awkward confronting this? What is my attitude towards this? Am I being titillated by what I see in front of me?
[...]

KJ You got some flack from feminists at that time.

RF Because of the use of the women as objects, yeah. I mean, a little later on it got a little more sophisticated, but the fact was that the women in the plays were generally passive. Things were being done to them. Rhoda was always being tortured, you know. In 'Boulevard de Paris.' In 'Rhoda in Potatoland,' in most of those plays Rhoda was always put in the most awkward, degrading positions, in a sense. Not necessarily only sexual, but she seemed to be a victim, continually.

KJ So how did you respond to the criticism?

RF I said you're right. I realize that I've been conditioned by my society, and I realize I tend to think of women in those terms. Or tend to somewhat objectify women, to think of women as powerless, that is reflected in my work. What

should one do? I'm reflecting honestly the way I've been made by my society. That was my response in those days. And I'm being factual and honest about what goes on in most twentieth century male minds at this point.
KJ: Kate didn't feel uncomfortable with this?
RF: You know, we didn't talk about it too much. And she ... well, I can't answer for her. But we didn't talk about it too much, and obviously she wasn't too unhappy with it, and in many ways it reflected ways that she understood that women were pictured, and she'd been pictured all her life by the society in which she existed. But of course I slowly changed, and a lot of those feminists who attacked me have been very pleased, or said they've been very pleased, in the last few years to see that the Rhoda character, and the other female characters seemed to be becoming much more willful, and much more dominant psychologically in the plays.

Manheim seldom discusses her approach to acting, but in light of Dolan's critique her exchange with Richard Schechner in 1987 allows room for her own agency in the construction of 'woman' and thus complicates issues of gender in O-HT performance:

Schechner How do you feel about enacting a male consciousness? In the earlier plays you were often naked, an object, and Richard says he wrote those plays by lifting his unconscious right out of his notebooks. You were a big part of that conscious manifestation of Richard Foreman's unconscious. You were both yourself, Kate Manheim, and a figment of this man's unconscious.
Manheim Yeah.
Schechner How does it feel to enact for 17 years the female of a male?
Manheim I didn't think of it that way. I thought of it as a way to get over certain shynesses, particularly about being naked and about speaking out loud. It was sort of my way of getting over certain difficulties. I knew it was the story of our life but I didn't question it in terms of woman and man. Now I'm questioning it a lot but I'm not quite sure I'd put it in terms of sexes.
Schechner How would you put it?

Manheim I've become so sexless over the years, it's another thing I'll have to work on.

Schechner Not so much in *Radio* [*Film Is Evil: Radio Is Good*, 1987] but in the other plays I've seen you in, sexless is the last word I'd use to describe if not you then your persona. But again, it's a male version of sexy – all black silk stockings, the garter belt, the merry widow bra.

Manheim But just a minute, this male gaze, it must not have only to do with Richard because all these costumes were my idea. Richard never said put on a black garter belt …

Schechner Which piece was it, *Sophia* [1973], where you were sitting on the bench – ?

Manheim There I was pretty much completely naked. And it's only since *The Cure* [1986] that I wanted to show the bottom of my legs. Before, even in *Sophia*, there were boots or knee socks. I was always ashamed of the muscles in my calves …

Schechner So this image of Rhoda or Sophia is really Kate Manheim's, not Richard Foreman's? But Richard says that he puts on stage as much as possible what's in his head. If the garter belts are not his cup of tea, if you are selecting the dresses, covering or uncovering the calves – then you are controlling the stage image. The words may be Foreman's, but these plays are so strongly pictorial – what is seen of the female is from you, is your construction.

Manheim Well, yeah. These plays are my way of living my life.

Finally, Neal Swettenham interviewed 'post-Manheim' actors working on a 2004 Foreman show, King Cowboy Rufus, *and relates how performers new to Foreman's theatre find their way into his texts and characters:*[35]

We should begin by laying down one important marker: with reference to Michael Kirby's careful taxonomy of 'acting and not-acting,' Foreman's performers are definitely actors.[36] They have dialogue to speak, 'characters' to explore, worlds to inhabit: this is not a theatre of performers who are essentially 'being themselves,' while executing a series of tasks. The problems arise because that text is *so* unusual, those characters are so fragmented and apparently unmotivated (at least in the Stanislavskian sense), and the worlds inhabited are so remote from any conventional theatrical landscape.

... Along with making audiences dizzy, this also makes life very difficult for the actors. Juliana Francis, the actress playing Suzie, who has worked with Foreman on three previous occasions, describes the experience as:

> Totally disorienting. I've always done experimental work, but I come from a Meisner background, which is very Method ... I find that Richard's work is the most resistant to more traditional acting techniques.

... The specific 'quality' that Foreman seems to be looking for is that of being constantly 'off-balance' both physically and mentally. Juliana Francis describes this as a 'kind of oscillation that he wants you to arrive at, so you never really are in a kind of state that makes you feel secure' ...:

> I remember the first two shows I had to just keep thinking in terms of things like organic brain injury. I just couldn't figure out how to create the behavior in a way that I could understand and that fulfilled what he was asking for us to do. I would give myself impediments, like I would pretend that I had certain kinds of like temporal lobe injuries to justify the kind of behavior that he was pushing us towards ...

NOTES

1 Introduction to the 1970s

1 Robert Patrick, *Kennedy's Children: A Play in Two Acts* (New York: Random House, 1976), 13.

2 Bruce J. Schulman, *The Seventies: The Great Shift in American Culture, Society, and Politics* (New York: Free Press, 2001). Schulman introduces the term 'southernization' in his *From Cotton Belt to the Sunbelt: Federal Policy, Economic Development, and the Transformation of the South, 1938–1980* (Durham, NC: Duke University Press, 1994), and deploys it as a central concept for the 'great shift' in the later book.

3 Jefferson Cowie, *Stayin' Alive: The 1970s and the Last Days of the Working Class* (New York: New Press, distributed by Perseus Distribution, 2010), 77–8.

4 Beth L. Bailey and David R. Farber, *America in the Seventies*, Cultureamerica (Lawrence: University Press of Kansas, 2004), 109.

5 Schulman, *The Seventies*, 68–77.

6 David Frum, *How We Got Here: The 70's, the Decade That Brought You Modern Life, for Better or Worse* (New York: Basic Books, 2000), 251.

7 See David Heathcote, *The 70s House* (New York: Wiley & Sons, 2005).

8 Schulman, *The Seventies*, 148.

9 This account is indebted to Allen J. Matusow, *The Unraveling of America: A History of Liberalism in the 1960s* (Athens: University of Georgia Press, 2009).

10 Daniel Bell, *The End of Ideology. On the Exhaustion of Political Ideas in the Fifties* (Glencoe, IL: Free Press, 1960).

11 For a revealing and more nuanced review of 1950s America, one that substantially questions the image of a passive college

generation, see David Halberstam, *The Fifties* (New York: Random House, 1994).

12 Sean Wilentz, *The Age of Reagan: A History, 1974–2008* (New York: Harper, 2008).

13 Bruce J. Schulman, *From Cotton Belt to Sunbelt: Federal Policy, Economic Development, and the Transformation of the South, 1938–1980* (Durham, NC: Duke University Press, 1994).

14 Richard Hofstadter, *The Paranoid Style in American Politics, and Other Essays* (New York: Knopf, 1965).

15 In this respect, Kevin Phillips's work proved prophetic. See Kevin Phillips, *The Emerging Republican Majority* (Garden City, NY: Anchor Books, 1970).

16 See Francis Wheen, *Strange Days Indeed: The 1970s: The Golden Age of Paranoia* (New York: PublicAffairs, 2010)

2 American Theatre in the 1970s

1 David Frum, *How We Got Here: The 70's, the Decade That Brought You Modern Life, for Better or Worse* (New York: Basic Books, 2000).

2 Todd Gitlin, 'From Universality to Difference: Notes on the Fragmentation of the Idea of the Left', *Contention: Debates in Society, Culture, and Science* 2 (2) (1993): 15–40.

3 Jefferson Cowie, *Stayin' Alive: The 1970s and the Last Days of the Working Class* (New York: New Press, distributed by Perseus Distribution, 2010).

4 Beth L. Bailey and David R. Farber, *America in the Seventies*, Cultureamerica (Lawrence: University Press of Kansas, 2004), 1.

5 Howard Juncker, 'Who Erased the Seventies?', *Esquire* 88 (December 1977): 154. See also Peter N. Carroll, *It Seemed Like Nothing Happened: America in the 1970s* (New Brunswick, NJ: Rutgers University Press, 1990).

6 Bruce J. Schulman, *The Seventies: The Great Shift in American Culture, Society, and Politics* (New York: Free Press, 2001), xi.

7 George Packer, 'The Decade Nobody Knows', *New York Times*, 10 June 2001, http://www.nytimes.com/2001/06/10/books/the-decade-nobody-knows.html (accessed 13 December 2015).

8 Ibid.

9   Schulman, *The Seventies*, 53–77.
10 Matthew Charles Roudané, *American Drama since 1960: A Critical History* (New York and London: Twayne Publishers, Prentice Hall International, 1996), 19.
11 Mark Fearnow, '1970–1990: Disillusionment, Identity and Discovery', in David Krasner (ed.), *A Companion to Twentieth-Century American Drama*, Blackwell Companions to Literature and Culture (Malden, MA: Blackwell, 2005), 423.
12 Samuel L. Leiter, *Ten Seasons: New York Theatre in the Seventies* (New York: Greenwood Press, 1986), xi.
13 James Harding and Cindy Rosenthal, *Restaging the Sixties: Radical Theaters and Their Legacies* (Ann Arbor: University of Michigan Press, 2006).
14 Sally Banes, *Greenwich Village 1963: Avant-Garde Performance and the Effervescent Body* (Durham, NC: Duke University Press, 1993).
15 Allan Tannenbaum, *New York in the 70s: Soho Blues: A Personal Photographic Diary* (New York: Overlook Duckworth, 2012).
16 Leiter, *Ten Seasons*, 1–2.
17 Glen Fowler, 'Union "Guide" to "Fear City" Is Banned by a Court Order', *New York Times*, 13 June 1975.
18 See Jonathan Mahler, *Ladies and Gentlemen, the Bronx Is Burning: 1977, Baseball, Politics, and the Battle for the Soul of a City* (New York: Farrar, Straus and Giroux, 2005).
19 The report was commissioned by the New York Cultural Commission. William J. Baumol, *Study of the New York Theater* (New York: New York City Cultural Council, 1972).
20 Gerald M. Berkowitz, *New Broadways: Theatre across America: Approaching a New Millennium*, rev. edn (New York: Applause, 1997), 212.
21 Leiter, *Ten Seasons*, 4.
22 Gerald M. Berkowitz, *American Drama of the Twentieth Century*, Longman Literature in English Series (London and New York: Longman, 1992), 121.
23 Leiter, *Ten Seasons*, 5.
24 Arnold Aronson, 'American Theatre in Context: 1945–Present', in Don B. Wilmeth and C. W. E. Bigsby, *The Cambridge History of American Theatre* (Cambridge: Cambridge University Press, 2000), 106.

25 Berkowitz, *New Broadways*, 32.
26 C. W. E. Bigsby, *A Critical Introduction to Twentieth-Century American Drama*, Vol. 3, *Beyond Broadway* (Cambridge: Cambridge University Press, 1985), 24.
27 Even as Papp sought to support publicly writers from marginalized identity groups, the Public was rocked by strikes and protests by Latino/a and Asian-American actors who rose up against what they considered to be token efforts to include equal ethnic representation in the Public's shows. As well, Notzake Shange recalls that when *for colored girls* reached the Public 'they took out all my Puerto Ricans, and when I wanted them to include Asians they looked at me like I had lost my mind!'. See Will Power, 'Catching Up with Ntozake Shange', https://www.tcg.org/publications/at/Apr07/shange.cfm (accessed 13 December 2015).
28 Mel Gussow, 'Off- and Off-Off-Broadway', in Wilmeth and Bigsby, *The Cambridge History of American Theatre*, 198.
29 Leiter, *Ten Seasons*, 26. It is estimated that *A Chorus Line* brought more than $40 million to the New York Shakespeare Festival.
30 Martin Gottfried, 'What shall it profit a theatre if …?', *New York Times*, 23 August 1970, sec. 2: 1+, http://search.proquest.com.ezproxy.library.wisc.edu/docview/117965802?accountid=465 (accessed 10 December 2015).
31 Ibid., 63.
32 For information regarding Off- and Off-Off-Broadway theatre, see David Crespy, *Off-Off-Broadway Explosion: How Provocative Playwrights of the 1960s Ignited a New American Theater* (New York: Back Stage Books, 2003); Stephen J. Bottoms, *Playing Underground: A Critical History of the 1960s Off-Off-Broadway Movement*, Theater: Theory/Text/Performance (Ann Arbor: University of Michigan Press, 2004); Christopher Olsen, *Off-Off-Broadway: The Second Wave, 1968–1980* (CreateSpace Independent Publishing Platform, 2011).
33 Bottoms, *Playing Underground*, 344.
34 Elenore Lester, 'The Pass-the-Hat Theater Circuit', *New York Times*, 5 December 1965, http://search.proquest.com.ezproxy.library.wisc.edu/docview/116782281?accountid=465 (accessed 10 December 2015).
35 See Sally Banes, 'Institutionalizing Avant-Garde Performance: A Hidden History of University Patronage in the United States', in James Harding, *Contours of the Theatrical Avant-Garde* (Ann Arbor: University of Michigan Press, 2000), 217–38.

36 During the 1960s almost a million white residents of New York left the city, and the pace accelerated in the early 1970s before levelling off mid-decade. See Stuart W. Little, *After the Fact: Conflict and Consensus: A Report on the First American Congress of Theatre* (New York: Arno, 1975), 18.

37 Christopher Olsen, *Off-Off-Broadway*, 260–5.

38 Ibid., 264.

39 For histories of the regional theatre movement, see the following: Joseph Wesley Zeigler, *Regional Theatre: The Revolutionary Stage* (New York: Da Capo Press, 1977); Stuart W. Little, *Off-Broadway: The Prophetic Theater* (New York: Coward, 1972); Berkowitz, *New Broadways*.

40 Berkowitz (*New Broadways*, 102) elegantly summarizes the differences between the commercial and non-commercial theatres:

> The fact is that every regional resident theatre company loses money, and loses big. According to annual surveys by the Theatre Communications Group, total earned income (primarily for ticket sales, but also including royalties, theatre rentals, merchandising, etc.) averages between 50 and 65 percent of expenses, with some theatres making as little as one-third of their expenses at the box office. When that happens on Broadway a show closes and its backers lose their money, just as if they had invested in a company that went bankrupt. In the resident theatres for the most part, the company happily continues operation, with the missing 35 or 66 percent being made up by sources who believe that the arts aren't *supposed* to be profitable and who don't expect to be repaid.

41 Zeigler, *Regional Theatre*, 188.

42 Berkowitz lists, as examples, Paddy Chayevsky's *The Latent Heterosexual*, Albee's *Box-Mao-Box*, Robert Anderson's *Solitaire/Double Solitaire* and several plays by the long-standing supporters of the resident theatre movement, Jerome Lawrence and Robert E. Lee, particularly *The Night Thoreau Spent in Jail*. Berkowitz, *New Broadways*, 96–7.

43 Philip C. Kolin and Colby H. Kullman, *Speaking on Stage: Interviews with Contemporary American Playwrights* (Tuscaloosa: University of Alabama Press, 1996), 162.

44 Leiter, *Ten Seasons*, 57.

45 Ibid.

46 The terminological and ideological debate did not cease, as evidenced by Robert Brustein's continued commentary as late as 1988. See Robert Brustein, 'The Siren Song of Broadway is a Warning', *New York Times*, 22 May 1988, http://search.proquest.com.ezproxy.library.wisc.edu/docview/110520933?accountid=465 (accessed 14 December 2015).

47 Ibid., 33.

48 For the history of the resident non-profit professional theatre beyond 1970, see Martha LoMonaco, 'Regional/Resident Theatre', in Wilmeth and Bigsby, *The Cambridge History of American Theatre*, 242–6; and Berkowitz, *New Broadways*, 108–23.

49 Miller would return, triumphantly, to Broadway in the 1990s after a series of notable revivals renewed interest in his contemporary work. After London openings and regional American premieres, *The Ride Down Mount Morgan* had a successful run in 1999–2000, the same year the 50th anniversary of *Death of a Salesman* occasioned a Broadway revival starring Brian Dennehy. See June Schlueter, 'American Drama of the 1990s On and Off-Broadway', in Krasner, *A Companion to Twentieth-Century American Drama*, 504–17.

50 Brenda Murphy, 'Albee's Threnodies', in Stephen J. Bottoms, *The Cambridge Companion to Edward Albee* (Cambridge: Cambridge University Press, 2005), 91–107.

51 Bigsby, *Beyond Broadway*, 371.

52 Ibid., 373.

53 Fearnow, 'Disillusionment', in Krasner, *A Companion to Twentieth-Century American Drama*, 427.

54 C. W. E. Bigsby, *Contemporary American Playwrights* (Cambridge: Cambridge University Press, 1999), 20.

55 Krasner, *A Companion to Twentieth-Century American Drama*, 101.

56 Matthew Roudané, 'Plays and Playwrights Since 1970', in Wilmeth and Bigsby, *The Cambridge History of American Theatre*, 57.

57 Leiter, *Ten Seasons*, 101.

58 Raymond Knapp, *The American Musical and the Formation of National Identity* (Princeton, NJ: Princeton University Press, 2006).

59 John Degan, 'Musical Theatre Since World War II', in Wilmeth and Bigsby, *The Cambridge History of American Theatre*, 450.

60 Leiter, *Ten Seasons*, 102.

61 Ibid., 85.
62 Laurence Maslon, 'Broadway', in Wilmeth and Bigsby, *The Cambridge History of American Theatre*, 181. The production was aided, near the end of its run, by a 14-week engagement with Richard Burton in the title role, which led to the making of the 1977 film.
63 See Bigsby, *Beyond Broadway*, 39–62. Berkowitz, *New Broadways*, 140–7.
64 Robert Nov Gordon, *The Purpose of Playing: Modern Acting Theories in Perspective* (Ann Arbor: University of Michigan Press, 2006).
65 William W. Demastes, *Realism and the American Dramatic Tradition* (Tuscaloosa: University of Alabama Press, 2015).
66 Berkowitz, *New Broadways*, 147.
67 Ibid., 167. Mark Fearnow provides a good sampling of both realist and 'new realist' plays that succeeded on Broadway and Off-Broadway in his overview of the period, 'Disillusionment', in Krasner, *A Companion to Twentieth-Century American Drama*, 1.
68 For a fuller discussion, see Mamet's essay 'Realism', in David Mamet, *Writing in Restaurants* (London: Faber, 1988, 1986). See also Michael Quinn, 'Anti-Theatricality and American Ideology: Mamet's Performative Realism', in William W. Demastes, *Realism and the American Dramatic Tradition* (Tuscaloosa: University of Alabama Press, 1996), 235–54.
69 Mamet's *The Woods* also played in 1977 Off-Broadway at the St Nicholas Theatre, starring Peter Weller and Patti Lupone. Back in Chicago, *A Life in the Theatre* was produced at the Goodman Theatre. For a full account of Mamet's meteoric rise in American theatre during the decade, see Johan Callens, 'The Seventies', in C. W. E. Bigsby, *The Cambridge Companion to David Mamet*, Cambridge Companions to Literature (Cambridge and New York: Cambridge University Press, 2004), 41–56.
70 Toby Zinman, 'David Mamet', in *The Methuen Drama Guide to Contemporary American Playwrights* (London: Methuen, 2014), 161.
71 Richard Gottlieb. 'The "Engine" that Drives Playwright David Mamet', *New York Times*, 15 January 1978, D4.
72 C. W. E. Bigsby, *Modern American Drama, 1945–2000* (Cambridge and New York: Cambridge University Press, 2000), 196.

73 See also David Mamet, *The Secret Knowledge: On the Dismantling of American Culture* (New York: Sentinel, 2011). Here, Mamet disavows his earlier liberalism and makes a case for neoliberal capitalism.

74 Quoted in Bottoms, *Playing Underground*, 346.

75 Ibid., 346–7.

76 Arnold Aronson, 'American Theatre in Context', in Wilmeth and Bigsby, *The Cambridge History of American Theatre*, 109. Walter J. Meserve, *An Outline History of American Drama*, 2nd edn (New York: Feedback Theatrebooks and Prospero Press, 1994), 375–80. For a brief overview of earlier American ethnic theatres, see Rachel Shteir, 'Ethnic Theatre in America', in Krasner, *A Companion to Twentieth-Century American Drama*, 18–33.

77 Ann Haugo, 'Native American Drama', in *A Companion to Twentieth-Century American Drama*, 334–51.

78 Bigsby, *A Critical Introduction to Twentieth-Century American Drama*, 3; *Beyond Broadway*, 343–54.

79 Jon D. Rossini, 'Teatro', in Suzanne Bost and Frances R. Aparicio, *The Routledge Companion to Latino/a Literature* (London and New York: Routledge, 2013), 275–86.

80 See Tiffany Ana Lopez, 'Writing Beyond Borders: A Survey of US Latino/a Drama', in Krasner, *A Companion to Twentieth-Century American Drama*, 370–87.

81 Bigsby, *Beyond Broadway*, 395.

82 Leiter, *Ten Seasons*, 103.

83 Stewart F. Lane, *Black Broadway: African Americans on the Great White Way* (Garden City Park, NY: Square One Publishers, 2015), 210.

84 Aronson, 'American Theatre in Context', in Wilmeth and Bigsby, *The Cambridge History of American Theatre*, 131.

85 Samuel O'Connell, 'Fragmented Musicals and 1970s Soul Aesthetic', in Harvey Young (ed.), *The Cambridge Companion to African American Theatre* (online), Cambridge Companions to Literature, 155–73 (Cambridge: Cambridge University Press, 2012), http://dx.doi.org.ezproxy.library.wisc.edu/10.1017/CCO9781139062107 (accessed 11 December 2015). Tellingly, these significant works are not mentioned in Stuart Lane's *Black Broadway*.

86 Ed Bullins incorporated music into a number of his plays, and composed the musical *Home Boy* (produced by the Perry Street Theatre) in 1976.

87 Laurance Maslon, 'Broadway', in Wilmeth and Bigsby, *The Cambridge History of American Theatre*, 181.

88 The live television production of the show in December 2015 (starring Queen Latifah) registered more than 11 million viewers.

89 Mike Sell, 'The Drama of the Black Arts Movement', in Krasner, *A Companion to Twentieth-Century American Drama*, 263–84.

90 See Marc Robinson's chapter on Kennedy in Marc Robinson, *The Other American Drama* (Baltimore, MD: Johns Hopkins University Press, 1997).

91 See for instance Elizabeth Pittman, 'Historical Memory and Embodied Politics as Public Interventions in Amiri Barak's *Slave Ship*', *prefix* 1 (1) (2010): 34. Baraka's engagement with black nationalism began around 1965, following the assassination of Malcolm X, and led to his founding of the Black Arts Repertory Theatre that year. Also relevant was his conversion to Islam in 1968 when he changed his name from LeRoi Jones to Imamu Amiri Baraka.

92 Mike Sell (ed.), *Ed Bullins: Twelve Plays and Selected Writings* (Ann Arbor: University of Michigan Press, 2006).

93 See Sell, 'Drama of the Black Arts Movement', in Krasner, *A Companion to Twentieth-Century American Drama*, 268–9.

94 Roudané, 'Plays and Playwrights Since 1970', in Wilmeth and Bigsby, *The Cambridge History of American Theatre*, 393.

95 John Simon, 'On Stage: "Enuf" Is Not Enough', *New Leader* 59 (14) (1976).

96 It should be noted that, throughout the decade, ritual forms were being explored by many playwrights associated with the Black Arts Movement, such as Baraka, Marvin X and Adrienne Kennedy. See Sell, 'Drama of the Black Arts Movement', in Krasner, *A Companion to Twentieth-Century American Drama*, 271–2.

97 Shange was co-creator, with Jessica Hagedorn and Thulani Davis, of *Where the Mississippi Meets the Amazon*, produced at the Public's Cabaret Theatre in 1977.

98 Leiter, *Ten Seasons*, 83.

99 Ibid., 84.

100 Dinah Luise Leavitt, *Feminist Theatre Groups* (Jefferson, NC: McFarland, 1980); Susan M. Steadman, *Dramatic Re-Visions: An Annotated Bibliography of Feminism and Theatre, 1972–1988* (Chicago: American Library Association, 1991); Charlotte Canning, *Feminist Theaters in the U.S.A.: Staging Women's*

Experience, Gender in Performance (London and New York: Routledge, 1996). See also Olsen, *Off-Off Broadway: The Second Wave*, 151–66.

101 Marvin Carlson, 'Alternative Theatre', in Wilmeth and Bigsby, *The Cambridge History of American Theatre*, 249–93.

102 Erhen Fordyce, 'Experimental Drama at the End of the Century', in David Krasner, *A Companion to Twentieth-Century American Drama* (Malden, MA: Blackwell, 2005), 537–51.

103 Ibid., 276.

104 Bonnie Marranca et al., *The Theatre of Images* (New York: Drama Book Specialists, 1977).

105 Iris Fischer-Smith, *Mabou Mines: Making Avant-Garde Theater in the 1970s* (Ann Arbor: University of Michigan Press, 2010).

106 Mike Vanden Heuvel, 'A Different Kind of Pomo: The Performance Group and the Mixed Legacy of Authentic Performance', in Harding and Rosenthal, *Restaging the Sixties: Radical Theaters and Their Legacies*, 332–52.

107 Berkowitz, *American Drama of the Twentieth Century*, 166.

108 See Fearnow, 'Disillusionment', in Krasner, *A Companion to Twentieth-Century American Drama*, 424–5.

109 Jeffrey Ullom, *The Humana Festival: The History of New Plays at Actors Theatre of Louisville* (Carbondale, IL: Southern Illinois University Press, 2008), 46.

3 David Rabe's Plays of the 1970s

1 Clive Barnes, 'Theater: "Training of Pavlo Hummel"', *New York Times*, 21 May 1971, 25, http://search.proquest.com.ezproxy.library.wisc.edu/docview/119161270?accountid=465 (accessed 17 March 2016).

2 Robert Brustein, 'The Crack in the Chimney: Reflections on Contemporary American Playwriting', *Theater* 9 (2) (1978): 21–9.

3 William W. Demastes and Michael Vanden Heuvel, 'The Hurlyburly Lies of the Causalist Mind: Chaos and the Realism of Rabe and Shepard', in William W. Demastes, *Realism and the American Dramatic Tradition* (Tuscaloosa: University of Alabama Press, 1996), 259.

4 Toby Silverman Zinman, 'What's Wrong with This Picture?

David Rabe's Comic-Strip Plays', in David Rabe and Toby Silverman Zinman, *David Rabe: A Casebook* (New York: Garland, 1991), 31.

5   Ibid., 33.
6   James J. Christy, 'Remembering Bones', in ibid., 120. Christy notes that the MA programme Rabe completed at Villanova was 'dedicated to the development of the original script and to the examination and presentation of the new theatre of Europe which was then dominated by Brecht', and that department 'had a reputation for being avant, especially in its enthusiasm for Brecht'.
7   Sigmund Freud, 'The Uncanny', in Sigmund Freud, *General Psychological Theory: Papers on Metapsychology* (New York: Touchstone, 2008), 129.
8   Ibid., 123–4.
9   Ibid., 156.
10 Walter Benn Michaels, *The Gold Standard and the Logic of Naturalism: American Literature at the Turn of the Century*, New Historicism: Studies in Cultural Poetics (Berkeley: University of California Press, 1987), 173.
11 Arthur Miller, *Timebends: A Life* (New York: Grove Press, 1987), 114.
12 Toby Silverman Zinman, 'Interview', in Rabe and Zinman, *David Rabe: A Casebook*, 4.
13 Craig Werner, 'Primal Screams and Nonsense Rhymes: David Rabe's Revolt', *Educational Theatre Journal* 30 (4) (1978). Werner writes that Rabe's 'rebel characters ultimately fail, but they struggle to articulate their own experience and establish human contact' (518), 517–29.
14 *The Basic Training of Pavlo Hummel* in David Rabe, *Plays: 1* (London: Methuen, 2002), 56. All further references are to this volume and are cited parenthetically.
15 *Sticks and Bones* in ibid., 106. All further references are to this volume and are cited parenthetically.
16 Pamela Cooper, 'David Rabe's "Sticks and Bones": The Adventures of Ozzie and Harriet', *Modern Drama* 24 (4) (1986): 613–25. Cooper notes that the very title of the play comments on the *real* effects of words: 'The title suggests the children's rhyme: "Sticks and stones can break my bones but names can never harm me." Rabe gives the verse ironic effect, for it disclaims the power of psychological violence which the play affirms' (623).

17 Oddly (perhaps), in 1973 Rabe collaborated with Joseph Papp and director Robert Downey on what Cooper called 'a censored and radically altered film script' for a televised version of the play, which aired on CBS (ibid., 613).

18 *Streamers* in Rabe, *Plays: 1*, 153. All further references are to this volume and are cited parenthetically.

19 Robert J. Andreach, *Drawing Upon the Past: Classical Theatre in the Contemporary American Theatre* (New York and Oxford: Peter Lang, 2003), 131.

20 Ibid., 111.

21 Quoted in Andreach, *Drawing Upon the Past*, 131.

22 Les Wade, 'David Rabe and the Female Figure: The Body in the Boom Boom Room', *Text and Performance Quarterly* 12 (1) (1992): 40.

23 Ibid., 52.

24 Stephen Watt, *In Mass Culture's Image: The Subject of (in) Rabe's Boom Boom Rooms* (New York: Garland, 1991), 54.

25 Ibid., 67.

26 Zinman, 'Interview', in Rabe and Zinman, *David Rabe: A Casebook*, 9.

4 Sam Shepard

1 Stanley Kauffmann, 'What Price Freedom?', in Bonnie Marranca, *American Dreams: The Imagination of Sam Shepard* (New York: Performing Arts Journal Publications, 1981), 106.

2 For an excellent study of the Off-Off-Broadway movement and Shepard's place in it, see Stephen J. Bottoms, *Playing Underground: A Critical History of the 1960s Off-Off-Broadway Movement*, Theater: Theory/Text/Performance (Ann Arbor: University of Michigan Press, 2004).

3 Matthew Charles Roudané, *American Drama since 1960: A Critical History* (New York and London: Twayne Publishers, Prentice Hall International, 1996), 207–8.

4 Sam Shepard, 'Visualization, Language and the Inner Library', in Marranca, *American Dreams*, 217.

5 Herbert Blau, 'The American Dream in American Gothic: The

Plays of Sam Shepard and Adrienne Kennedy', *Modern Drama* 27 (4) (1984): 524.

6   Philip C. Kolin, *American Playwrights since 1945: A Guide to Scholarship, Criticism, and Performance* (New York: Greenwood Press, 1988), 395.

7   Thomas Adler, 'Repetition and Regression in *Curse of the Starving Class* and *Buried Child*', in Matthew Charles Roudané, *The Cambridge Companion to Sam Shepard* (Cambridge and New York: Cambridge University Press, 2002), 111.

8   For additional historical context, see Leslie A. Wade, *Sam Shepard and the American Theatre*, Contributions in Drama and Theatre Studies (Westport, CT: Greenwood Press, 1997).

9   For a fuller contextualization of Shepard's work within American socioeconomic and cultural history, see ibid.

10 John Hellmann, *American Myth and the Legacy of Vietnam* (New York: Columbia University Press, 1986).

11 See Wade, *Sam Shepard*, 95–6.

12 Blau, 'American Gothic', 526.

13 David J. DeRose, *Sam Shepard* (New York and Toronto: Twayne, 1992), 96.

14 C. W. E. Bigsby, *Modern American Drama, 1945–2000* (Cambridge and New York: Cambridge University Press, 2000), 163.

15 Carol Rosen. '"Emotional Territory": An Interview with Sam Shepard', *Modern Drama* 36 (1) (1993): 5.

16 Ibid.

17 Carol Rosen, *Sam Shepard: A 'Poetic Rodeo'* (New York: Palgrave Macmillan, 2004), 123.

18 Rosen, 'Emotional Territory', 5.

19 Sam Shepard and Joseph Chaikin, *Seven Plays* (Toronto and New York: Bantam Books, 1981), 174.

20 For autobiographical details, see James A. Crank, *Understanding Sam Shepard*, Understanding Contemporary American Literature (Columbia: University of South Carolina Press, 2012), 39–41.

21 Bottoms, *Theatre of Sam Shepard*, 152.

22 Benedict Nightingale, 'Only When We Laugh', *New Statesman*, 29 April 1977, 577; Charles Marowitz, 'Is This Shepard or Saroyan?', *New York Times*, 15 May 1977, 3.

23 Harold Clurman, 'Review of "Curse of the Starving Class"', *Nation*, 25 March 1978, 348.
24 Martin Duberman, 'The Great White Way', *Harper's* (May 1978): 79–80, 83–7.
25 Crank, *Understanding Sam Shepard*, 38. He also notes that the 1985 revival 'led to an embarrassing cable television remake in 1994' (39).
26 Bottoms, *Theatre of Sam Shepard*, 158.
27 Michael Taav, *A Body across the Map: The Father–Son Plays of Sam Shepard*, Artists and Issues in the Theatre (New York: Peter Lang, 2000), 37.
28 Adler, 'Repetition and Regression', 117.
29 Rosen, *Sam Shepard*, 127.
30 Kleb, 'Sam Shepard', 397.
31 Lynda Hart, *Sam Shepard's Metaphorical Stages*, Contributions in Drama and Theatre Studies (Westport, CT: Greenwood Press, 1987), 75–6.
32 Bottoms, *Theatre of Sam Shepard*, 178. See also Tucker Orbison, 'Authorization and Subversion of Myth in Shepard's *Buried Child*', *Modern Drama* 37 (3) (1994): 509–20; and Bert Cardullo, *American Drama/Critics: Writings and Readings* (Newcastle: Cambridge Scholars, 2007), 119.
33 Hart, *Metaphorical Stages*, 80.
34 Orbison, 'Authorization and Subversion', 509.
35 Steven Putzel and Suzanne Westfall, 'The Back Side of Myth: Sam Shepard's Subversion of Mythic Codes in *Buried Child*', *Journal of Dramatic Theory and Criticism* 4 (1) (1989): 121.
36 Thomas Nash, 'Sam Shepard's *Buried Child*: The Ironic Use of Folklore', *Modern Drama* 26 (4) (1983): 486–91.
37 Taav, *A Body across the Map*, 56.
38 Wade, *Sam Shepard and the American Theatre*, 102.
39 Ibid.
40 Taav, *A Body across the Map*, 63–4.
41 See Una Chaudhuri's interpretation of the scene, in which 'this unearthed body is the sign that retroactively engages the literalist, superficial code of the play, devalorizing such mythemes as the corn (= fertility), the haircut (= castration), the lost leg (= impotence). Brought to the surface, the body exemplifies a

discourse of surface, whereby meanings are produced by the lateral associations of intertextuality rather than the deep resonances of myth.' Una Chaudhuri, *Staging Place: The Geography of Modern Drama*, Theater: Theory/Text/Performance (Ann Arbor: University of Michigan Press, 1995), 111.

42 See Crank, *Understanding Sam Shepard*, 61–4.
43 Putzel and Westfall, 'Back Side of Myth', 109.
44 Crank, *Understanding Sam Shepard*, 87–8.
45 Don Shewey, 'The True Story of "True West"', *Village Voice*, 30 November 1982, 115.
46 See Crank, *Understanding Sam Shepard*, 85–6; Wade, *Sam Shepard and the American Theatre*, 108–9; and Shewey, ibid.
47 See Crank, *Understanding Sam Shepard*, 61–2.
48 Ibid., 91.
49 Wade, *Sam Shepard and the American Theatre*, 104.
50 Tucker Orbison, 'Mythic Levels in Shepard's *True West*', *Modern Drama* 27 (4) (1984): 517.
51 Wade, *Sam Shepard and the American Theatre*, 131.
52 Ibid., 132.
53 For Shepard's 'late phase' and a revealing study of Shepard's remediations of past themes and styles in work after 1988, see Shannon Blake Skelton, '"Days with Age Hanging Off Me Like Dry Moss": The Late Work of Sam Shepard, 1988–2010', Order No. 3589179, University of Wisconsin – Madison, 2013 (Ann Arbor: ProQuest, Web, 6 July 2015). Similar material is included in his book *The Late Work of Sam Shepard* (Methuen Drama, 2016).

5 Ntozake Shange

1 Ntozake Shange, *for colored girls who have considered suicide, when the rainbow is enuf: a choreopoem* (Toronto and New York: Bantam, 1980), 9. All further references are to this volume and cited parenthetically.
2 Claudia Tate, *Black Women Writers at Work* (New York: Continuum, 1983), 149.
3 Stella Dong, '*Publishers Weekly* Interviews Ntozake Shange', *Publishers Weekly*, 3 May 1985, 75.

4   Henry Blackwell, 'An Interview with Ntozake Shange', *Black American Literature* 13 (4) (1979): 135.
5   Ntozake Shange, 'Ntozake Shange Interviews Herself', *Ms.*, December 1977, 72.
6   Margaret B. Wilkerson (ed.), *9 Plays by Black Women* (New York: Continuum International Publishing Group, 1984), 239.
7   Tate, *Black Women Writers at Work*, 154.
8   John Simon, 'Enuf Is Not Enough', *New Leader,* July 1976, 21.
9   Clive Barnes, 'Clive Barnes on *For Colored Girls* ... by Ntozake Shange', in Ben Brantley (ed.), *The New York Times Book of Broadway: On the Aisle for the Unforgettable Plays of the Last Century* (New York: St Martin's Press, 2001), 198.
10 Appears in the review section of Ntozake Shange and Ifa Bayeza's *Some Sing, Some Cry: A Novel* (2010).
11 Ibid.,14–15.
12 Paul C. Harrison, 'Mother/Word. Black Theatre in the African Continuum: Word/Song as Method', in Paul C. Harrison (ed.), *Totem Voices: Plays from the Black World Repertory* (New York: Grove Press, 1989), xlii.
13 Shange, *for colored girls*, 2–3.
14 Mervyn Rothstein, 'Women Playwrights: Themes and Variations', *New York Times*, 7 May 1989, http://www.nytimes.com/1989/05/07/theater/theater-women-playwrights-themes-and-variations.html (accessed 21 January 2016).
15 Diana Martha Louis, 'Bitch You Must Be Crazy: Representations of Mental Illness in Ntozake Shange's *for colored girls who have considered suicide /when the rainbow is enuf* (1976)', *Western Journal of Black Studies* 37 (3) (2013): 198–9.
16 See Marilyn Stasio, 'Shange Casts a Mixed Spell', *New York Post*, 5 June 1979, 107–8; Steven Winn, 'Shange's Sometimes Provocative Spell', *San Francisco Chronicle*, 26 March 1985, 44; John Simon, 'Fainting Spell', *New York Magazine*, 30 July 1979, 57; Onye Wambu, 'Broken Spell', *The Voice* (April 1985).
17 Sterling A. Brown, 'Negro Character as Seen by White Authors', *Journal of Negro Education* 2 (2) (1993): 179–203.
18 Karen Cronacher, 'Unmasking the Minstrel Mask's Black Magic in Ntozake Shange's "spell #7"', *Theatre Journal* 44 (2) (1992): 178.
19 *spell #7* in Ntozake Shange, *Three Pieces* (New York: St Martin's

Press, 1981), 125. All further references are to this volume and cited parenthetically.

20 Lynda Murdin, 'The Colors of Bitterness', *The Standard* (1985): '*Spell Number* #7 demands and fully expects sympathy for the various characters depicted by a group of actors and artists gathered in a Manhattan bar, but conveys no compassion itself for those beyond black society ... Ms. Shange insults us all: suggesting no promotion of racial harmony herself, she expects the same attitude from others.' See also Suzie Mackenzie, 'Spell #7 (Donmar Warehouse)', *Time Out*, April 1985. Mackenzie registered this same defensive posturing about what Shange offers for the psychological and emotional health of black actors and black people, posing the question, 'Can't you celebrate being black without denigrating being white?'

21 Ibid., 113.

22 Ntozake Shange, *boogie woogie landscapes* in ibid., 113. All further references are to this volume and cited parenthetically.

23 Judith Weinrub, 'A Touring Black Troupe Begins Its Journey', *Washington Star*, 15 June 1980.

24 Shange, *Three Pieces*, book jacket.

25 Joseph McLellan, *Washington Post* 20 June 1980, C6, called the piece a 'Bungled *boogie*', and Judith Martin, *Washington Post* 27 June 1980, C4, called the choreopoem 'A Scattered *Landscape*'. Martin, like others, found the dream structure aesthetically unsatisfying: 'What is lacking is organization of this material. There is no point of view ... The playwright does not abide by her own definition and observe any limitations of character place.' On the other hand, C. W. E. Bigsby, in *A Critical Introduction to Twentieth-Century American Drama (Volume 3: Beyond Broadway)* (Cambridge: Cambridge University Press, 1985), describes *boogie*: 'A lament for the forces which conspire to limit the freedom of women, to deform their sensibility, and damage their spirit, it is, nonetheless, a lyrical celebration. And this is the paradox with which Ntozake Shange has saddled herself. The grace of movement, the polyphony of sound, the shaping power of poetry inevitably resist the threat of anarchy which she observes' (413–14).

26 Sharon Blake, 'Pitt's Kuntu Repertory Theatre Presents Lavender Lizards and Lilac Landmines: Layla's Dream', *University of Pittsburgh News Services*, 18 March 2008. http://www.news.pitt.edu/news/

pitts-kuntu-repertory-theatre-presents-lavender-lizards-and-lilac-landmines-laylas-dream (accessed 28 September 2016).

27   Scott C. Morgan, 'Theater: Lavender Lizards and Lilac Landmines: Layla's Dream', *Windy City Times*, 23 February 2005. http://www.windycitymediagroup.com/lgbt/Theater-Lavender-Lizards-and-Lilac-Landmines-Laylas-Dream/7489.html (accessed 28 September 2016).

28   Shange, *Three Pieces*, 125.

29   Rita Williams-Garcia, 'Giving Thanks', *The Horn Book Magazine* (November/December 2011), 63.

30   For example, *Daddy Says* appears in *New Plays from the Black Theatre*, edited by Woodie King, Jr, (Chicago: Third World Press, 1989), *for colored girls* in Clive Barnes' *Best American Plays, 1974–1982* (New York: Crown Publishers, 1983) and *Totem Voices: Plays from the Black World Repertory*, edited by Paul Carter Harrison (New York: Grove Press, 1988). *The Resurrection of the Daughter: Liliane* appears in *Moon Marked and Touched by Sun: Plays by African-American Women*, edited by Sydne Mahone (New York: Theatre Communications Group, 1994), and *spell #7* in *9 Plays by Black Women*, edited by Margaret B. Wilkerson (New York: New American Library, 1986). *for colored girls*, *spell #7* and *The Love Space Demands* appear in the Contemporary Dramatists volume *Ntozake Shange Plays: One* (London: Methuen Drama, 1992).

31   Michael Earley and Philippa Keil (eds), *The Contemporary Monologue: Women* (London: Routledge, 1995), 65.

32   Ibid., back cover.

33   Will Power, 'Catching Up with Ntozake Shange: An Interview', *American Theatre* (April 2007), 31.

34   Anna D. Smith, *Fires in the Mirror: Crown Heights, Brooklyn, and Other Identities* (New York: Bantam Doubleday Dell Publishing Group, Inc., 1993), xv.

35   See, for instance, James Able et al.'s *For Colored Guys Who Have Considered Suicide and Found No Rainbow: A Choreopoem/Drama* (Baltimore, MD: New Poets Series, Inc., 1986), Keith Antar Mason's *for black boys who have considered homicide when the streets were too much* (New York: Plume, 1993), Keith Boykin's edited collection *For Colored Boys Who Have Considered Suicide When the Rainbow Is Still Not Enough: Coming of Age, Coming Out, and Coming Home* (New York: Magnus Books, 2012), Robert Styles's *Not Just for Colored Boys: Our Struggle* (Rolest Publishing, Inc., 2011), D. L. Simon's *For Colored Guys: A Gospel Stage Play*

	(2011), Kristiana Colón's *bt I cd only whisper* (2006) and Erika and Ntare Ali Gault's *Ain't She Brave* (2014).
36	Roger Ebert, 'For Colored Girls', *Roger Ebert*, 3 November 2010, http://www.rogerebert.com/reviews/for-colored-girls-2010 (accessed 17 March 2016).
37	Kirk Honeycutt, 'For Colored Girls: Film Review', *Hollywood Reporter*, 21 October 2010, http://www.hollywoodreporter.com/review/colored-girls-film-review-32056 (accessed 22 October 2015).
38	The film's soundtrack of 13 tunes, *For Colored Girls: Music From and Inspired by the Original Motion Picture* (2010), includes accomplished singers Macy Gray, Janelle Monae, Nina Simone, Ledisi, Leona Lewis, Estelle, Gladys Knight, Lalah Hathaway, Sharon Jones and the Dap Kings.
39	Personal interview, 27 August 1986.
40	It is not unsurprising then that many, especially women of colour, have embraced and celebrated Shange's individual poems to protest, document and legitimize their lived experiences. For instance, the website *Miss Moon's Musings* is a feminist blog that includes at least two poems from *for colored girls* to communicate realities about the lives of women of colour. 'stuff' and 'no assistance' are printed on the site along with videos of recorded performances of them (http://missmoonsmusings.blogspot.com/2010/01/dope-somebody-almost-walked-off-wid.html), while 'sorry' is highlighted on the website *AfroPoets* (http://www.afropoets.net/ntozakeshange.html) (both accessed 17 March 2016).
41	Felicia R. Lee, 'Schomburg Center Plans Exhibition on "For Colored Girls"', *New York Times*, 8 September 2014.
42	Susana Morris, 'Ntozake Shange's "for colored girls" Turns 40', *About News*, http://womensissues.about.com/od/artscreativity/fl/Ntozake-Shangersquos-for-colored-girls-Turns-40.htm (accessed 17 March 2016).
43	Personal email, 25 March 2015.

6 Richard Foreman

1	Richard Foreman, 'Ontological-Hysteric Theatre', http://www.ontological.com/notebooks.html (accessed 17 March 2016).

2   Richard Foreman, *Plays and Manifestoes* (New York: New York University Press, 1976), 19.
3   David Savran, 'Both Halves of Richard Foreman: The Playwright. Interview with David Savran', 1987, in Gerald Rabkin, *Richard Foreman*, Paj Books Art + Performance (Baltimore: Johns Hopkins University Press, 1999), 118.
4   Ibid., 118–19.
5   Richard Foreman, 'The Carrot and the Stick', in Rabkin, *Richard Foreman*, 170.
6   Richard Foreman and Ken Jordan, *Unbalancing Acts: The Theater of Richard Foreman* (New York: Pantheon Books, 1992), 38–9.
7   Ibid., 64.
8   Bonnie Marranca (ed.), *The Theatre of Images* (New York: Drama Book Specialists, 1977), 13–14.
9   Foreman and Jordan, *Unbalancing Acts*, 55.
10 Richard Schechner, 'The Decline and Fall of the (American) Avant-Garde', *Performing Arts Journal* 5 (2) (1981): 50.
11 Rabkin, *Richard Foreman*, 115.
12 Ibid., 47.
13 Ibid., 42.
14 Foreman and Jordan, *Unbalancing Acts*, 41–2.
15 Rabkin, *Richard Foreman*, 24.
16 Foreman and Jordan, *Unbalancing Acts*, 17.
17 Ibid., 54.
18 Peter Handke, *Kaspar and Other Plays* (New York: Farrar, Straus, 1969), 7.
19 Richard Foreman, 'How I Write My (Plays: Self)', *The Drama Review: TDR* 21 (4) (1977): 5–24.
20 Foreman and Jordan, *Unbalancing Acts: The Theater of Richard Foreman*, 12.
21 Ibid., 13.
22 William Burroughs, 'The Cut Up Method', in Leroi Jones (ed.), *The Moderns: An Anthology of New Writing in America* (New York: Corinth Books, 1963), 347.
23 Both essays are found in Richard Schechner, *Public Domain; Essays on the Theater* (Indianapolis: Bobbs-Merrill, 1969).

24 Ed Bullins and New Lafayette Theatre, *The New Lafayette Theatre Presents* (Garden City, NY: Anchor Press, 1974).
25 Richard Foreman, *Sophia: The Cliffs/ 35+ Year Retrospective – Ontological-Hysteric Theater*, DVD, produced by Jay Sanders, Tzadik, 2009.
26 T. S. Eliot, *Selected Essays* (New York: Harcourt, 1950), 124–5.
27 Foreman, *Plays and Manifestoes*, 130. All subsequent quotations are from this edition and cited parenthetically.
28 Marranca, *The Theatre of Images*, 12–13. All subsequent quotations are from this edition.
29 Foreman and Jordan, *Unbalancing Acts*, 14.
30 Rabkin, *Richard Foreman*, 71.
31 Richard Foreman, *The Manifestos and Essays* (New York: Theatre Communications Group, 2013), 53.
32 *Plays and Manifestoes*, 207.
33 Rabkin, *Richard Foreman*, 101.
34 Ibid., 124.

Afterword

1 The lack of identifiably conservative (rather than 'Conservative') playwrights in America is an ongoing topic of discussion. A *New York Times* article entitled 'Liberal Views Dominate Footlights' is representative: it begins, 'During this election season theatregoers in New York can see a dozen or so overtly political plays, about Iraq, Washington corruption, feminism or immigration; what they won't see are any with a conservative perspective.' Patricia Cohen, 'Liberal Views Dominate Footlights', *New York Times*, 15 October 2008, http://search.proquest.com.ezproxy.library.wisc.edu/docview/897753884?accountid=465 (accessed 17 March 2016). To date, there is no American equivalent to John Bull's study of conservative and right wing theatre in Britain. See John Bull, *Stage Right: Crisis and Recovery in British Contemporary Mainstream Theatre* (New York: St Martin's Press, 1994).
2 *The Methuen Drama Guide to Contemporary American Playwrights* (London: Methuen Drama, 2014), xiv.
3 Shannon Blake Skelton, '"Days with Age Hanging Off Me Like

Dry Moss": The Late Work of Sam Shepard, 1988–2010', PhD diss., University of Wisconsin-Madison, 2013.

4   See the earlier chapter in this book on Shepard for information regarding these revisions. Shepard hoped to see his 1994 play, *Simpatico*, staged on Broadway, but efforts to raise the more than $800,000 needed to stage it fell short.

5   Leslie A. Wade, *Sam Shepard and the American Theatre* (Westport, CT: Greenwood Press, 1997), 159.

6   In Matthew Charles Roudané, *The Cambridge Companion to Sam Shepard* (Cambridge and New York: Cambridge University Press, 2002), 287–8.

7   Rosen, *Sam Shepard*, 152.

8   Wade, *Sam Shepard and the American Theatre*, 259.

9   James A. Crank, *Understanding Sam Shepard* (Columbia: University of South Carolina Press, 2012), 112.

10 See Shannon Blake Skelton, *The Late Work of Sam Shepard* (London: Methuen Drama, 2016).

11 Chad Hammett (ed.), *2 Prospectors: The Letters of Sam Shepard & Johnny Dark*, 1st edn (Austin: University of Texas Press, 2013).

12 This was a trope used by Reagan as far back as a speech by that title in 1970 made while Governor of California, and repeated in his declaration of his first candidacy for the Republican presidential nomination in 1976. He also evoked the phrase at key points during his two terms as President. See Bernard von Bothmer, *Framing the Sixties: The Use and Abuse of a Decade from Ronald Reagan to George W. Bush* (Amherst: University of Massachusetts Press, 2010), 35.

13 Philip C. Kolin, *David Rabe: A Stage History and a Primary and Secondary Bibliography*, Garland Reference Library of the Humanities (New York: Garland, 1988), 99.

14 For instance, Rabe does not appear in *The Methuen Drama Guide to Contemporary American Playwrights*. In Roudané's *Drama Since 1960* (Twayne, 1996), only his work through to *Hurlyburly* is covered in detail. The last scholarly book devoted to Rabe was Zinman's *David Rabe: A Casebook* (New York: Garland, 1991).

15 David Savran, 'Ambivalence, Utopia, and a Queer Sort of Materialism: How "Angels in America" Reconstructs the Nation', *Theatre Journal* 47 (2) (1995), 207–27.

16 Charles Isherwood, 'The Burden of a World of Pain', *New York*

Times, 17 November 2015, www.lexisnexis.com/hottopics/lnacademic (accessed 2 January 2016).

17 Chris Jones, 'David Rabe at Gift Theatre: A Debut from the Bard of Vietnam Era', *Chicago Tribune*, 10 September 2015, http://www.chicagotribune.com/entertainment/theater/ct-ae-0913-fall-theater-profile-20150910-column.html (accessed 17 March 2016).

18 Sandra L. Richards, 'Conflicting Impulses in the Plays of Ntozake Shange', *Black American Literature Forum* 17 (2) (1983): 73. Frantz Fanon, *Studies in a Dying Colonialism* (New York: Monthly Review Press, 1965). Shange quotes the passage in the preface to Ntozake Shange, *Three Pieces* (New York: St Martin's Press, 1981), xiii.

19 Hilton Als, 'Color Vision: Ntozake Shange's Outspoken Art', *New Yorker* 86 (35) (2010), http://www.newyorker.com/magazine/2010/11/08/color-vision (accessed 26 October 2015).

20 P. Jane Splawn, 'An Intimate Talk with Ntozake Shange: An Interview', in Jacqueline Bobo, *Black Women Film and Video Artists*, Afi Film Readers (New York: Routledge, 1998), 189–206.

21 Will Power, 'Catching up with Ntozake Shange: Her Innovations in Stage Verse and Movement Have Inspired a New Generation (Interview)', *American Theatre* 24 (4) (2007), https://www.tcg.org/publications/at/Apr07/shange.cfm (accessed 17 March 2016).

22 Ibid.

23 Richard Foreman and Ken Jordan, *Unbalancing Acts: The Theater of Richard Foreman* (New York: Pantheon Books, 1992), 85.

24 The phrase comes from Jerome J. McGann, *Radiant Textuality: Literature after the World Wide Web*, 1st edn (New York: Palgrave, 2001).

Documents

1 Samuel L. Leiter, *Ten Seasons: New York Theatre in the Seventies* (New York: Greenwood Press, 1986). See also *Thirty Years After: New Essays on Vietnam War Literature, Film, and Art* (Newcastle upon Tyne: Cambridge Scholars, 2009).

2 Michael Herr, *Dispatches* (New York: Knopf, 1977), 19–20.

3 Joseph Wesley Zeigler, *Regional Theatre: The Revolutionary Stage* (New York: Da Capo, 1977), 228–9.

4   David Savran, *In Their Own Words: Contemporary American Playwrights* (New York: Theatre Communications Group, 1988), 202–3.

5   Helen Epstein, *Joe Papp: An American Life* (New York: Da Capo, 1996), 275, 280–1.

6   Albin Krebs, 'Paley, C. B. S. Chairman, Personally Vetoed Showing of "Sticks and Bones"', *New York Times*, 20 March 1973, 78.

7   Sam Shepard, 'Language, Visualization, and the Inner Library', in Bonnie Marranca, *American Dreams: The Imagination of Sam Shepard* (New York: Performing Arts Journal Publications, 1981), 217.

8   John Glore, 'The Canonization of Mojo Rootforce: Sam Shepard Live at the Pantheon', *Theater* 12 (3) (1981): 57.

9   Sam Shepard, *Rolling Thunder Logbook* (New York: Penguin Books, 1978), 31.

10 Robert Brustein, 'The Crack in the Chimney: Reflections on Contemporary American Playwriting', *Theater* 9 (2) (1978): 24.

11 William Demastes and Michael Vanden Heuvel, 'The Hurlyburly Lies of the Causalist Mind: Chaos and the Realism of Rabe and Shepard', in William W. Demastes, *Realism and the American Dramatic Tradition* (Tuscaloosa: University of Alabama Press, 1996), 267.

12 Bonnie Marranca, 'Alphabetical Shepard: The Play of Words', in Marranca, *American Dreams: The Imagination of Sam Shepard*, 20–1.

13 See also Marc Robinson, 'Joseph Chaikin and Sam Shepard in Collaboration', in Matthew Roudané (ed.), *The Cambridge Companion to Sam Shepard* (Cambridge and New York: Cambridge University Press, 2002), 83–110.

14 Eileen Blumenthal, *Joseph Chaikin: Exploring at the Boundaries of Theater*, Directors in Perspective (Cambridge and New York: Cambridge University Press, 1984), 176–7.

15 Jeannette R. Malkin, *Memory-Theater and Postmodern Drama* (Ann Arbor, University of Michigan Press, 1999), 119.

16 From Samuel Beckett, 'Enueg II', in Samuel Beckett, *Echo's Bones, and Other Precipitates* (Paris: Europa Press, 1935), 262, 101.

17 From Brecht's 'Alles Wandelt Sich' ('Everything Changes'), in Bertolt Brecht, Reinhold Grimm and Caroline Molina y Vedia, *Bertolt Brecht: Poetry and Prose*, German Library (New York: Continuum, 2003), 125.

18 Robert Staples, 'The Myth of Black Macho: A Response to Angry Black Feminists', *Black Scholar* 10 (1979), 24–32. See also the response by Neal A. Lester, 'Shange's Men: *For Colored Girls* Revisited, and Movement Beyond', *African American Review* 26 (2) (1992), 319–28.

19 Sandra Hollin Flowers, 'Colored Girls: Textbook for the Eighties', *Black American Literature Forum* 15 (2) (1981) 52. Hilton Als, 'Color Vision: Ntozake Shange's Outspoken Art', *New Yorker* 86 (35) (2010), http://www.newyorker.com/magazine/2010/11/08/color-vision.

20 Andrea Benton Rushing, 'For Colored Girls: Suicide or Struggle', *Massachusetts Review: A Quarterly of Literature, the Arts and Public Affairs* 22 (3) (1981), 545.

21 Serena Anderlini, 'Drama or Performance Art? An Interview with Ntozake Shange', *Journal of Dramatic Theory and Criticism* 6 (1) (1991), 85–97.

22 Ntozake Shange, 'A Foreword to *Three Pieces*,' reprinted in Ntozake Shange, *See No Evil: Prefaces, Essays & Accounts, 1976–1983* (San Francisco: Momo's Press, 1984), 18.

23 'Ntozake Shange Interviews Herself', *Ms.* 6 (1977), 34–5, 70–2.

24 Gerald Rabkin, *Richard Foreman*, Paj Books Art + Performance (Baltimore: Johns Hopkins University Press, 1999).

25 Richard Foreman, 'Ontological-Hysteric Theatre', http://www.ontological.com/notebooks.html (accessed 17 March 2016).

26 See, as one example, Marc Robinson, *The Other American Drama* (Baltimore: Johns Hopkins University Press, 1997).

27 Lehmann's note reads 'As cited in E. Fuchs, Elinor Fuchs, *The Death of Character: Perspectives on Theater after Modernism* (Indianapolis: Indiana University Press, 1996). p. 93.'

28 Ibid., 102.

29 Bonnie Marranca, *Ecologies of Theater: Essays at the Century Turning* (Baltimore: Johns Hopkins University Press, 1996).

30 Guy Scarpetta, 'Richard Foreman's Scenography: Examples from His Work in France', *The Drama Review* 28 (2) (102) (1984), 23.

31 Don Shewey, 'Richard Foreman Remains Provocative', *New York Times*, 15 May 1983, http://www.nytimes.com/1983/05/15/theater/richard-foreman-remains-provocative.html?pagewanted=all (accessed 12 December 2015)

32 Ibid.

33 Jill Dolan, *The Feminist Spectator as Critic*, Theater and Dramatic Studies (Ann Arbor, MI: UMI Research Press, 1988), 51.

34 Ken Jordan, 'Interview with Richard Foreman', 1990, http://www.ontological.com/Interviews/InterviewWithKenJordan1990.html (accessed 16 March 2016).

35 Neal Swettenham, 'The Actor's Problem: Performing the Plays of Richard Foreman', *New Theatre Quarterly* 24 (1) (93) (2008), 68.

36 Michael Kirby, 'On Acting and Non-Acting', in Phillip B. Zarrilli, *Acting (Re)Considered: A Theoretical and Practical Guide* (London and New York: Routledge, 2002), 43–58.

BIBLIOGRAPHY

Books on America in the 1970s

Bailey, Beth L. and David R. Farber. *America in the Seventies.* Cultureamerica. Lawrence: University Press of Kansas, 2004.

Berkowitz, Edward D. *Something Happened: A Political and Cultural Overview of the Seventies.* New York: Columbia University Press, 2006.

Booker, Christopher. *The Seventies: The Decade That Changed the Future.* New York: Stein and Day, 1981.

Frum, David. *How We Got Here: The 70's, the Decade That Brought You Modern Life, for Better or Worse.* New York: Basic Books, 2000.

Sagert, Kelly Boyer. *The 1970s.* American Popular Culture through History. Westport, CT: Greenwood Press, 2007.

Sandbrook, Dominic. *Mad as Hell: The Crisis of the 1970s and the Rise of the Populist Right.* New York: Alfred A. Knopf, 2011.

Schulman, Bruce J. *The Seventies: The Great Shift in American Culture, Society, and Politics.* New York: Free Press, 2001.

Schulman, Bruce J. and Julian E. Zelizer. *Rightward Bound: Making America Conservative in the 1970s.* Cambridge, MA: Harvard University Press, 2008.

Tannenbaum, Allan. *New York in the 70s: Soho Blues: A Personal Photographic Diary.* New York: Overlook Duckworth, 2012.

Wilentz, Sean. *The Age of Reagan: A History, 1974–2008.* New York: Harper, 2008.

Books on American theatre

Berkowitz, Gerald M. *American Drama of the Twentieth Century.* Longman Literature in English Series. London and New York: Longman, 1992.

Berkowitz, Gerald M. *New Broadways: Theatre across America: Approaching a New Millennium*. Rev. edn. New York: Applause, 1997.

Bigsby, C. W. E. *A Critical Introduction to Twentieth-Century American Drama*. Vol. 3, *Beyond Broadway*. Cambridge: Cambridge University Press, 1985.

Bigsby, C. W. E. *Contemporary American Playwrights*. Cambridge: Cambridge University Press, 1999.

Bigsby, C. W. E. *Modern American Drama, 1945–2000*. Cambridge and New York: Cambridge University Press, 2000.

Brantley, Ben. *The New York Times Book of Broadway: On the Aisle for the Unforgettable Plays of the Last Century*. New York: St Martin's Press, 2001.

Bryer, Jackson R. and Mary C. Hartig, eds. *The Facts on File Companion to American Drama*. 2nd edn. New York: Facts On File, 2010.

Kolin, Philip C. *American Playwrights since 1945: A Guide to Scholarship, Criticism, and Performance*. New York: Greenwood Press, 1988.

Krasner, David. *A Companion to Twentieth-Century American Drama*. Blackwell Companions to Literature and Culture. Malden, MA: Blackwell, 2005.

Krasner, David. *American Drama 1945–2000: An Introduction*. Blackwell Introductions to Literature. Malden, MA, and Oxford: Blackwell, 2006.

Middeke, Martin, Peter Paul Schnierer, Christopher Innes and Matthew C. Roudané, eds. *The Methuen Drama Guide to Contemporary American Playwrights*. London: Methuen Drama, 2014.

Robinson, Marc. *The Other American Drama*. Baltimore: Johns Hopkins University Press, 1997.

Roudané, Matthew Charles. *American Drama since 1960: A Critical History*. New York and London: Twayne Publishers, Prentice Hall International, 1996.

Wilmeth, Don B. and C. W. E. Bigsby. *The Cambridge History of American Theatre*. Cambridge: Cambridge University Press, 2000.

Books on American theatre in the 1970s

Bottoms, Stephen J. *Playing Underground: A Critical History of the 1960s Off-Off-Broadway Movement*. Theater: Theory/Text/Performance. Ann Arbor: University of Michigan Press, 2004.

Canning, Charlotte. *Feminist Theaters in the U.S.A.: Staging Women's

Experience. Gender in Performance. London and New York: Routledge, 1996.
Cohn, Ruby. *New American Dramatists, 1960–1980*. Grove Press Modern Dramatists. New York: Grove Press, 1982.
Demastes, William W. *Realism and the American Dramatic Tradition*. Tuscaloosa: University of Alabama Press, 1996.
Epstein, Helen. *Joe Papp: An American Life*. New York: Da Capo, 1996.
Hoffman, Ted, ed. *Famous American Plays of the 1970's*. New York: Dell, 1981.
King, Woodie. *Black Theater: The Making of a Movement*. San Francisco: California Newsreel, 1978.
Leavitt, Dinah Luise. *Feminist Theatre Groups*. Jefferson, NC: McFarland, 1980.
Lee, Esther Kim. *A History of Asian American Theatre*. Cambridge Studies in American Theatre and Drama. Cambridge and New York: Cambridge University Press, 2006.
Leiter, Samuel L. *Ten Seasons: New York Theatre in the Seventies*. Contributions in Drama and Theatre Studies. New York: Greenwood Press, 1986.
Marranca, Bonnie, Richard Foreman, Lee Breuer and Robert Wilson. *The Theatre of Images*. New York: Drama Book Specialists, 1977.
Reston, James Jr, ed. *Coming to Terms: American Plays & the Vietnam War*. New York: Theatre Communications Group, 1985.

The playwrights

David Rabe

Plays

The Basic Training of Pavlo Hummel. New York: Viking Press, 1971.
Sticks and Bones. New York: Viking Press, 1973.
In the Boom Boom Room. New York: Random House, 1975.
The Orphan. New York: Samuel French, 1975.
Streamers. New York: Knopf, 1977.
Hurlyburly. Chicago: Grove Press, 1985.
Goose and Tomtom. Chicago: Grove Press, 1987.
Those the River Keeps. New York: Grove Weidenfeld, 1991.
A Question of Mercy. New York: Grove Press, 1998.
The Dog Problem. New York: Samuel French, 2002.

The Black Monk. New York: Samuel French, 2004.
An Early History of Fire. New York: Samuel French, 2013.

Screenplays

I'm Dancing As Fast As I Can. Paramount, 1982.
Streamers. United Artists, 1983.
Casualties of War. Columbia, 1989.
State of Grace. Orion, 1990.
The Firm. Paramount, 1993.
Hurlyburly. Fine Line Features, 1998.

Fiction

Recital of the Dog. New York: Grove Press, 1992.
A Primitive Heart: Stories. New York: Grove Press, 2005.
Dinosaurs on the Roof. New York: Simon & Schuster, 2008.
Girl by the Road at Night: A Novel of Vietnam. New York: Simon & Schuster, 2010.

Recommended books

Kolin, Philip C. *David Rabe: A Stage History and Primary and Secondary Bibliography*. New York: Garland, 1988.
Zinman, Toby Silverman, ed. *David Rabe: A Casebook*. Casebooks on Modern Dramatists. Gen. ed. Kimball King. New York: Garland, 1991.

Sam Shepard

Plays

Operation Sidewinder: A Play in Two Acts. Indianapolis: Bobbs-Merrill, 1970.
The Tooth of Crime and Geography of a Horse Dreamer: Two Plays. London: Faber, 1974.
Angel City & Other Plays. New York: Urizen Books, 1976.
Four Two-Act Plays. New York: Urizen Books, 1980.
States of Shock; Far North; Silent Tongue: A Play and Two Screenplays. London: Methuen Drama, 1993.
Plays 1. London: Methuen Drama, 1996.

Plays 2. London: Methuen, 1996.
Plays 3. London: Methuen, 1996.
Simpatico: A Play in Three Acts. New York: Vintage Books, 1996.
The Late Henry Moss; Eyes for Consuela; When the World Was Green: Three Plays. New York: Vintage Books, 2002.
The God of Hell: A Play. New York: Vintage Books, 2005.
Sam Shepard: Seven Plays. New York: Dial Press, 2005.
Buried Child: A Play. Revised edition. New York: Vintage Books, 2006.
Tooth of Crime: (Second Dance): A Play with Music in Two Acts. Revised edition. New York: Vintage Books, 2006.
Kicking a Dead Horse. New York: Dramatists Play Service, Inc., 2009.
Fifteen One-Act Plays. New York: Vintage Books, 2012.
Heartless: A Play. New York: Vintage Books, 2013.

Fiction and non-fiction

Rolling Thunder Logbook. New York: Viking Press, 1977.
Motel Chronicles. San Francisco: City Lights Books, 1982.
Cruising Paradise: Tales. New York: Knopf, distributed by Random House, 1996.
Great Dream of Heaven: Stories. New York: Knopf, distributed by Random House, 2002.
Day out of Days: Stories. New York: Alfred A. Knopf, 2010.

Recommended books

Bottoms, Stephen J. *The Theatre of Sam Shepard: States of Crisis*. Cambridge and New York: Cambridge University Press, 1998.
Callens, Johan. *Dis/Figuring Sam Shepard*. Brussels and New York: Peter Lang, 2007.
Crank, James A. *Understanding Sam Shepard*. Columbia: University of South Carolina Press, 2012.
DeRose, David J. *Sam Shepard*. New York and Toronto: Twayne, 1992.
Graham, Laura J. *Sam Shepard: Theme, Image, and the Director*. New York: Peter Lang, 1995.
Hart, Lynda. *Sam Shepard's Metaphorical Stages*. Westport, CT: Greenwood Press, 1987.
King, Kimball. *Sam Shepard: A Casebook*. New York: Garland, 1988.
LC Off-Air Taping Collection (Library of Congress). *Sam Shepard – Stalking Himself, Great Performances*. Arlington, VA: PBS, 1998.
Marranca, Bonnie. *American Dreams: The Imagination of Sam Shepard*. New York: Performing Arts Journal Publications, 1981.

Mottram, Ron. *Inner Landscapes: The Theater of Sam Shepard*. Columbia: University of Missouri Press, 1984.
Oumano, Elena. *Sam Shepard: The Life and Work of an American Dreamer*. 1st edition. New York: St Martin's Press, 1986.
Roudané, Matthew Charles, ed. *The Cambridge Companion to Sam Shepard*. Cambridge and New York: Cambridge University Press, 2002.
Skelton, Shannon Blake. *The Late Work of Sam Shepard*. London: Methuen Drama, 2016.
Taav, Michael. *A Body across the Map: The Father–Son Plays of Sam Shepard*. New York: Peter Lang, 2000.
Tucker, Martin. *Sam Shepard*. New York: Continuum, 1992.
Wade, Leslie A. *Sam Shepard and the American Theatre*. Westport, CT: Greenwood Press, 1997.
Wilcox, Leonard. *Rereading Shepard: Contemporary Critical Essays on the Plays of Sam Shepard*. New York: St Martin's Press, 1993.

Ntozake Shange

Plays

For Colored Girls Who Have Considered Suicide, When the Rainbow Is Enuf: A Choreopoem. New York: MacMillan, 1977.
A Photograph: Lovers in Motion. New York and London: S. French, 1981.
Spell #7: A Theater Piece in Two Acts. New York: S. French, 1981.
Three Pieces. New York: Penguin, 1982.
From Okra to Greens: A Different Kinda Love Story: A Play with Music & Dance. New York: S. French, 1985.
Spell Number Seven. Women's Playhouse Plays. London: Methuen, 1985.
The Love Space Demands: A Continuing Saga. New York: St Martin's Press, 1991.
Plays, One. Methuen World Dramatists. London: Methuen Drama, 1992.
Three Pieces. New York: St Martin's Press, 1992.
For Colored Girls Who Have Considered Suicide, When the Rainbow Is Enuf: A Choreopoem. 1st Scribner trade paperback edition. New York: Scribner, 2010.
Shange, Ntozake and Michael Sporn. *Whitewash*. New York: Walker & Co., 1997.

Selected poetry

Melissa & Smith. St Paul, MN: Bookslinger Editions, 1976.
Nappy Edges. New York: St Martin's Press, 1978.
A Daughter's Geography. New York: St Martin's Press, 1983.
Ridin' the Moon in Texas: Word Paintings. New York: St Martin's Press, 1987.
Shange, Ntozake, Romare Bearden and Linda Sunshine. *I Live in Music: Poem*. New York: Welcome Enterprises, 1994.

Novels

Sassafrass, Cypress & Indigo: A Novel. New York: St Martin's Press, 1982.
Betsey Brown: A Novel. New York: St Martin's Press, 1985.
Liliane: Resurrection of the Daughter. New York: St Martin's Press, 1994.
If I Can Cook, You Know God Can. Boston: Beacon Press, 1998.

Fiction for children

Shange, Ntozake and Kadir Nelson. *Ellington Was Not a Street*. New York: Simon & Schuster Books for Young Readers, 2004.
Shange, Ntozake and Edel Rodriguez. *Muhammad Ali, the Man Who Could Float Like a Butterfly and Sting Like a Bee*. New York: Jump at the Sun/Hyperion Books for Children, 2002.
Shange, Ntozake and Michael Sporn. *Whitewash*. New York: Walker & Co., 1997.

Recommended books

Effiong, Philip U. *In Search of a Model for African-American Drama: A Study of Selected Plays by Lorraine Hansberry, Amiri Baraka, and Ntozake Shange*. Lanham, MD and Plymouth: University Press of America, 2000.
Lester, Neal A. *Ntozake Shange: A Critical Study of the Plays*. New York: Garland, 1995.
Olaniyan, Tejumola. *Scars of Conquest/Masks of Resistance: The Invention of Cultural Identities in African, African-American, and Caribbean Drama*. New York: Oxford University Press, 1995.
Sharadha, Y. S. *Black Women's Writing: Quest for Identity in the*

Plays of Lorraine Hansberry and Ntozake Shange. London: Sangam, 1998.

Splawn, P. Jane. 'Rites of Passage in the Writing of Ntozake Shange: The Poetry, Drama, and Novels'. PhD dissertation, University of Wisconsin-Madison, 1988.

Tate, Claudia. *Black Women Writers at Work*. New York: Continuum, 1983.

Richard Foreman

Plays

Plays and Manifestoes. New York: New York University Press, 1976.
Reverberation Machines: The Later Plays and Essays. Barrytown, NY: Station Hill, 1985.
My Head Was a Sledgehammer: Six Plays. Woodstock, NY: Overlook Press, 1995.
Paradise Hotel: And Other Plays. Woodstock, NY: Overlook Press, 2001.
Bad Boy Nietzsche and Other Plays. New York: Theatre Communications Group, 2007.
The Manifestos and Essays. New York: Theatre Communications Group, 2013.
Foreman, Richard and Ken Jordan. *Unbalancing Acts: The Theater of Richard Foreman*. New York: Pantheon Books, 1992.
Silverman, Stanley and Richard Foreman. *Love & Science: Selected Music-Theatre Texts*. New York: Theatre Communications Group, 1991.

Screenplays and films

Out of Body Travel. American Dance Festival. New York: Electronic Arts Intermix. VHS video; VHS tape, 1976.
City Archives. Maja Bjornson; Jim Cada; Walker Art Center; Minnesota Public Programing Corporation. New York: Electronic Arts Intermix, Inc, 1978.
Strong Medicine. New York: Ontological-Hysteric Theatre, 1981.
Once Every Day. New York: Picture Art Films, 2012.

Performance DVDs

Many of Foreman's productions have been filmed and are available at the New York Public Library for the Performing Arts. A list of available titles can be found at the Ontological-Hysteric Theatre Website (see below).

Foreman, Richard, Bob Fleischner, Andrew Noren, Margot Breier, Linda Patton, Kate Manheim, Jim Hoberman, et al. *Richard Foreman Ontological-Hysteric Theater*. Vol. 1, *Sophia: The Cliffs*. New York: Tzadik, 2009.

Foreman, Richard, John Zorn, Mike Patton, Trevor Dunn, Joey Baron, Karl Allen, Benjamin Forster, et al. *Richard Foreman Ontological-Hysteric Theater*. Vol. 2, *Astronome: A Night at the Opera: A Disturbing Initiation*. New York: Tzadik, 2010.

Recommended books

Aronson, Arnold. *Looking into the Abyss: Essays on Scenography*. Theater/Theory/Text/Performance. Ann Arbor: University of Michigan Press, 2005.

Davy, Kate. *Richard Foreman and the Ontological-Hysteric Theatre*. Theater and Dramatic Studies. Ann Arbor, MI: UMI Research Press, 1981.

Doczy, Kriszta and Richard Foreman. *Foreman Planet: Interview with Richard Foreman* (DVD). South Freemantle, Western Australia: Contemporary Arts Media, 2003.

Marranca, Bonnie. *The Theatre of Images*. 1st edn. New York: Drama Book Specialists, 1977.

Rabkin, Gerald. *Richard Foreman*. Art + Performance. Baltimore: Johns Hopkins University Press, 1999.

Robinson, Marc. *The Other American Drama*. Baltimore: Johns Hopkins University Press, 1997.

Web resources

General

American Theatre: http://www.americantheatre.org/
American Theater Web: http://www.americantheaterweb.com

Digital Librarian: Performing Arts: http://www.digital-librarian.com/performing.html
Doollee Database of Modern Playwrights (post-1956): http://www.doollee.com/
Theatre Communications Group: http://www.tcg.org/
Theatre History on the Web: http://www.videoccasions-nw.com/history/jack.html

New York Theatre

Broadway Database: Off-Off-Broadway: http://www.broadwayworld.com/off-off-broadway/
Broadway League: https://www.broadwayleague.com/
Internet Broadway Database: http://www.ibdb.com/
Off-Off-Broadway Review: http://www.oobr.com/
Playbill New York City Theatre Database: http://www.playbillvault.com/index.html

Regional/resident/university theatre

American Alliance for Theatre and Education: http://www.aate.com/
American Association of Community Theatre: http://www.aact.org/
University/Resident Theatre Association: http://urta.com/

Richard Foreman

Nobody Zone: http://nobodyzone.com/
Ontological-Hysteric Theatre Website: http://www.ontological.com/

Ntozake Shange

https://www.poets.org/poetsorg/poet/ntozake-shange

Sam Shepard

Sam Shepard Website: http://www.sam-shepard.com/

INDEX

abortion, 8, 10, 29, 35, 143–4, 194, 224
absurdism, 49, 93, 217
Academy Awards, 6, 33, 196
Actors Theatre of Louisville, Humana Festival, 60, 82, 88, 250
Actors' Equity Association (AEA), 49, 54, 57, 73
Akalaitis, Joanne, 82
Albee, Edward
   All Over, 42, 59, 125
   Counting the Ways, 59
   Delicate Balance, A, 59
   Lady from Dubuque, The, 59
   Who's Afraid of Virginia Woolf?, 59
   Zoo Story, The, 49, 59
Ali, Muhammad, 21, 23, 273
All in the Family, 28, 34
Alley Theatre (Houston), 55
alternative theatre, 47, 52–4, 83–7, 250
Altman, Robert, 19, 34, 186, 200
American Century, 26
American dream, 14, 20, 27, 59, 62, 252–3, 264–5, 271
American frontier, 25, 117, 126, 134–6, 139
Apocalypse Now, 33, 200
Archie Bunker, 1, 34
Arena Stage (Washington, DC), 55–6

Aronson, Arnold, 49, 78, 243, 248
Artaud, Antonin, 215
Ayckbourn, Alan, 68

Bach, Richard: *Jonathan Livingston Seagull*, 16–17
Bakke v. Regents of the University of California, 11, 32
Baraka, Amiri (LeRoi Jones), 70, 78–9, 180, 249, 273
Barnes, Clive, 92, 145, 250, 256, 258
Basquiat, Michel, 18
Baumol Report, 46
Beck, Julian, 84, 180
Beckett, Samuel, 86, 184, 265
Belushi, John, 34
Bennett, Michael, 66 *see also Chorus Line, A*
Beverley, Trazana, 81
Bicentennial, 1, 22, 31
Black Arts Movement, 43, 78–9, 81, 249
Black Panthers, 41, 117, 181
Bovasso, Julie, 48, 82
Brecht, Bertolt, 166, 180, 222, 265
Breuer, Lee, 85, 269
Broadway, 42–74, 76–85, 87–9, 92–3, 113–16, 132, 134–5, 141–2, 145, 155, 160, 163, 168, 171–2, 174, 193–4,

INDEX

196, 202, 209, 223, 227, 243–50, 252, 256, 258, 262, 268, 276
Brustein, Robert, 93, 217, 246, 250, 264
Bullins, Ed
   Clara's Ole Man, 80
   Duplex, The, 80
   Fabulous Miss Marie, The, 80
   Goin' a Buffalo, 80
   Taking of Miss Janie, The, 69, 78, 80, 193
Burroughs, William, 177, 261

Caffe Cino, 61, 73, 168, 181
Cage, John, 84, 118, 171–3, 177–9, 186
Carlos, Laurie, 162, 204
Carmines, Al, 73
Carter, James Earl, 1, 6, 31–3, 139
Carter, Paul, 146, 258
Chaikin, Joseph, 79, 84, 114–15, 219–20, 253, 265
Cherry Lane Theatre, 59, 61, 72, 79, 134
Childress, Alice, 79
Childs, Lucinda, 85, 173
Chin, Frank: *Chickencoop Chinaman*, 75
choreopoem, 81–2, 143–5, 147–9, 151, 153–5, 157–9, 161–3, 199, 202–3, 206–7, 224, 256–7, 259, 272
Christian Right, 34, 41, 194–5
Cino, Joe, 73
Circle in the Square, 56, 63
Circle Rep, 61, 69
civil rights, 8, 11, 24, 30, 33, 41, 75, 89, 117
Cleveland Playhouse, 55
Clurman, Harold, 122, 254

commercial theatre, 44, 46, 51, 59–60, 76, 87, 154, 168
computers, 1, 31, 37
concept musical, 65–6 *see also* musical
consciousness raising, 66
Cook, Ralph, 73
Cowie, Jefferson, 6, 40, 241–2

Dark, Johnny, 199, 221, 262
disco, 1, 13–14, 21, 36
divorce, 8–10, 16, 34
Drama Desk Awards, 62, 69, 92
Drexler, Rosalyn, 82–3
Durang, Christopher, 44
Dylan, Bob, 6, 12, 20, 216

Earth Day, 4, 28, 42
East Village, 52, 86, 114, 192
environmental movement, 4–5, 18, 42, 70 *see also* Earth Day

Fanon, Frantz, 202, 263
Farber, David, 40
Feingold, Michael, 190
feminism, 8–9, 17, 28, 43, 81–4, 112, 144, 148–53, 160–1, 163, 195 *see also* National Organization for Women (NOW)
Fichandler, Zelda, 55
film, 6, 10, 13, 19–21, 23, 26, 32–4, 44, 47, 50, 60, 63, 67, 75, 80, 86, 98, 102, 104, 109, 113–14, 116, 126, 134, 139, 142, 153, 161–2, 168, 174–6, 181–2, 186, 191–2, 195–6, 199–206, 208, 216, 221, 238, 247, 252, 259, 263–4, 274
Foote, Horton, 194

INDEX

Ford Foundation, 52, 55
Ford, Gerald, 1, 30–1
Foreman, Richard
   Pandering to the Masses, 165, 172, 174–5, 183, 185–7, 189, 191
   Rhoda in Potatoland (Her Fall-Starts), 165, 172, 188, 190, 236, 260
   Sophia = Wisdom (The Cliffs), 165, 174–5, 182–3, 189, 234, 260–1, 275
   Strong Medicine, 168, 175–6, 274
Fornes, Maria Irene: *Fefu and Her Friends*, 74, 83
Fosse, Bob
   Chicago, 66
   Liza with a 'Z', 66
   Pippin, 65–6, 77
Frum, David, 11, 39, 241–2
Fuller, Charles
   Brownsville Raid, The, 81
   Soldier's Play, A, 80
   Zooman and the Sign, 81

gay rights, 8–9, 89, 193
Geiogamah, Hanay, 75
Gelber, Jack, 75
Gielgud, John, 59, 68
Gitlin, Todd, 39, 242
Glass, Philip, 14, 85–6, 168, 173
Godfather, The, 20–1
Godspell, 69, 194
Goldwater, Barry, 26, 180
Goodman Theatre, 62, 247
Gordone, Charles: *No Place to Be Somebody*, 76
Gray, Spalding, 86
Greenwich Village, 81, 113, 132, 140, 243
Guare, John

   Bosoms and Neglect, 62
   House of Blue Leaves, 51, 62
   Landscape of the Body, 62
   Lydie Breeze, 62
   Marco Polo Sings a Solo, 62
   Six Degrees of Separation, 62, 194
Gurney, A. R., 44, 194
Gussow, Mel, 51, 244

Hagedorn, Jessica, 146, 249
Haley, Alex, 15, 35
Hamlisch, Marvin, 64, 66
Handke, Peter, 177, 261
Hansberry, Lorraine
   Les Blancs, 77
   Raisin in the Sun, A, 41, 76, 160
Happenings, 43, 85, 114, 168
Hare, David, 47, 68
Herr, Michael: *Dispatches*, 207, 264
High Modernism, 18, 86, 180
hip-hop, 14, 159, 204
Home Box Office (HBO), 33
Horovitz, Israel
   Art of Dining, The, 82
   Indian Wants the Bronx, The, 70
Howe, Tina: *Museum*, 12, 82, 88, 160
Hwang, David Henry: *FOB*, 75

Inge, William, 58
Innaurato, Albert *Gemini*, 69

jazz, 6, 14, 36, 114–15, 118–19, 183, 189, 216, 219
Jenkin, Len, 84
Johnson, Lyndon, 26, 52
Jones, Margo, 55–6, 88
Jory, John, 88
Judson Poets Theatre, 74, 232

Katz, Leon: *Dracula: Sabbat*, 73
Kennedy, Adrienne
   Movie Star Has to Dream in Black and White, A, 79
   Wedding Band, 79
King, Martin Luther, 41
King, Woodie, 79, 258
Kopit, Arthur
   Indians, 59, 222
   Nine, 8, 22, 27, 31, 60, 66, 76
   Oh Dad, Poor Dad, Mamma's Hung You in the Closet and I'm Feelin' So Sad, 62
   Wings, 24, 60

La MaMa, 52, 61, 73, 75, 84, 114, 168, 181, 232
Lange, Jessica, 196, 222
Lawrence, Jerome, 87, 245
League of Resident Theatres (LORT), 57
LeCompte, Elizabeth, 43, 82, 86
Lee, Robert Edwin, 87, 245
Left, New, 26
Left, Old, 25
Leiter, Samuel, 43, 45, 48, 51, 57, 64, 67, 76, 82
Lewitin, Margot, 83
liberal consensus, 24–7, 41, 89
liberalism, 6, 24, 70, 194–5, 241, 248
Lincoln Center, 46, 78, 92, 115, 209
Linney, Romulus, 44
Living Theater
   Brig, The, 70, 210
   Connection, The, 70
   Paradise Now!, 180
Ludlam, Charles, 43, 74

Mabou Mines
   B. Beaver Animation, 86
   Red Horse Animation, 86
   Shaggy Dog Animation, 86
Maciunas, George, 182
Magic Theatre (San Francisco), 74, 83, 115, 132, 134, 220
Malaczech, Ruth, 85, 175
malaise, 13, 26, 33, 42, 117, 139, 198, 201
Malcolm X, 41, 249
Malik, Terence, 126, 195
Malina, Judith, 48, 84, 180
Mamet, David
   American Buffalo, 62–3, 72–3, 194–5
   Duck Variations, The, 72
   Glengarry Glen Ross, 194
   Oleanna, 195
   Sexual Perversity in Chicago, 72
   Water Engine, The, 72
Manheim, Kate, 174–5, 187, 233, 237–8, 275
Manson, Charles, 31, 117
Mark Taper Forum (Los Angeles), 69, 76, 142
Marowitz, Charles, 121, 254
Marranca, Bonnie, 85, 116, 219, 232, 250, 252, 260, 264, 266
Mason, Marshall, 61, 69
McNally, Terence
   Bad Habits, 60
   Lady of the Camellias, The, 60
   Lips Together, Teeth Apart, 61
   Love! Valor! Compassion!, 61
   Masterclass, 61
   Ritz, The, 60
Me Decade, 1, 23, 33, 66, 117
Medoff, Mark: *When You Comin' Back, Red Ryder?*, 69
Mee, Charles, 84
Mekas, Jonas, 182, 205
memory, 3, 34, 111, 124, 130, 135, 140, 155, 183, 198, 204, 220–1, 249, 265

Miller, Arthur
   Creation of the World and Other Business, The, 58
   Crucible, The, 70
   Death of a Salesman, 95, 246
   Price, The, 58
   Theatre Essays, 58
Miller, Jason: *That Championship Season*, 209
minimalism, 14, 18, 85, 183
Monk, Meredith, 84
Moral Majority, 33
'Morning in America', 139, 199
Moses, Gilbert, 78–9
Mosher, Gregory, 62
musical, 14, 46–7, 53, 57–8, 60, 62, 64–9, 76–9, 81, 88, 142, 145, 168, 194, 200, 207, 209, 219–20, 227, 246, 248 *see also* concept musical
My Lai Massacre, 28, 96, 104
myth, 72, 75–6, 97–8, 100, 103, 113–14, 117–23, 126–7, 129, 131–2, 135–40, 148, 180, 184, 197, 199, 204, 207–8, 216–18, 223, 231, 253–5, 265

NASA, 35–7, 139
National Endowment for the Arts (NEA), 17
National Endowment for the Humanities (NEH), 18, 57
National Organization for Women (NOW), 9
naturalism, 61, 93–5, 116, 129, 218, 251
New Federal Theatre, 69, 79–81, 204
New Journalism, 36, 207
New Lafayette Theatre, 78, 80, 261

new realism, 116
New Right, 6, 10, 25–6, 39–40
New York Shakespeare Festival, 50–1, 92, 142, 244
Nightingale, Benedict, 121, 254
Nobel Prize, 16
Norman, Marsha: *Getting Out*, 82, 88

O'Horgan, Tom, 47, 73
O'Neill, Eugene, 44, 58, 70, 114–16, 127, 140
Obie Awards, 80, 142, 168, 181
Off-Broadway, 42–4, 46, 48–62, 64–74, 76–80, 82–3, 87–8, 92, 113–16, 134–5, 141–2, 168, 174, 194, 196, 209, 244–7, 252, 268, 276
Off-Off-Broadway, 42–4, 46, 48, 50–4, 57, 61, 70–1, 73–4, 79–80, 83, 88, 113–14, 116, 135, 168, 196, 244–5, 252, 268, 276
Off-Off-Broadway Alliance, 52, 54
oil
   embargo, 2, 30, 32
   OPEC, 2, 27, 30
Olympics, 21–2, 228
Ontological-Hysteric Theater, 43, 165–92, 205, 229, 233, 235 *see also* Foreman, Richard
Open Theater 84 *see also* Chaikin, Joseph
   Nightwalk, 84
   Purlie Victorious, 76–7
   Serpent, The, 84, 102, 193
   Terminal, 84
Owens, Rochelle, 83

Pacino, Al, 63, 69, 92
Papp, Joseph, 50, 66, 92–3, 134, 142, 209, 252, 264, 269

Patrick, Robert, 1, 193, 241
Pentagon Papers, 36, 116
performance art, 18, 43–4, 85, 88, 168, 172, 226, 265
Performance Group, 43, 53, 69, 86, 172, 180–1, 232, 250
Performing Garage, 86, 181, 191
Perry, Tyler, 161, 204
Pinero, Miguel: *Short Eyes*, 76
Ping Chong, 43, 52, 75, 84
Pinter, Harold, 68, 102, 127
Playwrights Horizon, 69
pornography, 9, 45–6
Postmodern, 18, 75, 85–6, 96, 111, 121, 176, 184, 220–1, 231, 265
Prince, Hal, 64, 66
proposition 13, 1, 32
Public Theater, 50, 66, 75, 79, 92–3, 141–2
Pulitzer Prize, 10, 16, 59, 61, 66, 75, 88, 113–14, 132, 195
punk, 12, 14, 20, 26

Quiet Generation, 25, 54

Rabe, David
  Basic Training of Pavlo Hummel, The, 92, 97–101, 111, 199, 213, 250
  Hurlyburly, 111, 199–201, 214, 251, 263–4, 269–70
  In the Boom Boom Room, 92–3, 111, 252, 269
  Orphan, The, 92–3, 110, 269
  Sticks and Bones, 91–2, 96, 101, 103–5, 111–12, 209–14, 250–1, 264, 269
  Streamers, 91–3, 96, 106, 108, 110, 200, 210, 250, 252, 269–70
Rabe, Lilly, 200
race relations, 6, 10–11, 20, 34, 41, 76, 80, 148, 150–7, 201, 225
Rambo, 199–200
Reagan, Ronald, 25–6, 32, 139, 263
realism, 61, 69–72, 84, 87, 93–4, 116, 118, 121–2, 126, 130, 132–3, 137–8, 140, 146, 162, 174, 177, 197, 202, 217–18, 247, 251, 264, 269
  see also new realism
regional theatre
  not-for-profit, 50, 76, 88
  resident theatre, 51–3, 55–7, 74, 79, 87–8, 245–6, 276
Reich, Steve, 14, 173
Richards, Lloyd, 75
ritual, 66, 79, 117–19, 122–3, 125, 160, 170, 180, 214, 233, 249
Rolling Thunder Revue, 216, 264, 271
Roots, 1, 15, 35, 52, 55, 62, 65, 86, 126, 136, 188
Ruhl, Sarah, 84
Rust Belt, 7

Sackler, Howard: *Great White Hope, The*, 56, 76
Sanchez, Sonia, 78, 226
Saturday Night Live, 1, 34
scenic writing, 171, 232
Schechner, Richard, 43, 53, 86, 172, 180, 188, 237, 260–1
school busing, 10, 30, 41
Schulman, Bruce, 11, 20, 40
science, 16, 36–7, 167, 242, 274
Scorsese, Martin, 20, 63
Second World War, 24, 27, 41, 64, 96, 103, 139
Shange, Ntozake
  boogie woogie landscapes, 141–2, 155–8, 163

for colored girls who have considered suicide/when the rainbow is enuf, 77, 81, 141, 144–8, 158, 161, 256, 259, 265
From Okra to Greens, 82, 142, 203, 272
Lavender Lizards and Lilac Landmines, 157, 258
Photograph, A, 81–2, 141, 272
spell #7, 82, 141–2, 148–51, 154–5, 159, 163, 227–8, 256–8, 272
Shawn, Wallace, 50
Shepard, Sam
  Buried Child, 113–14, 116, 126, 128–32, 135, 139, 195–6, 221, 252–4, 271
  Curse of the Starving Class, 113, 116, 120–1, 125–6, 130–2, 215, 252–4
  Fool for Love, 134, 196–7
  Inacoma, 115
  Late Henry Moss, The, 134, 271
  Motel Chronicles, 196, 271
  Savage/Love, 116, 219
  States of Shock, 196, 198, 270
  Tongues, 116, 220
  Tooth of Crime, The, 70, 115–17, 131, 270
  True West, 113, 116, 132–6, 195, 197, 218, 252, 255
Shuberts, 35, 46–7, 66, 68
Simon, John, 81, 145, 249, 256–7
Simon, Neil
  Chapter Two, 63
  Gingerbread Lady, The, 63
  God's Favorite, 63
  Plaza Suite, 63
  Prisoner of Second Avenue, The, 63
  Sunshine Boys, The, 63

  They're Playing Our Song, 63–4
Smith, Michael, 53, 73
Sondheim, Stephen
  Company, 11, 34–5, 43, 52–5, 57–8, 62, 65, 67, 71, 73–5, 79, 81, 83–4, 86–7, 114, 123, 180, 228, 232, 245
  Follies, 67
  Little Night Music, A, 67
  Pacific Overtures, 64, 67
  Sweeney Todd, 67
Soviet Union, 22, 140
Split Britches, 83
Springsteen, Bruce, 14
Squat Theatre, 43, 55, 84, 166
St. Mark's, 79, 166, 171, 175, 191–2
stagflation, 2, 27–8, 40
Stein, Gertrude, 168–9, 178, 180, 231–2
Steppenwolf Theatre (Chicago), 57, 63, 132, 134, 196
Stewart, Ellen, 52–3, 61, 75
Stoppard, Tom, 68
Sun Belt, 7, 22, 25–6, 29, 41
Supreme Court, 7-8, 10, 21, 29, 32
Swados, Elizabeth, 66

Tavel, Ronald, 74
Taxi Driver, 19–20, 63
television, 6, 9, 14–15, 17, 21–3, 26, 33–5, 46, 66, 96, 104, 116, 129, 133, 153, 162, 209–12, 233, 249, 254
Terry, Megan, 74, 83
Theatre Genesis, 73, 114
Theatre of the Ridiculous, 43
Toffler, Alvin, 15, 28
Tony Awards, 78, 88, 92, 141, 209

Valdez, Luis, 75

Van Peebles, Melvin
  Ain't Supposed to Die a Natural Death, 78
  Don't Play Us Cheap, 78
Venturi, Robert, 18
Vietnam, 3, 14–16, 25–7, 29–34, 59–61, 69, 75, 91–3, 96–101, 104–6, 109–12, 116–17, 148, 180, 198, 200, 207–8, 210–12, 217
Village Voice, 53, 73, 114, 223, 255
Vivian Beaumont Theatre, 46, 93

Walker, Joseph: *River Niger, The*, 77
Ward, Douglas Turner, 77
Wasserstein, Wendy: *Uncommon Women and Others*, 82
Watergate, 27, 29, 33, 36, 116
Webber, Andrew Lloyd: *Jesus Christ Superstar*, 65, 77
Weller, Michael, 193
Wellman, Mac, 84
Wilder, Thornton, 231
Williams, Samm-Art, 72, 77
Williams, Tennessee
  Small Craft Warnings, 58
  Summer and Smoke, 56, 58
Wilson, August, 85
Wilson, Doric, 74

Wilson, Lanford
  Balm in Gilead, 61
  Fifth of July, The, 61, 193
  Gingham Dog, 61
  Hot L Baltimore, The, 61
  Madness of Lady Bright, The, 61
  Mound Builders, The, 61
  Rimers of Eldritch, The, 61
  Serenading Louie, 61
  Talley and Son, 61
  Talley's Folly, 61
Wilson, Robert
  Byrd Hoffman School of Byrds, 43, 85
  Deafman Glance, 66, 85
  Einstein on the Beach, 14, 66, 85
  Letter to Queen Victoria, A, 85
Wiz, The, 78, 228
Woodruff, Robert, 122, 132
Wooster Group
  Nayatt School, 86
  Rumstick Road, 86
  Sakonnet Point, 86
working class, 241–2
Wounded Knee, 29

Yankowitz, Susan, 82
Young, Harvey, 248

www.ingramcontent.com/pod-product-compliance
Lightning Source LLC
Chambersburg PA
CBHW070019010526
44117CB00011B/1632